Matti Steinitz

Afro-Latin Soul Music and the Rise of Black Power Cosmopolitanism

American Frictions

Editors
Carsten Junker
Julia Roth
Darieck Scott

Editoral Board
Arjun Appadurai, New York University
Mita Banerjee, University of Mainz
Tomasz Basiuk, University of Warsaw
Isabel Caldeira, University of Coimbra

Volume 1

Matti Steinitz

Afro-Latin Soul Music and the Rise of Black Power Cosmopolitanism

Hemispheric Soulscapes between Spanish Harlem, Black Rio and Panama

DE GRUYTER

ISBN 978-3-11-066450-8
e-ISBN (PDF) 978-3-11-066555-0
e-ISBN (EPUB) 978-3-11-066459-1
ISSN 2698-5349

Library of Congress Control Number: 2024943394

Bibliographic information published by the Deutsche Nationalbibliothek
The Deutsche Nationalbibliothek lists this publication in the Deutsche Nationalbibliografie;
detailed bibliographic data are available on the Internet at http://dnb.dnb.de.

© 2025 Walter de Gruyter GmbH, Berlin/Boston

www.degruyter.com
Questions about General Product Safety Regulation:
productsafety@degruyterbrill.com

Acknowledgements

In many ways, the making of this book was a multi-stop journey that would not have started nor come to a conclusion without the support and trust of a number of people. To begin with, I would like to mention Sergio Costa of the Institute for Latin American Studies at the Free University of Berlin, who encouraged me to remain in academia after completing my master's degree. Based on my research interest in the North-South dialogues between black movements and cultures in the Americas, he recommended me to have a look at the Center for InterAmerican Studies at the Bielefeld University. Fortunately, I followed his advice and came into contact with Wilfried Raussert, co-founder of the center, who was enthusiastic about my idea of writing a dissertation on soul and Black Power in Latin America under his supervision. Without his friendship, complicity, and belief in the project, this book would not have been written – thank you, Willy.

In a joint effort, Willy and I laid the foundation for the project by first convincing the German Research Foundation (DFG) that it was worthy of support. The DFG funding enabled us to launch the Black Americas Network in 2016, which now brings together over 100 researchers, activists and artists whose work is related to the Afro-diasporic presence in the Americas. Within the framework of the network, we organized two conferences – "Entangled Black Americas" (2017) and "Black Power – Movements, Cultures and Resistance in the Black Americas" (2018) – at which important impulses and contacts for this project were generated. The dialogues with network members such as Afua Cooper from Canada, Angel Perea Escobar from Colombia, Angel Quintero Rivera from Puerto Rico, Ariel Abreu from Cuba, and Carlos Alberto Medeiros from Brazil (whose insights can also be found in our edited volume *Black Power in Hemispheric Perspective*, 2022) were very helpful in getting an idea of the inter-American dimensions of the movement that this book is about. I am also grateful to Alejandro de la Fuente and George Reid Andrews for giving me the opportunity to discuss my findings at the 2018 Mark Claster Mamolen Dissertation Workshop of the Afro-Latin American Research Institute at Harvard University.

Infinite gratitude is due to the people who shared their experiences and opened doors for me during my travels tracing the routes of soul music in the Americas. One of these door openers was Luis "Lucho" Ogilvie, whom I met in Rio Abajo, Panama City's historically Afro-Caribbean neighborhood. Upon returning from New York to his native Panama, it was here that he opened *Lucho's Place*, which had become a central meeting place for the local black community. I knew that I was at the right spot when I noticed that, unlike the other bars on the block, which played cumbia, salsa and reggaeton, the speakers outside Lucho's

https://doi.org/10.1515/9783110665550-001

VI —— Acknowledgements

Place blasted James Brown, The Temptations, Otis Redding and other soul greats from the 1960s and 1970s. Lucho's contacts included protagonists of Panama's vibrant soul scene, such as Ernie King (Kabir) of The Festivals and Carlos Brown of The Exciters, who had performed at Johnny B's and other clubs on the very same block a few decades earlier. It was Lucho who got me in touch with these and some other Panamanian musicians, with whom I conducted many of the interviews for this book. *Gracias*, Lucho.

Another key figure in my focus on Panama was the record collector Roberto Ernesto "Beto" Gyemant, whose compilation "Panama! Latin, Calypso and Funk on the Isthmus 1965–75" (Soundway, 2006) with its insightful liner notes was my first source of information about soul music in a country where I hadn't expected to find it. After unsuccessfully trying to reach Beto for some time, we met by a wild coincidence when we both had an appointment with the late Afro-Panamanian community organizer Ines Sealy at the Waikiki Restaurant in Parque Lefevre. To his delight, I told him that his pioneering work as a record digger had actually inspired me to write part of my dissertation on Panama's soul scene. Thank you, Beto!

I am also forever grateful to Melva Lowe de Goodin, who not only shared her memories and important photos and documents from the 1960s and 1970s with me, but also introduced me to *Museo Afroantillano* and the members of SAMAAP (*Society of Friends of the West Indian Museum of Panama*) which she co-founded in 1981. The meetings with Alberto Barrow, Gerardo Maloney, Bruce Codrington, and the visit organized by Luis Pulido Ritter to Carlos Russell one year before his death, were also crucial to my analysis of Panama's significance as a location for hemispheric black activism. I would also like to thank Lloyd Gallimore and Billy Herron of The Beachers, Francisco "Bush" Buckley, Alfredito Payne, and the *combos* musicians I met in the city of Colón: Mauro García (Los Caballeros de Colón), Carlos Grenald (The Silvertones), and Alejandro Duncan (Hermanos Duncan). My archival research at Panama's *Biblioteca Nacional* wouldn't have been as fruitful without the invaluable support of Mario García Hudson, coordinator of the library's *Centro Audiovisual*.

In New York, again, I was fortunate enough to get the support of various key people for my project. First and foremost, I would like to thank Joe Bataan for the lessons he taught me on the emergence of *Afro-Latin Soul* between Black and Spanish Harlem – there couldn't have been a better teacher. The interviews with Young Lords founders and organizers such as Felipe Luciano, Denise Oliver and Carlos Aponte, as well as the musicians Benny Bonilla, Henry Pucho Brown and Bobby Sanabria and the poet Papoleto Melendez were extremely helpful in my endeavor to analyze the interethnic dialogues that shaped New York in the 1960s and 1970s. I would also like to thank Omar Ruiz, who, as a researcher at the Center for Puerto

Rican Studies, introduced me to Centro's wonderful library and its manager Aníbal Arocho, who deserves special thanks for providing me with a wealth of precious material – in particular a box of notes and documents from the late Juan Flores, on whose groundbreaking studies on the connection between Latin Boogaloo and *afrolatinidad* this book builds. Two other New York residents should not go unmentioned here. During our interview, Tito Johnson taught me a lot about his childhood and youth in Colón and the translocal connections between Panama and Brooklyn. DJ Mr. Finewine deserves special thanks, because the archive of his weekly show "Downtown Soulville", which has been broadcast on WFMU since 1995, got me through the most difficult and lonely hours of this project.

I owe a great deal to my friends Asfilófio de Oliveira Filho aka Dom Filó and Carlos Alberto Medeiros for helping me to understand the importance of soul for the Afro-Brazilian movement during my stay in Rio de Janeiro. From day one, Filó and Medeiros took the time to show me sites of Black Rio like the Renascença Clube and put me in touch with protagonists of the scene. I would also like to thank interview partners such as Dr. Sidney Alma Negra, Carlos Dafé, Sir Dema, as well as some protagonists who upheld the legacy of Rio's soul movement before unfortunately passing away much too early, such as the singer Gerson King Combo, the DJs Paulinho from the *Black Power* sound system and Bira from *JB Soul*. The exchange with researchers such as Paulina Alberto, Michael Hanchard, and Amilcar Pereira, was also extremely helpful in analyzing soul in Brazil.

I would like to express my gratitude to my colleagues at Bielefeld University, Alexa Kenter, Diana Fulger, Julia Andres, Mariya Nikolova, Gigi Adair, Brian Rozema, Atahualpa García, Nadine Pollvogt, Philipp Wolfesberger, Olaf Kaltmeier, and especially Julia Roth, who has supported my work from the very beginning and with whom we were able to gather important insights into the significance of popular music for social movements in the African diaspora in the project *#hiphophavanaberlin* (2022). In her role as editor of the American Frictions series, Julia invited me to publish my work in this context, for which I would like to thank her and her co-editors Carsten Junker and Darick Scott. Thanks to this invitation, I had the great fortune to meet Julie Miess, who was responsible for the editing process at DeGruyter and who, along with her colleagues, showed me an almost infinite amount of patience and understanding during the process.

I would also like to thank my parents, grandparents and those friends who never stopped believing, even when the goal seemed very distant. Above all, I would like to dedicate this book to my wife and most loyal supporter, Nina, and to our children, Etta and Avi, who had to endure my long stays abroad and my not always pleasant presence at home. I couldn't have made this journey without you.

Contents

Acknowledgements —— V

Introduction —— 1

1   Theorizing Hemispheric Black Transnationalism —— 29
1.1   Transnational Turns: From Black Studies to African Diaspora Studies —— 30
1.2   Beyond Binaries: Black (Inter) Nationalism, Gilroy, and his Critics —— 37
1.3   Black Cosmopolitanism —— 42
1.4   Overcoming Invisibility: Afro-Latin America in Transnational Perspectives —— 49
1.5   Towards Hemispheric Black Studies —— 52

2   "It's a New Day" – Black Liberation and the Politics of Soul —— 56
2.1   Soul Music, Cultural Nationalism and the Black Arts Movement —— 57
2.2   James Brown, Soul Brother No. 1 —— 61
2.3   Soul Style: "Black is beautiful" —— 64
2.4   "Right on!" Black Panthers, Soul, and the Universal Dream of Freedom —— 67
2.5   "Message from the Soul Sisters": Black Feminist Perspectives —— 71
2.6   "What happened to soul?" Debates in the Post-Soul Era —— 74

3   Spanish Harlem: Latin Boogaloo and Black-Nuyorican Coalition-Building —— 79
3.1   "Alliance of Survival": The Making of Spanish Harlem —— 80
3.2   The Roots of Afro-Latin Soul —— 85
3.3   The Latin Boogaloo Era (1966 – 1969) —— 91
3.4   Joe Bataan: "Young, Gifted, and Brown" —— 102
3.5   Black Power in El Barrio: Nuyorican Poets and Young Lords —— 110

4   Panama: Soul, Black Internationalism and Afro-Caribbean Liberation at the Hemispheric Crossroads —— 116
4.1   Colón: Global Traffic and Black Cosmopolitanism —— 117
4.2   Racism, Nationalism, and West Indian-African American Alliances in the Era of Decolonization —— 122
4.3   The 1950s and Beyond: Afro-Panamanian Community Building in New York —— 127
4.4   The Turbulent 1960s: Anti-Imperialism and Black Power in Panama —— 131

X — Contents

4.5   Panama Soul: From Nights of Fun to Combos Nacionales —— **135**
4.6   The Exciters: Soul Music and Black Empowerment —— **144**
4.7   The 1970s: Torrijos, Afro-Panamanian Activism and the Fear of Black Power —— **150**

5   Black Rio: Raising Consciousness on the Dancefloor —— 158
5.1   *Democracia Racial* and the Politics of Comparative Race Relations —— **158**
5.2   From Harlem to Rio: Toni Tornado —— **160**
5.3   Bailes Soul: Rio Becomes *Black* —— **162**
5.4   Soul, Empowerment and *movimento negro* —— **163**

6   Soul vs. *cultura nacional*: Race, Nation, and *anti-Afro-Americanism* in Latin American Identity Discourses —— 169
6.1   Latin Boogaloo: Between "African Americanness" and *latinidad* —— **170**
6.2   Afro-Caribbean Transnationalism and the Boundaries of *panameñidad* —— **174**
6.3   Black Rio: Soul as a Threat to National Security and *democracia racial* —— **183**
6.4   Analyzing Soul in Latin American Contexts —— **187**

Conclusion —— 191

Sources —— 197

Appendix —— 216

Index —— 233

Introduction

Joe Panama was born in the Bronx in 1936 under the name David George Preud-homme Jr. His father was raised as the son of French-Caribbean migrant workers in the U.S.-controlled Panama Canal Zone, from where he moved to New York. Preudhomme Jr.'s mother, a woman from the Dominican Republic, had encouraged him to learn to play the piano at the age of five. As a teenager, he adopted the stage name "Joe Panama" and formed a band with which he performed at clubs such as the Savoy Ballroom in Harlem and the Blue Morocco in the Bronx (Fig. 1), where mambo and Latin jazz were popular with African American audiences at the time. Influenced by pioneers of New York's vibrant 1940s and 1950s Latin music scene such as Machito, Mario Bauzá and Tito Puente, Joe Panama's band fused Latin American, Caribbean, and African American genres such as son, mambo, cha-cha-cha, jazz and R&B. In probably the only article ever published about Joe Panama, Lynne Duke writes in the *Los Angeles Times:* "He was never a star. But he had a name back in the 1950s, '60s, even '70s. With timbales, vibes, conga, bass, piano and vocalist, the Joe Panama Sextet swirled in the musical ferment that, for a time, built a bridge between black and brown New York."

Among the musicians who integrated the Joe Panama Sextet in the early 1950s was Jimmy Sabater, a timbales player and vocalist, who grew up as a son to Afro-Puerto Rican immigrants in the eastern section of Harlem, also known as Spanish Harlem or El Barrio. Sabater recruited his friend Gilberto "Sunny" Calderón, who also belonged to the first generation of *Nuyoricans*, New York-born Puerto Rican migrants, to become Joe Panama's conga player (Fig. 2). In 1955, after an argument with Joe Panama, Calderón took over the band, eventually renaming it to "Joe Cuba Sextet" (Salazar 237). A decade after the split, the Joe Cuba Sextet, with Jimmy Sabater as a front singer, released "Bang! Bang!" (1966), widely recognized as the first big hit of the Latin boogaloo era that brought together New York's Puerto Rican and African American youth on the dancefloors by fusing Afro-Latin styles with R&B and soul music. Other musicians who integrated Joe Panama's band in the 1950s included Henry "Pucho" Brown, an Harlem-born African American who became known as a master of Latin percussion with his band Pucho & The Latin Soul Brothers in the 1960s (Fig. 3). Pucho described the new cross-over sound that emerged from the dialogues between New York-based African Americans and Caribbean migrants as "cha-cha with a backbeat" (P. Brown). Just like his father's country of origin, which had developed into a diasporic crossroads with the construction of the Panama Canal, Joe Panama's band also became a contact zone of musicians from the United States, the Caribbean, and Latin America. Although its success was short-lived and limited to the local Harlem club scene, Joe Panama's

https://doi.org/10.1515/9783110665550-002

2 —— Introduction

band, brought together by different waves of hemispheric migration, proved to be a hotbed of musicians who would become protagonists in the emergence of what he defined as the "New York Afro-Latin Soul Sound" on the sleeves of his only album *The Explosive Side of Joe Panama* (1967).

While Joe Cuba, Jimmy Sabater, and Henry "Pucho" Brown achieved stardom with their fusions of African American and Afro-Latin genres in the mid-to-late 1960s, Joe Panama never gained the visibility of his alumni. Nevertheless, some of the songs featured on his 1967 album – such as the ode to Muhammad Ali "What's My Name?" and "Soul Sister" – gave voice to the spirit of connectedness with African American expressions that had taken hold of many Caribbean and Latin American migrants in these turbulent years. In 1971, Joe Panama resurfaced with the single "My People" for the New York-based Latin music label Tico. In this fast, percussion-driven Latin soul song, Panama conveys a sense of pride in the way African American popular culture and freedom struggles became the focus of public attention during the Civil Rights and Black Power era:

> Things are really coming to light, my people
> They say they gonna make things right, my people
> The newspaper, radio, and TV,
> I'm talking about a true place in history,
> For all the world to see, talking about my people
> The dancing and the grooving,
> The rhythm and the moving, my people
> My free will, and hip-dealing, hypnotizing sex appeal, my people
> The doctor, the lawyer, the Indian chief
> The rich man, poor man, and the thief
> They are all talking 'bout my people
> The hard sweat, the toil, and the misery, my people
> The love they have for all humanity, my people
> The proud and humble way we go,
> To let the whole world know we know
> Talking 'bout my people
> Let me talk 'bout my people
> Martin Luther King, my people
> Malcolm X, my people
> Marcus Garvey, my people
> John and Robert Kennedy, my people
> James Brown, Ray Charles, Bill Cosby, Sammy Davis, and Aretha
> My people
> (Joe Panama, "My People", 1971)

With "My People", Joe Panama addressed the national and global impact of African American politics, culture, music, and style in the 1960s and 1970s ("... they are all talking 'bout my people"), paying tribute to black movement leaders such as Marcus Garvey, Malcolm X, and Martin Luther King (interestingly including the Kennedy brothers) and soul singers such us James Brown, Aretha Franklin, and Ray Charles who took center stage in the era. Joe Panama's "My People" expressed the widespread sense of identification, admiration, and solidarity with the African American freedom struggle and its cultural expressions that emerged among people of color from across the Americas against the backdrop of sit-ins and freedom rides in the Deep South and urban rebellions in the North and West of the United States. In the 1960s, soul music became a conduit for this affinity.

Focusing on the hemispheric diffusion of soul as a genre and a discourse of "black resilience" (Lordi), this study examines how this new form became a platform for the transnational and translocal identification with the African American freedom struggle and its cultural manifestations among Caribbean and Afro-Latin American youths in New York, Panama, and Brazil. Addressing the perception of soul as the sound of a new black assertiveness not only in the USA, but also in Latin America and the Caribbean, the book interrogates the role of black popular music in the making of interethnic alliances and the border-crossing appeal of the U.S. black movement. As the investigation demonstrates, young people from across the hemisphere saw African American activists, writers, actors, athletes, entertainers, artists and musicians as role models who had managed to survive and thrive "in the belly of the beast," enduring life and practicing heroic resistance in a country with an infamous record of racist violence and oppression. Afro-Puerto Rican scholar Miriám Jiménez Román hinted at this sense of connectedness with the Civil Rights and Black Power movements among many Caribbean and Latin American migrant activists in the USA when she noted that "African Americans have always been in the vanguard" (qtd. in W. Guzmán). This affinity transcended U.S. borders, as can be observed in the works of Afro-Latin American writers such as Nicolás Guillén, Nancy Morejón, Manuel Zapata Olivella, Quince Duncan, and Carlos Guillermo Wilson, who portrayed U.S. blacks "as martyrs and as symbols of resistance, model figures in the fight against racism in this hemisphere" (Jackson 116).

Though literature was an important medium for the articulation of pan-Afro-American sensibilities, its impact, limited to small circles of intellectuals, couldn't match the mass appeal of artists like James Brown, Aretha Franklin, and The Temptations. As the concept of *hemispheric soulscapes* shall illustrate, soul became an effective message carrier, creating a sense of solidarity and identification with the African American freedom struggle that manifested itself in the popularization of Black Power slogans and symbols across the Americas. Hence, I propose to conceive of these flows as an expression of hemispheric black transnationalism understood as the practice through which Afro-diasporic musicians, DJs, activists, artists, movements, and discourses in the Americas have traveled and "related to one an-

4 —— Introduction

other beyond the boundaries of white nationhood" (Swan 209). This study traces these inter-American flows through the lens of soul.

Afro-Latin Soul: Concepts, Pioneers, Protagonists

Mapping the emergence of youth movements and hybrid styles that resulted from cross-cultural dialogues between African Americans, Afro-Latin Americans, and Caribbean migrants in the soul era, this investigation focuses on three geographically, culturally, and linguistically distant sites whose Afro-diasporic histories are interwoven through migration processes and the mobility of cultural products and political ideas: New York, Panama, and Rio de Janeiro.

As a center of "hemispheric transculturation" (Lao-Montes and Davila 18) and crucial contact zone between African Americans and migrants from Latin America and the Caribbean, New York's intercultural environment was the logical site for the initial spark that led to the first Afro-Latin American adaptations of R&B and soul music with recordings such as Mongo Santamaría's "Watermelon Man" and Ray Barretto's "El Watusi", both released in 1963. In the mid-to-late 1960s, Nuyorican musicians like Joe Cuba, Johnny Colón, and Pete Rodriguez answered the growing demand for a fusion of Afro-Cuban styles with the dynamic sounds of soul with a new crossover sound promoted as *Latin boogaloo* or *Latin soul*, upsetting the established order of the traditional New York Latin music scene. While the boogaloo era only lasted from 1966 to 1969, the term Latin soul encompasses a broader phenomenon, as Juan Flores, whose groundbreaking work was a key inspiration for this study, argues: "Latin soul ... understood expansively as all intersections of 'Latin' and African American vernacular musical styles, boasts a long tradition ranging back to earlier in the twentieth century and proceeding to the present... [and] is ultimately expressive of the social interactions between US Latinos and African Americans in the New York setting" (*Salsa Rising* 150–151).

While the role of New York as a starting point for the soul-based dialogues between intersecting African American, Afro-Latin American and Caribbean diasporas is also discussed in detail here, this study is the first to take a look at the hemispheric dimensions of a cross-cultural dialogue that found its expression in the emergence of Latin soul (and Latin funk) scenes throughout the Caribbean, Central and South America. Whereas Latin soul is referred to here as the specific label with which a new genre was first promoted in the 1960s New York context, I propose *Afro-Latin Soul* (first used on the sleeve notes of the mentioned Joe Panama LP) as an alternative umbrella term to describe the crossover styles and movements that emerged from the sonic dialogues between African Americans, Afro-Latin Americans and Caribbean migrants in the soul era. Making sense of the interrelated emergence of soul scenes in different Afro-Latin American contexts across the region, the term Afro-Latin Soul takes into account the "decidedly non-Black – and in significant ways discursively anti-Black" (Flores and Jiménez 325) connotations of "Latino" identity constructions. The concept of Afro-Latin Soul pays tribute to the fact that many of the pioneers who set these dialogues in motion crossed the lines between soul as a signifier of U.S. blackness and *afrolatinidad* as a new identity construction, which emerged as a reaction to the denial of black identities in Latin American contexts. Thus, the notion of Afro-Latin Soul is situated in the context of recent interventions that call for the bridging of existing demarcations between African American and Afro-Latin American Studies by putting concepts from both disciplines, such as *soul* and *afrolatinidad*, into dialogue with each other, as Regina Mills and Trent Masiki proposed in a special issue of *The Black Scholar* on "Post-Soul and Afro-Latinidades" (2022).

The broader concept of Afro-Latin Soul helps to relate the New York Latin boogaloo scene to the emergence of new styles and movements in other Afro-Latin American contexts where soul music also functioned as a lingua franca of interethnic dialogues. Like Nuyoricans, the descendants of Anglophone Caribbean labor migrants in Panama had developed a similarly close relationship with U.S. black popular culture, nurtured by interactions with African American GIs who were stationed in the U.S.-controlled Canal Zone, the constant arrival of ships from the north and the large-scale migration of Afro-Panamanians to New York in the 1950s and beyond. In the late 1960s, these ties gave birth to the so-called *combos nacionales*, a range of local bands such as The Exciters, Los Soul Fantastic and The Fabulosos Festivals, which transformed Panama into the site of Central America's most vibrant soul scene in the 1960s and 1970s. Undoubtedly, one of the most significant manifestation of the popularity of U.S. black music and movements among the Afro-Latin American youth of this era was in Brazil, where, in the early to mid-1970s, the *Black Rio* movement brought together hundreds of thousands of young Afro-Brazilians at the so-called *bailes black* – popular parties organized by sound systems such as *Alma Negra, Black Power* and *Soul Grand Prix* where only imported soul music from the United States was played.

This study addresses the experiences of some of the protagonists of Afro-Latin Soul – a new generation of Afro-Latin Americans and Caribbean migrants, who, like Joe Panama and his bandmates, came of age in the "global 1960s" (Brown and Lison), when the images of the Civil Rights and Black Power movements were omnipresent in the news and the sounds of soul conquered dancefloors and airwaves. Although they lived in, and moved between, different urban settings in the Americas – the United States, the Caribbean, Central and South America – they had more in common than their mostly Afro-Latin American background and their upbringing in times of revolutionary change. As this study examines the relationship between popular music and social movements, it is no coincidence that most of its protagonists were musicians or activists in these years, in some cases both. As is argued throughout this study, they were also agents of black internationalism and cosmopolitanism: Informed by experiences of forced and voluntary migrations and intercultural encounters with other diasporic communities, many of them had developed a consciousness of belonging to a transnational community that made transcending the boundaries prescribed by nation and ethnicity a central element of their political activism and cultural productions. In the 1960s and 1970s, they were in their teens or twenties and passionate lovers of soul as one of the most popular Afro-diasporic genres of the time. In fact, the phrase "Soul music was our music," expressed in English, Spanish, or Portuguese, but always with the emphasis on "our", came up in the course of most of the interviews I conducted tracing the hemispheric routes of soul. While this book demonstrates that the initial expressions of these interethnic dialogues through soul emerged in the streets and clubs of New York, it shows that they also occurred in places like Panama and Brazil, where African American influence became similarly strong in the age of Black Power.

Very much in tune with the spirit of parallel and intersecting anti-authoritarian, anti-racist and anti-colonial youth rebellions that shaped the era, the musicians, activists, dancers, and DJs who enriched this study with their invaluable insights, were not into accepting established orders and traditions. Performers such as Joe Bataan, Benny Bonilla and Henry "Pucho" Brown from New York, Carlos Brown, Ralph Weeks and Ernie King from Panama, as well as Dr. Sidney Alma Negra, Gerson King Combo and Carlos Dafé from Brazil stood out precisely because they disrupted the essentialist expectations of the kinds of musical traditions that Afrodescendants from the Caribbean, Latin America and the USA should represent in their respective contexts. Addressing the social and political significance of Afro-Latin Soul, the study not only draws on the testimonies of performers but also of activists such as New York-based Young Lords founding members Denise Oliver and Felipe Luciano, Afro-Panamanian movement veterans Melva Lowe de Goodin, Alberto Barrow, and Gerardo Maloney as well as Afro-Brazilian community leaders Dom Filó and Carlos Alberto Medeiros who saw the potential of soul music to mobilize young people of color through identification with the African American freedom struggle. To many of these pioneers, soul music became a way to voice dissent with the status quo in societies that were shaped by diverse, often veiled, forms of anti-black racism. Their rebellious acts of boundary-crossing through engagement with African American politics and culture defied the diverging notions of what it meant to be black and Latino in the United States, the Caribbean, and Latin America.

Hemispheric Soulscapes

This hemispheric account of soul demonstrates that the inequalities caused by racism, capitalism and imperialism contributed significantly to some key factors for the development of transnational networks among Afro-diasporic communities in the Americas. Focusing on the emergence of Afro-Latin soul scenes in New York, Panama, and Rio de Janeiro, this study argues that the proliferation of soul in the inter-American context was a result of the emergence of transnational, translocal, and transcultural connections that were rooted in some of the developments that shaped hemispheric relations in the 20th century. Initially, US racism and imperialism sparked large migratory movements from the Deep South and the Caribbean, leading to encounters between African Americans and Caribbean migrants in contact zones such as New York and Panama. Against the backdrop of the global 1960s youth revolt, the transnationalization of US popular culture contributed to the spread of African American influences in geographically distant places such as Rio de Janeiro.

To analyze the appropriation of political, cultural, and aesthetic manifestations of the African American freedom struggle by Afro-Latin American youth movements through the consumption and translation of soul music, I propose the concept of *hemispheric soulscapes*. I argue that by connecting Afrodescendants in the Americas across national, cultural, ideological, and linguistic boundaries in their struggles against different forms of white supremacy, hemispheric soulscapes provided diasporic youth across the region with a common language of black assertiveness that became a significant factor in the forging of anti-racist movements and networks of solidarity. As I will show, the practices of hemispheric black transnationalism associated with the dissemination of soul represented a break with homogenizing identity discourses such as *latinidad, mestizaje* and *democracia racial* and contributed to the emergence of new notions of *afrolatinidad*.

The book interrogates the ways in which cultural goods and the political messages they conveyed could spread in culturally and linguistically contrasting contexts. What resistances to these exchange processes emerged, and how did the various forms of appropriation of soul played out in the selected sites? What was the role of soul in the emergence of local versions of Black Power? What explains the potential of soul to transcend constructed national and ethnic boundaries and shape social movements? It will be shown that the proliferation of soul and its centrality to the articulation of new Afro-diasporic identity discourses was not so much the result of common African roots, but rather an expression of the shared experience of exclusion and the quest for emancipation from white supremacy mediated through this musical genre. Thus, the book explores how soul was instrumental in creating a sense of solidarity and identification between Afrodescendants who lived in contexts where racism took very different forms. By examining the reception of the genre in different hemispheric contexts, this study aims to show how its adaptation represented a way for Afro-diasporic youth to challenge paternalistic and folkloristic identity ascriptions within the framework of "national cultures". Drawing on current debates about the mobility of Afro-diasporic movements and cultures and the varying connotations of race and blackness in the Americas, the study takes a comparative look at parallels and differences in manifestations of these hemispheric dialogues in the Black Power era, providing insights into the highly diverse forms of racial subordination and resistance strategies employed by Afro-diasporic communities in the Western hemisphere.

Drawing on the model of "scapes", introduced by Appadurai (33–36), the notion of hemispheric soulscapes intends to make sense of the flows between diverse communities, cultural products and political ideas across national and ethnic boundaries in the context of globalization. Appadurai's idea of "ethnoscapes" (33) is useful to describe the imagined networks between Afro-diasporic communities in the United States, the Caribbean, and Latin America in which the cultural transfers and translocal interactions under study take place. The "mediascape" (35) in focus here is constituted by 1960s and early 1970s soul music and the related representations of blackness. It describes the connection between different communities, sometimes far apart from each other, through the consumption of the same media products, whereby reception, interpretation, and connotation can take on different forms among different consumers. The model of "mediascapes" helps to discern the emergence of "diasporic public spheres" (ibid.) in which media products and their consumers can no longer be confined to local, regional or national units, but continuously transcend them, as also addressed in the concept of "transversal consumer cultures" (Thiess and Raab). The "flows" that emerge in this context enable the accelerated bridging of spatial and cultural boundaries, leading to an increased mutual influence of local practices and discourses in different contexts. Here, so-called "ideoscapes" (Appadurai 36) also come into play, describing the global spread of ideologies such as black (inter-) nationalism and their locally strongly divergent contexts of meaning. With the help of this model, the various forms of appropriation and translation and the associated possibility of articulating resistance against the respective hegemonic social relations that the consumption of the cultural products and political discourses entailed will be captured.

By focusing on the dissemination of soul in its musical and political significance for the popularization of "Black Power" in Latin American contexts, this study deals with a chapter of cultural globalization that has received little attention to date. It is situated within the context of Transnational American Studies (Fisher Fishkin; Fluck, Pease & Rowe; Davis) and Inter-American Studies (Kaltmeier; Raussert "Mobilizing") which provide a useful frame of reference due to their focus on capturing the mobility (Kunow) and the multidirectional transculturation processes that characterize the Americas. Of importance here is the much-discussed relationship between globalization and "Americanization" and the question of why and how US culture, black popular culture specifically, is being received in a wide variety of local contexts worldwide. In contradiction to the cultural imperialism thesis, according to which globalization (or "Americanization") produces cultural homogenization and contributes to the consolidation of the status quo, many studies underline the significant role "that African American musical forms have played in challenging hegemonic local identities, and establishing new kinds of cultural alliances between the marginalized and dispossessed in widely separated societies" (Stokes 303). Arguing in the same direction, Livio Sansone has discerned a "globalization of blackness" (1): an ongoing process of cultural transfer between highly mobile Afro-diasporic communities in which black popular culture from the U.S. occupied a prominent position as a major focus of identification. Lorgia García Peña critically reflects on the ambiguous character of this "hegemonic blackness" that is intrinsically linked to "US colonialism and cultural dominance around the world" while acknowledging that at the same time "US history and radical struggles for freedom have afforded many people a lingua franca with which to articulate and translate blackness" (237). Paul Gilroy was among the first to emphasize how knowledge of the black movement in the U.S. "was transmitted into Black ghettos and communities all over the world by Afro-American music" (*Union Jack* 171), where it functioned as a "source of cultural and political raw material" (228) for new diasporic identity constructions. The globalizing character of U.S. culture has been explained with the dominant African American influence in U.S. popular music and its rebellious potential which facilitated the identification of non-white people abroad (Reichardt). Contradicting the cultural imperialism thesis that globalization (or "Americanization") produces cultural homogenization and contributes to the consolidation of the status quo, this study contributes to research on the significant role of African American musical forms in the articulation of counter-hegemonic and oppositional identity discourses and the detachment from nationalist and ethnocentric attributions in the African diaspora and beyond.

The influence of music on social movements and ethnic identity formation associated with the "migration of sounds" (Raussert *Cornbread and Cuchifritos*) is the focus of this study on the inter-American dimensions of soul and its role in the dissemination of messages and symbolisms associated with Black Power. The existing literature on the transnational spread of African American popular culture mostly focuses on hip-hop (Mitchell) while the significance of soul as an important precursor is often mentioned only tangentially. By examining the routes of soul and the socio-political dynamics associated with the appropriation of this genre in various hemispheric contexts in the 1960s and 1970s, this study promises new insights into a period that was formative for the emergence of border-crossing flows in the Americas.

Through the concept of *hemispheric soulscapes*, this book situates soul as a central connecting element within the transnational and translocal circuits that have shaped different waves of black popular music in the 20th century. In many ways, the internationalization of soul built on preexisting Afro-diasporic networks that played an important role in the emergence of jazz in the first half of the 20th century. Lara Putnam describes how circum-Caribbean migrations paved the way for the "border-crossing spread of black-identified music and dance in this era" that "reflected a different kind of black internationalism" (*Radical Moves* 4). The trajectory of Afro-Caribbean-descended Panamanian Luis Russell who became the band leader of Louis Armstrong's orchestra after migrating from Colón to New Orleans speaks to the relevance of Panama and the Caribbean in the making of jazz (Pérez Price). The genre also provided a platform for fusions with Afro-Cuban rhythms that were at the core of sonic dialogues between New York-based African American, Afro-Cuban and Puerto Rican musicians like Arsenio Rodriguez, Chano Pozo, Machito, Mario Bauzá, Tito Puente, and Dizzy Gillespie that resulted in styles such as Latin jazz and mambo (García; Moreno). Continuing these exchanges, the Latin boogaloo broke with prevailing models of Latin music traditions while at the same time providing a bridge that connected young Nuyoricans with their Afro-Latin roots in ways that gave birth to salsa as a new Pan-Caribbean genre in the early 1970s (Flores *Salsa Rising*). The increased use of Afro-Latin elements in rhythm and blues, soul and funk, described as "the latin tinge" (Storms) as well as the joint appearance of the Fania All Stars, James Brown, Bill Withers and others at the Zaire '74 festival before the "rumble in the jungle" between Muhammad Ali and George Foreman epitomized the reciprocity of cultural exchange between African American and Latin American expressions. Against the backdrop of the anti-colonial revolution that swept the African continent in the 1960s, soul and salsa also became extremely popular in urban centers like Accra, Bamako, Dakar, Kinshasa, Johannesburg, Nairobi and Lagos where influences from the African diaspora resulted in the emergence of new styles like rumba congolaise, township jive, highlife, and afrobeat. The contributions of afrobeat musician Fela Kuti who fused Black Power ideology, pan-Africanism, James Brown-style funk rhythms and local genres are most significant in this context (Stewart).

Calypso as an important platform for political commentary popularized by artists from across the Caribbean like Mighty Sparrow, Harry Belafonte, and Lord Panama in the 1950s and 1960s was also shaped by influences from U.S. black popular music from the United States and gave birth to *soca*, a term derived from the "So-ul of Ca-lypso". In the same vein, the emergence of reggae, defined as "Jamaican soul music" by Stephen Davis represented a creative appropriation of African American soul styles as shown in the earliest releases of Bob Marley and the Wailers and other reggae artist (Fared). In the 1970s, reggae itself became the focal point of a transnational Afro-diasporic culture that also contributed to to the birth of new Afro-Latin American forms such as samba reggae in northeastern Brazil and *reggae en español* in Panama, which is now recognized as the genre that gave birth to reggaetón (Rivera et. al; Rivera-Rideau; Twickel). Next to the sampling of soul and funk records, techniques of "cut'n'mix" (Hebdidge), dubbing, and "toasting" derived from Jamaican soundsystem culture were key elements in the late 1970s emergence of hip-hop as a global youth movement that resulted from the cross-cultural dialogues between African American, Jamaican and Puerto Rican youth in the South Bronx and Harlem (Rivera *New York Ricans*). Samba pioneer Pixinguinha's experiments with jazz in the fist half of the 20th century, the significant impact of soul, reggae, and hip-hop on Afro-Brazilian movements as well as the early 2000s emergence of baile funk in Rio de Janeiro underline Brazil's role as a site were genres from across the diaspora, and Black America specifically, were combined and reinvented. George Yudice has defined the ways the translation of black popular music from the United States and the Caribbean has provided Afro-Latin youth with means to articulate opposition with the local racial hierarchies as "transbarrio sampling from one subaltern group to another" (131). As the influence of Caribbean and Brazilian styles in soul, funk, and hip-hop demonstrate, hemispheric flows in the Black Americas have always been multidirectional and transversal rather than representing a mere north-south cultural homogenization.

Black Power Cosmopolitanism and Anti-Afro-Americanism in Latin America

This book addresses the interrelatedness between the emergence of Afro-Latin Soul scenes and the popularization of Black Power influences from the U.S. among Afro-Latin American youth in the 1960s and 1970s, arguing that the related creative appropriations of slogans and symbols from a different national and ethnic context constituted cosmopolitan practices. These hemispheric flows are situated in the context of the global circulation and translation of African American cultural products and discourses in the 1960s and 1970s that I propose to define as *Black Power cosmopolitanism.* This concept draws on different reinterpretations of a "cosmopolitanism from below" (Ingram; Kurusawa) such as Ifeoma Nwankwo's "black cosmopolitanism", Kwame Appiah's "rooted cosmopolitanism", Nico Slate's "colored cosmopolitanism", Nina Glick-Schiller's "diasporic cosmopolitanism", and Daphne Brook's "sonic cosmopolitanism." The concept of Black Power cosmopolitanism runs counter to conventional wisdom according to which the essentialized and U.S-centered notions of blackness associated with Black Power seem to be antithetical to the universalist tenets of cosmopolitanism. Black Power is often portrayed as an era of retreat to ethnic particularism and nationalism and a symbol of the failure of Martin Luther King's universal dream of freedom – the "evil twin" (751) of the Civil Rights Movement, as Peniel Joseph put it. While 1960s and 1970s black cultural nationalism and Afrocentrism were indeed characterized by essentialism and racial exceptionalism, Black Power was broader and its scope neither limited to the African American community nor to the US national context. Contrary to one-dimensional readings of the movement as separatist, the manifestations of black-brown solidarity, interethnic coalition-building and hemispheric dialogues addressed in this book demonstrate that the Black Power movement transcended narrow ethnic nationalisms. Importantly, Black Power provided other marginalized communities in the U.S. and abroad with powerful symbols of resistance and self-affirmation in their local struggles for emancipation. Thus, Black Power cosmopolitanism conceptualizes how activists, musicians, and intellectuals throughout the African diaspora confronted the exclusionary and repressive character of the nation-states they lived in by selectively adopting elements of Black Power ideology from the U.S. in their search for models of identification and allies beyond the nation. Situated within the context of research on the role of African American forms in the making of a black global culture, this study interrogates the hemispheric dimensions of soul as a conduit of Black Power cosmopolitanism between the mid-1960s and mid-1970s.

While the transnational dimensions of Black Power have been addressed at length in research on its interrelatedness with Third World liberation movements and the emergence of Afro-diasporic countercultures in the 1960s and 1970s (Plummer; Quinn; Slate; Swan), its impact in Latin America remains somewhat underexplored. With the exception of Brazil, where there is a growing body of studies that deal with the dialogues between Afro-Brazilian and African American intellectuals and activists (Alberto; Hanchard, Medeiros; Seigel), the significance of these interactions in other local and national contexts has been downplayed or denied altogether. As recent scholarship and activist accounts suggest, the movement did, however, have a key influence on the rise of black movements throughout the region in the 1970s and beyond (Abreu; Andrews "Black Movements;" Paschel 232 – 236; Perea; Steinitz and Raussert). The present study aims to advance ongoing efforts of mapping these pan-Afro-American dialogues in the western hemisphere.

One explanation for the underrepresentation of Black Power in research on Latin America lies in the fact that the expression of solidarity with African American struggles through the appropriation of symbolic representations of black pride by Afro-Latin American youth collided with the widespread racial exceptionalism of identity discourses such as *latinidad, mestizaje* and *democracia racial.* These discourses were based on the idea that racism was a problem exclusive to the United States, while race did not play any relevant role in the allegedly exemplary Latin American multiracial democracies (Stam and Shohat). As the militant anti-racism associated with Black Power was perceived as a serious threat to these nationalist ideologies, it is not surprising then that its advocates, both in the ruling Latin American classes and in leftist intellectual circles, received the diffusion of ideas, slogans and sounds related to the U.S. black movement with hostility. What the present study on the reception of soul in Latin America reveals is that this hostile stance, that I describe as *anti-Afro-Americanism,* claimed to be anti-imperialist but was at the same time a covert form of racism, that projected the fear of a black rebellion onto the United States.

U.S. imperialism and the related asymmetries in United States-Latin American relations played a key role in the emergence of anti-Afro-Americanism. Due to its status as a hotbed of white supremacy at home and its imperialist policies abroad, Latin American and African American radicals alike regarded the United States as a common enemy that had to be defeated in the struggle for liberation. At the same time, some of the most important impulses for the global wave of youth rebellions that shaped the 1960s and 1970s originated in U.S. counterculture and the related anti-war, students, women's, gay, and black movements. In Latin America, where the increased U.S. interference during the Cold War era led to a widely shared sentiment of anti-imperialism and anti-(US)-Americanism, elites and intellectuals often didn't make such a distinction between imperialist foreign policies and the transnational appeal of U.S.-based counterhegemonic movements. The widespread rejection of soul and other African American influences by Latin American elites and intellectuals was justified as a response to the interventionist and imperial policies with which the United States dominated the hemisphere economically, politically, and militarily since the early 20th century. Through this lens, the diffusion of U.S. counterculture as in the popularization of soul was interpreted as another element in a strategy to undermine Latin America's sovereignty. The significant role of soul and other African American genres in the formation of counter-hegemonic Afro-Latin American movements and identies was perceived as a threat and rejected as a manifestation of U.S. cultural imperialism. Leading Latin American intellectuals like the Brazilian anthropologist Gilberto Freire even saw a conspiracy to import racism and disrupt the allegedly harmonious race relations by means of a commercial campaign to sell U.S. products, in this case records (Hanchard 115). The notion of anti-Afro-Americanism makes sense of how the racial implications of the demonization of soul and Black Power (the fear that Afro-Latin American communities might be incited by the subversive potential of these influences), were often disguised as anti-imperialism with nationalist rhetoric.

By tracing the hostile attitudes toward soul through analysis of the debates on national culture, authenticity and identity the genre sparked in the three contexts considered, this book provides insights into how the interplay of nationalism and racism has manifested itself in similar patterns of anti-Afro-Americanism in different Latin American contexts. Puerto Rican traditionalists and elites condemned the ways in which Nuyorican youth adopted the symbols, slogans, and sounds of African Americans as manifested in Latin boogaloo and the politics of the Young Lords because these expressions "violated the bounds that kept distinct what was Black and what was Latino" (Rivera 244). Similarly, the descendants of the Afro-Caribbean migrants who had built the Panama Canal challenged the self-image of Panama as a homogenous, Hispanic nation with their appropriation of African American soul styles that became a defining feature of the *combos nacionales.* In 1970s Brazil, a right-wing military regime feared that the Black Rio movement might inspire Afro-Brazilians to follow the example of black radicals from the United States and threaten national security. Here, as in other parts of Latin America, left-wing anti-imperialists were also part of this unlikely alliance against soul music and other manifestations of Black Power that would contaminate "authentic" national cultures and imperil harmonious race relations, as they feared. Black Power cosmopolitans such as the Afro-Latin soul musicians, DJs, and activists featured in this book, challenged these paternalistic and nationalist visons of popular culture in Latin America.

Black Internationalism and Hemispheric Migrations

Black Power and its hemispheric dissemination through soul music were deeply rooted in the practice of black internationalism. The transmission of liberation discourses through the consumption and appropriation of popular music that this study addresses is part and parcel of what Cedric Robinson has defined as the *black radical tradition:* a series of transnational and interrelated struggles for the emancipation of Afrodescendants in the Americas that date back to manifestations of slave resistance such as the Haiti Revolution, maroon societies, *palenques* and *quilombos,* and find its 20th century expressions in movements such as Pan-Africanism, *negritude,* and Black Power (Robinson). Although largely ignored in literature on world-history and social movements, black internationalism played a crucial role in global emancipation struggles and operated on a global scale centuries before "globalization" was declared a new phenomenon (West and Martin 2). Emphasizing the key role of black migrations, Brent Hayes Edwards defined black internationalism "as the imagination of a black international community" (243) that resulted from increased crossings of spatial and linguistic boundaries and a renewed skepticism of nation-states and nationalisms as points of reference after the disastrous world wars and the exclusion of Afrodescendants from Western national projects. Edwards argues that black internationalism was forged first and foremost by the ways Afro-diasporic intellectuals were "forced by the pressure of the times" to cross boundaries: "black radicalism necessarily emerges through boundary crossing—black radicalism is an internationalization" (243). Following this argument, it is no coincidence that the first decades of the 20th century, when world-historical developments such as an intensified imperialism of European empires and the emergence of the United States as a rising regional power, decolonization, and two world wars set in motion massive waves of migration, saw a significant rise in black internationalist activism. As Michael O. West and William G. Martin argue in their account of the making of a "Black International" in the early 20th century: "Everywhere, African peoples were crossing boundaries – regional, and provincial, national and imperial, continental and oceanic – on a scale unseen since the end of the Atlantic slave trade" (9). In the Americas, U.S. racism and imperialism as well as parallel "waves of decolonization" (D.L. Brown) propelled various black migrations that converged in locales such as New York City and Panma, converting these urban centers in hubs of the "Black International" and setting the stage for the intra-diasporic encounters that enabled the hemispheric spread of soul in the 1960s.

Starting in the early 20th century, New York became the main destination of parallel migration waves. Millions of African Americans, pushed by the persistence of racial subjugation and Jim Crow segregation in the Deep South, headed to the urban centers of the North in what is commonly referred to as the Great Migration. At the same time both, the British and the Hispanic Caribbean were the origins of other Great Migrations, also mainly black. Their main causes lay in the demise of the sugar industry in the 19th century and the accelerated push of the United States to replace the British and Spanish empires as dominant regional forces in the Caribbean and join the circle of European imperialist powers in their quest for global hegemony. The Spanish-American War of 1898 not only represented the first major first step of the U.S. on its path to empire, it also marked the beginning of a long history of migration to the United States by residents of the islands of Cuba and Puerto Rico, which became a U.S. colony as a consequence of the war. After 1917, when the Jones-Shafroth Act granted Puerto Ricans limited U.S. citizenship migration towards New York increased significantly. Simultaneously, large numbers of Anglophone Caribbean labor migrants also gravitated to New York where they initially settled in neighborhoods inhabited by African Americans. Thus, New York became a center of "hemispheric transculturation" (Laó-Montes and Dávila) where "immigrants encountered American blacks, creating in the encounter what has been called a transgeographical America" (786), as Earl Lewis put it in his influential essay on "overlapping diasporas". Hinting at the fact that a quarter of Harlem's population was of West Indian origin in the mid-1920s, Jason Parker argues that the convergence of "war, empire, race, and decolonization" turned Harlem into a a key node of the African diaspora in the Western Hemisphere that shaped 20th century black culture, politics, and protest significantly (98–99, 113). The protagonism of Caribbean immigrants and black internationalists who lived in or passed through New York illustrate both the role of the Caribbean as a region which "is produced by and produces a series of global transformative movements" (Boyce-Davies and Nixon 1) and the role of New York as a site for the emergence of intersections and dialogues between African Americans and Afrodescendants from other hemispheric contexts (Valdés; Meehan; Stephens; Guridy).

Late 19th and early 20th century labor migration from the British West Indies to Central America was similarly crucial for the emergence of a circum-Caribbean migratory sphere that connected Harlem with Kingston, Havana, Puerto Limón, Caracas, Port-of-Spain, and Colón, as outlined by Lara Putnam in *Radical Moves*. Driven by poor economic conditions in their home islands, thousands of Afro-Caribbean sojourners were recruited by the United Fruit Company which had acquired vast banana plantations in countries such Costa Rica, Guatemala, Nicaragua and Panama and relied on the readiness of the U.S. government to use military power to secure its trade interests in the respective countries. Again, U.S. imperialism, in the case of Central America also known as "big stick diplomacy," was an essential factor in the circular migrations that ensured the emergence of contact zones between Afro-descendants from the Caribbean, Latin America and the United States. The transnational activism of Marcus Garvey's UNIA in Harlem, Jamaica, Cuba, Puerto Rico, and Central American countries with Anglophone Afro-Caribbean migrant communities like Costa Rica and Panama represented a crucial step in the creation of a hemispheric sense of blackness upon which the regional spread of Black Power several decades later was built (Putnam "Nothing Matters").

By far the most consequential step in the U.S. assertion of regional hegemony over the Western Hemisphere was the decision of President Theodore Roosevelt to build the Panama Canal at the dawn of the 20th century. The megaproject, which created a navigable passage between the Caribbean and the Pacific and was carried out between 1904 and 1914, was made possible by the recruitment of 150.000 to 200.000 labor migrants of from the Caribbean, the majority of them from Jamaica and Barbados, who took charge of the most dangerous and demanding parts of the construction. This "most important modern migration of African descendants within Spanish America and the Caribbean" (Duke 75) and the subsequent settlement of Afro-Caribbean sojourners turned the U.S.-controlled Canal Zone and the surrounding Panamanian republic in another contact zone, where Afro-descendants from different hemispheric sites encountered and conflicting modes of racialization such as U.S. black-white dichotomy and Latin American *mestizaje* collided. Due to its location at the Caribbean gateway to the Panama Canal, it was especially the port city Colón which became a hub of black cosmopolitanism in the first half of the 20th century. A diverse black migrant population and the constant flow of incoming ships from the United States and the Caribbean created an environment shaped by border-crossing awareness of international developments related to matters of racial discrimination and black mobilizations. With *Panama in Black – Afro-Caribbean World Making in the Twentieth Century*, Kaysha Corinealdi has provided an insightful analysis of how translocal connections between Panama and New York became particularly strong as many Afro-Caribbean Panamanians continued their migratiory circuits from Panama to the United States. Colón's role as a key stronghold for Marcus Garvey's UNIA, visits by African American leaders such as Paul Robeson, the involvement of Afro-Caribbean *colonenses* such as writer Eric Walrond in the Harlem Renaissance and, as in the case of Louis Armstrong's bandleader Luis Russell, in the emergence of jazz, all speak to the city's status as an important, though often overlooked, site of the "Black International."

Building on the hemispheric imaginaries and networks that had emerged in the wake of migration waves in the first half of the 20th century, the traffic of ideas and sounds between New York and Panama was especially intense in the 1960s, when the interactions between the Anglophone Afro-Caribbean community and black GIs stationed in the Canal Zone – facilitated by the absence of linguistic barriers, the shared experience of racial discrimination, and the diffusion of black popular music from the U.S. – made sure that Black Power discourses arrived more quickly and directly than they did in other parts of Afro-Latin America. U.S.-inspired expressions of black consciousness in politics, culture, and soul music were an important source of information for the bourgeoning black movement in Panama and a main point of reference in the efforts of activists and writers like Carlos Russell, Gerardo Maloney, Melva Lowe de Goodin, Carlos Guillermo Wilson, Alberto Barrow and Alberto Smith to dismantle the widespread racism and anti-West Indian xenophobia in Panamanian society (Steinitz "Hemispheric Ambassador").

Soul Music in Transnational, and Hemispheric Perspectives

Based on an understanding of the political and cultural significance of soul for the African American freedom struggle in the United States, it is the purpose of this study to situate soul in the transnational context of popular music in the African diaspora and to generate insights for its hemispheric dimensions. Because of soul music's inherent transgression of the boundaries between nations, cultural expression and political manifestation, it has been described as a "dissident form of black expressive culture" and "diasporic black cultural practice" (Wald 147). Starting from the assumption that black music as a "source of empowerment, education, and "consciousness raising" (Eyerson and Jamison 78) that has often displayed an "emancipatory potential" (97), the analysis of soul as a platform for cultural resistance in the African diaspora builds on scholarship on the interrelatedness of black popular music and social movements. In *Freedom Dreams: The Black Radical Imagination,* Robin D.G. Kelley holds that black music "helped generate community pride, challenged racial self-hatred and built self-respect" by creating "a world of pleasure [...] to escape the everyday brutalities of capitalism, patriarchy, and white supremacy" (11–12). Angela Davis' observation that black music was instrumental in creating an "aesthetic community of resistance, which in turn encouraged and nurtured a political community of active struggle for freedom" (201) is of particular interest when addressing the role of soul music for the internationalization of the black freedom struggle.

The creative appropriation of soul in Afro-Latin contexts in the 1960s and 1970s is part of a broader phenomenon in which musical expressions accompanied, and often encouraged, struggles against oppression in the African diaspora from the days of slavery until the 21st century. While soul and other Afro-diasporic genres such as hip-hop and reggae reflected specific socio–political realities and consumer tastes in the local contexts of their origin, it was their mobility, their outstanding ability to transcend geographical and cultural boundaries that made them conduits of transnational movements and the articulation of new identity constructions (Raussert and Habell-Pallán; Steinitz and Suárez Ontaneda). Hinting at the connections between the mobility of sounds and movements as a distinct feature of black internationalist struggles, Shana Redmond has described collective music consumption in the African diaspora as "a method of rebellion" and participation within border-crossing liberation projects that is "strategically employed to develop identification between people who otherwise may be culturally, ideologically, or spatially separate or distinct from one another" (1–2). The emergence of soul as Black Power's most effective message carrier that provided marginalized communities abroad with powerful symbols of resistance and self-affirmation speaks to the primordial role of African American forms in the making of a black global culture.

Throughout the Western Hemisphere, the histories of movements, migrations, and new ethnic identity constructions are reflected in a great variety of popular music genres. In their assessment of the interrelationship between music and social movements in the Americas, Kaltmeier and Raussert argue that "music as medium for narrating the social" (2) has enhanced the emergence of inter-American imaginaries of protest. Despite the divergences between the various contexts, related to different forms of colonial domination and contrasting manifestations of racism and anti-racism, black popular music genres in the Americas converge in their function as platforms of anti-racist expression and resistance, but also as objects of folklorization, state co-optation and commercialization.

The diffusion and creative appropriation of musical genres across national, cultural and linguistic barriers has also been essential to the development of practices of black transnationalism that have been shaped by dialogues between diverse Afro-diasporic communities. The interrelated mobility of discourses and musical genres, closely linked to the expansion of the music industry and migration flows between the Caribbean, Latin America and the United States, is one of the characteristics of "traveling sounds" (Raussert and Miller Jones) in the Americas that challenge essentialist claims of their "purity" and "authenticity". Musical forms widely known as exclusively "black", "Caribbean" or "Latin" have been the product of cross-cultural interactions between Afro-diasporic communities in urban centers such as Colón, Havana, San Juan, Kingston, Rio de Janeiro, Salvador de Bahia, New Orleans and New York.

Studies on the transnational dimensions of soul have received crucial impulses by the pioneering contributions of Paul Gilroy. In *Ain't No Black in the Union Jack* he pointed out as early as 1987 that conscious soul songs like "Say It Loud" by James Brown "were all taken to the heart of black communities many miles from those in which they were created" (177). While the role of soul as a key factor in the making of a diasporic counterculture is acknowledged, there are only very few explicit references to the genre in his most important work, *The Black Atlantic*. Other scholars have taken Gilroy's cues and provided important insights into the importance of soul as a platform for black engagements with modernity in local contexts across the Atlantic world. Stressing the importance of the symbolic and aesthetic representations of blackness transported through the genre, these contributions reveal how "soul provided a cultural language through which people of African descent could speak about the horrors of slavery and colonialism while also serving as a source of cultural pride and political solidarity" (6), as Tanisha Ford has it. With *Liberated Threads – Black Women, Style, and the Global Politics of Soul*, a multi-sited study on the "liberatory potential of soul style" in London, New York

City, and Johannesburg, she contributed a rich analysis of how "a hip, chic urban soul culture" (3) served to "construct an aesthetic, political, and sonic representation of modern blackness" (10) throughout the African diaspora. In his account of James Brown's impact on local youth in 1960s Bamako, Manthia Diawara analyzes how African American soul culture became the major resource in the emergence of a "diaspora aesthetic" and the assumption of a new identity that was "secular and cosmopolitan", as it "united black youth through a common habitus of black pride, civil rights and self-determination" beyond national boundaries and the constraints of post-independence nationalism and anti-imperialism (253–254) In these and other studies, it becomes clear that soul was so attractive to black youth, activists, and musicians beyond U.S. borders primarily because it offered a way to break with traditionalist, folkloric, and nationalist notions of what black popular culture should and should not represent in various regional and national contexts.

Whereas the transnational dimensions of soul music and culture are specifically addressed in several studies with a focus on the relationships between Black America, Africa, the Anglophone Caribbean and its diasporas in Great Britain, research on the impact of African American popular culture in Afro-Latin American contexts mostly highlights the hemispheric dimensions of hip-hop as a key factor in the making of new Afro-diasporic identities across the region (Castillo-Garsow and Nichols; Saunders; Roth). Studies which deal with the key role of soul for the emergence of African American – Afro-Latino alliances in the Black Power era as important forerunner to the inter-American dissemination of hip-hop are, however, scarce and limited to specific local contexts. Centering Latin soul-boogaloo as an important precursor to salsa, Juan Flores was one of the first to address the significance of soul music for cultural and political alliances between African Americans and Puerto Rican migrants, and its implications for Afro-Latin identity formation *(From Bomba)*. In the same vein, the emergence of a "brown-eyed soul" scene in Los Angeles testifies to the interracial collaborations and alliances between Chicanas/os and African Americans in the 1960s and 1970s, as Luis Alvarez and David Widener point out. The ways these engagements with U.S. soul culture reverberated throughout the Hispanic Caribbean and Latin America in the 1960s and 1970s despite the rejection of local elites have been explored in the case of Puerto Rico where the popularization of the Afro as a symbol of Black empowerment among Afro-Puerto Ricans constituted a "direct affront to the island's racist ideologies and practices (83) as Yeidy Rivero put it. Whereas research on soul in Spanish-speaking contexts remains scarce, the number of studies on the Black Rio movement and the significance of soul and Black Power for the Brazil's *movimento negro* and the deconstruction of the myth of *democracia racial* has steadily increased since the pioneering studies of Michael Hanchard (1994) and Paulina Alberto (2009). More recent publications by Brazilian researchers speak to the continued relevance of the topic in academic debates on the meaning of international influences for Afro-Brazilian articulations (Sebadelhe and Peixoto; Diniz; Pedretti). Despite of these important contributions a comprehensive study on the inter-American diffusion of soul that takes a comparative look at its manifestations in different contexts not as isolated local phenomena, but as part of a movement relevant to the entire hemisphere, is still missing.

Questions, Gaps, and Limitations

The study addresses the question of how the circulation of soul music within a pan-Afro-American diasporic sphere that connected New York with Panama and Rio de Janeiro contributed to the emergence of antiracist mobilizations and new concepts of *afrolatinidad* in the age of Black Power (1965–1975). Building on existing scholarship on the meanings of soul in the United States and transnationally, this study interrogates how the emergence of translocal soul scenes in hemispheric urban settings, has shaped the forging of networks of solidarity between migrants from the Caribbean, Afro-Latin Americans and African Americans. While the crucial role of soul and Black Power as a source of inspiration for Afro-Latin American movements has been mentioned in overviews on the topic (Andrews 172; Guridy and Hooker 208–209; Paschel 232–233) and case studies on Brazil (Alberto; Hanchard *Orpheus;* Pedretti; Pereira; Vianna), it has not been addressed in a monograph from a hemispheric perspective.

Following the traces of soul music beyond the black community in the United States, this study addresses an understudied aspect of Afro-diasporic and inter-American flows that has not yet received sufficient attention given its importance in the emergence of new forms of cultural and political expression throughout the Black Americas. Whereas the relationship between the global circulation of soul music and the transnationalization of the black freedom struggle has been explored in African and Anglo-Caribbean diasporic contexts, its hemispheric dimensions in relation to Afro-Latin America have, with a few exceptions, remained a tangential reference in studies on popular music and social movements in the African diaspora. Considering that the popularization of soul and Black Power in Afro-Latin American settings preceded and, in many ways, heralded the diffusion of genres such as reggae, salsa, and hip-hop as important platforms for black articulations in Latin America from the late 1970s to the present, it seems a worthwhile endeavor to address these gaps. By doing so, the book contributes to ongoing efforts to overcome different exceptionalisms in African American and Latin American Studies that have manifested itself in "methodological nationalism" (Anthias; Glick Schiller "Beyond the Nation-State") in research on Afro-diasporic movements in the United States and Latin America. While African American Studies has often reproduced existing power dynamics by privileging the U.S. experience over other Afro-diasporic perspectives, it has become apparent that hemispheric approaches have also been rejected by many Latin Americanists who saw them as manifestations of the neocolonial patterns of domination and cultural imperialism that have long characterized the relationship between the U.S. and Latin America. Bridging demarcations between African American, Caribbean and Latin American Studies toward the advancement of Hemispheric Black Studies constitutes a main objective of my research.

While soul and the related symbolic representations of black pride are often considered manifestations of the quintessential African American experience in the U.S. context, I argue that a hemispheric perspective is necessary to detect how the meanings of soul music and culture have varied across the Americas. As will be shown throughout the study, a transnational and hemispheric approach is crucial for a full understanding of the manifold entanglements of Afro-descendant communities in the Caribbean, North and Latin America, that have been shaped by imperial U.S. policies and diverse racial regimes as well as cross-cultural dialogues, enabled through continued waves of migration and the mobility of cultural products. Aiming to complicate homogenizing and essentialist narratives of blackness and the prescribed meanings of black popular culture, this inter-American lens allows for insights into how the symbolic language provided by transnational soul culture offered young Afro-Latin Americans a model of diasporic identification as an attractive alternative to the exclusion and marginalization they experienced as Afrodescendants and/or immigrants in Latin America and the United States.

Whereas the translation of soul to Afro-Latin contexts as manifested in Latin boogaloo and Black Rio has been addressed in several case studies, the impact of the genre in Panama remains largely unexplored in scholarly texts. Studies on different dimensions of transnational community making between New York and Panama (Corinealdi) and the role of popular music in these processes (Putnam) have advanced our knowledge on how internationalism became a key strategy in the struggles of Panama's West Indian community against diverse forms of racism in the Canal Zone and the Panamanian republic. The question how these dynamics and the interrelations with African American politics and culture played out in Afro-Panamanian popular music and movements of the 1960s and 1970s has, however, only been addressed in a single article published in the context of this research project (Steinitz "Soulful Sancocho"). Generating new findings on the widespread reception of soul among Afro-Panamanians, the rise of the *combos nacionales* and its importance to the dissemination of Black Power discourses in this country constitutes a key desideratum of this study. Whereas the case of

New York is also addressed in detail, the Black Rio movement rather serves as an important comparative reference for further conclusions about the hemispheric significance of the genre. Thus, for the first time, different Afro-Latin soul scenes that so far have only been addressed locally, or not at all, will be analyzed from a hemispheric and translocal perspective which allows for the identification of unexplored differences, parallels, connections and intriguing intersections. As the trajectories of translocal actors such as Ralph Weeks, Joe Bataan, and Toni Tornado show, this becomes especially apparent in the mobilities and collaborations between Panamanian, Nuyorican, Afro-Brazilian, and African American musicians and activists to whom the language of soul became instrumental in the creation of hybrid styles and the forging of new alliances in the 1960s and 1970s.

This study also has serious limitations, specifically regarding the aspect of gender, which manifests itself in the underrepresentation of women throughout the following pages. The heavy preponderance of men in the scenes and movements discussed here, as well as among those interviewed for this study, is related to an important finding of these comparative studies. Although women participated in the evolving soul cultures as listeners, dancers and background singers, the examined scenes in all three locations were strictly male-dominated. While machismo, sexism, and patriarchy were also recurrent tropes in U.S. soul productions there is, however, a striking difference regarding the Latin American and Caribbean contexts. In the United States, female soul singers such as Nina Simone, Aretha Franklin, Gladys Knight, Roberta Flack, Diana Ross and many others were at the forefront of the genre, often challenging the prevalent sexism of male artists overtly. In Afro-Latin Soul, on the other hand, with the exception of very few recordings by La Lupe, there was no female artist who achieved a comparable degree of visibility. Accordingly, and despite my insistence, it was unfortunately not possible to find female performers of the genre, let alone interview them. The situation was different with the activists, where women already played an important role at that time, although the movements they participated in were, as in the USA, dominated by men. Thus, it was possible to take into account the insights of several female activists who, like Denise Oliver, Melva Lowe, and Selvia Miller played important roles in their movements. A further inquiry of women's agency in the 1960s and 1970s soul scenes and black movements that emerged across Latin America would be a significant and promising contribution for a better understanding of the era.

Motivations and Resources

The primary motivation for embarking on this project is related to my passion for soul music, to which I started to devote a lot of temporal (and financial) resources as a vinyl record collector long before entering academia. Unlike my friends who were more into punk, reggae and hip-hop, soul was an important source of inspiration for me already as a teenager when we were confronted with a strong rise of racism, nationalism and attacks by neo-Nazi groups in 1990s East Berlin. In 2002, I started to DJ under the label Black Atlantic Beatz, inspired by the lecture of Paul Gilroy's book. From the beginning I was interested not only in the music as such, but also in the social conditions these sounds reflected and the political movements they inspired and that were inspired by them. This interest intensified when I realized, during stays in Latin America, that soul music from the USA was an important resource for the emergence of new hybrid genres and anti-racist movements across the African diaspora. In the course of many hours spent in local record shops and journeys abroad, I created a personal archive of about 2000 soul, funk, afrobeat, highlife, Latin boogaloo, salsa, cumbia, samba, calypso, reggae, and hip-hop LPs and singles. These vinyl records represent the starting point and one of the most important resources for this study. In this sense, this study represents an attempt at "DJ scholarship" – a term coined by DJ Lynnée Denise to describe a "mix-mode research practice" in which DJs "assess, collect, organize, and provide access to music determined to have long-term value," using their record collections as historical archives (64).

In light of the scarcity of scholarly texts on the subject matter, I owe many of the things I learned about local music scenes in New York, Rio and Panama before travelling to the sites, to compilations such as *Latin Soul – New York Barrio Grooves 1966–1972* and *The NuYorican Funk Experience* (Nascente), *Latin Breakbeats, Basslines & Boogaloo* (Harmless), *Samba Soul 70!* (Ziriguiboom), *Black Rio – Brazil Soul Power 1971–1980* (Strut) and *Panama! Latin, Calypso and Funk on the Isthmus 1965–75* (Soundway). These records came with highly informative booklets and liner-notes crafted by dedicated compilers like Roberto Ernesto Gyemant, whose *Panama!* series first directed my attention to the *combos nacionales* and provided me with valuable background information on bands and labels. During my research stay in Colón, I met the DJ Noel Jones who ran a daily radio show in the 1960s and 1970s and granted me access to his rich record collection composed of *combos nacionales* releases from local Panamanian labels as Sally Ruth, Taboga, Loyola and Tamayo as well as imported soul and salsa records from U.S. labels as Motown, Stax, Chess, Atlantic, King, and Fania, giving insights into the eclectic and heterogeneous mixture of sounds that dominated Panama's airwaves in the era. My archive was significantly expanded by the acquisition of these and other records during my research stays in Panama, New York and Brazil, which allowed me to base my investigation on the original releases of vinyl records that were the primary medium for the transnational dissemination of soul. Since song lyrics and album covers played a key role in conveying the messages and images of Black Power, their analysis is an important aspect of my methodology. In addition to the purchased records, journals, newspapers, flyers, and advertisements from the period that I found in the archives of *Biblioteca Nacional de Panamá Ernesto J. Castillero* and *Museo Afro-Antillano* in Panama, Center For Puerto Rican Studies Library at Hunter College and the Schomburg Center for Research in Black Culture in Harlem were also taken into account.

Oral history interviews represent the most important source on which my study is based. During my field research, I conducted 62 semi-structured narrative interviews (not all of which could be taken into account here). My informants were mostly black musicians, DJs, activists, artists and intellectuals born between the early 1930s and 1950s, meaning that they were contemporary witnesses who had first-hand knowledge of the 1966–1976 time period under consideration here. The following questions guided my conversations with all of the interviewees: What were your first experiences with racism? What do you recall as being your first contact with African American culture and politics? How did you learn about the Civil Rights and Black Power movements? When did you first listen to soul music? What did it mean to you? In which ways did soul music and news from the African American freedom struggle change your attitude as a black person/an immigrant in a society dominated by whites? Do you recall instances in which listening to soul or showing symbols of Black Power such as the Afro resulted in discrimination or repression?

Methodology

The transgression of national, regional and ethnic divides under investigation here is also reflected in the methodology of this study. A combination of different methodological approaches will be used to conceptualize the mobility of cultural practices, identity discourses, and actors. The "multi-sited ethnography" approach introduced by George Marcus (1995) is particularly useful for the comparative study of the spread of a cultural phenomenon in different contexts. According to the principle of "follow the thing" (106), soul as a cultural practice and a concept is first analyzed in the context of its origin, the African American community in the U.S., to then follow its paths of diffusion, forms of reception and appropriation in Spanish Harlem, Panama, and Rio de Janeiro as the "sites" chosen for this investigation. True to Marcus's motto "follow the metaphor" (108), which also describes the search for traces of the circulation of signs, symbols, and discourses in different contexts, the project is also concerned with the dissemination of political messages and symbolic representations associated with Black Power, such as Afro hairstyles. To discern the ways linguistic barriers between the "sites" were bridged, visual and aesthetic expressions of Black Power conveyed through record covers, posters, photographs, and news clippings will be taken into consideration. The motto "follow the people" (106) also comes into play here, as an examination of the impact of travel and migration experiences on Afro-Latin American musicians and activists is of salient importance to the hemispheric and multidirectional dialogues addressed here. Based on an actor-centered approach the oral history interviews serve to reconstruct biographic trajectories central to the hemispheric spread of soul.

The multi-sited ethnography approach is combined here with the "scapes" model proposed by Appadurai (2000), which is the main source for the concept of *hemispheric soulscapes* proposed in this study. It allows for an identification of the "flows" through which the different "sites" and translocal actors are connected. Of importance here are "ethnoscapes," "mediascapes," and "ideoscapes" conceived as distinct spheres of life and how they intersect. Thus, cultural phenomena interconnected by "transversal flows" at different "sites" (Marcus) and within different intersecting "scapes" (Appadurai), caused by cultural globalization and migration, will be related to each other.

Crucial in this context is the further development of transnational approaches by adopting a *translocal* perspective, which places the analytical focus on the interactions between local contexts and thus provides an important frame of reference for the analysis of the significance of different urban spaces as sites of emergence of post-national identity constructions aimed at here (Freitag and Von Oppen). This project will examine the importance of "local-to-local relations" (Smith and Guarnizo) for the hemispheric circulation of soul and Black Power discourses between different sites of hemispheric transculturation, exploring how immigrants contributed to the emergence of translocal networks and the multidirectional flows of cultural practices and political discourses in the Americas. The study will focus on the importance of music as a key form of communication in the "transbarrio" dialogues (Yudice) that evolved between African American and Latin American contexts.

Since the analysis of the relationship between the proliferation of music and the formation of social movements is at the intersection of cultural studies, sociology, political science, and history, an interdisciplinary approach is proposed here. In particular, the envisaged investigation of the social and political implications of music production and consumption in the past requires the combination of research methods from cultural studies and history. This means that both documentary interviews with actors in the sense of an oral history approach as well as textual analyses of the archival material and analyses of the relevant discourses and ideologies are to be conducted.

In terms of a comprehensive analysis of this historical chapter in the dissemination of popular music, several dimensions will be examined: the role of musicians as essential actors; the discourses disseminated through the texts and aesthetic representations; the controversial debates on the meanings of "authentic" national culture triggered by the impact of "foreign" soul on Afro-Latino youth and the social practices of consuming soul (Storey). The focus is on how music can contribute to the translation of identity concepts into other local contexts. To examine the forms of resistance to racist hierarchies and paternalistic identity ascriptions that accompany the appropriation of soul, I draw on the concept of "contingent resistances" (Saukko), which focuses on the question of the specific effects of forms of resistance in particular local contexts and their relation to other places and developments. In this sense, this paper will analyze the forms of inequality and discrimination that were challenged by the appropriation of African American cultural practices and political messages in Latin American contexts in the 1960s and 1970s.

The Chapters

The first chapter, "Theorizing Hemispheric Black Transnationalism", outlines the main theoretical approaches, concepts, and debates that have guided this study and within which it is situated. Arguing that studies of the Afro-diasporic presence in the Americas are rooted in struggles for black liberation and have functioned as a site of dialogue on the contested relationship between race and nation that has shaped Afro-diasporic movements, the chapter traces the transnational turn in African American Studies. Centrally, it is about how the overcoming of nation-based approaches has enabled the development of new visions and concepts in African Diaspora Studies. Since black nationalism was the most important ideology of the Black Power movement, whose transnational dissemination is at issue here, particular attention is paid to the debate over its dual character as a tool of liberation and as an essentialist constraint triggered by Paul Gilroy's *Black Atlantic*. It is argued that transnational and hemispheric approaches from Afro-Latin American Studies and Inter-American Studies and concepts such as Black Cosmopolitanism and *afrolatinidad* are necessary to do justice to the complex realities of Afrodescendants in the Americas and the convergences and divergences that exist between them beyond the nation. Taking the widely held perception that soul music was the soundtrack of the Black Power movement as a point of departure, the second chapter discusses the meanings of soul music for the African American freedom struggle and its relationship with black nationalism. The diverging interpretations of the genre from black cultural nationalists and Black Arts Movement activists, who saw soul as the ultimate expression of the African American experience and celebrated artists like James Brown as the voice of black self-determination and masculinity, is contrasted with the visions of revolutionary black (inter-)nationalists like the Black Panthers who claimed soul to be the music of the proletarian masses and used it as a tool to mobilize an increasingly militant ghetto youth in their struggle against racism and capitalism. Challenging notions that reduce soul to the masculinist and essentialist tendencies within the Black Power movement, the pivotal role of soul as a site of female empowerment and universalist ideals of freedom and humanity is also discussed here. Chapter 3, 4 and 5 address the genesis and particularities in the emergence of Afro-Latin soul scenes in the contexts of New York, Panama and Rio de Janeiro as a result of diverse forms of interaction with U.S. black culture, resulting from and leading to increasing identification with the African American freedom struggle in the 1960s and 1970s. Based on interviews with musicians and activists, all three contexts demonstrate how U.S. imperial policies, migration processes, and the mobility of U.S. popular culture contributed to the emergence of urban contact zones in which soul functioned as a platform for the exchange of symbols and slogans that had empowering potential for diverse communities in their struggles for recognition and self-determination. Analyzing debates on national cultures and popular music in the three contexts considered, Chapter 6 discusses how and why the translation and appropriation of soul and the sense of connection to African American struggles conveyed through this genre was rejected by a broad alliance of nationalist and anti-imperialist elites and intellectuals – a cross-regional phenomenon defined here as anti-Afro-Americanism. In conclusion, based on the findings, it is argued that the cosmopolitan practice of appropriating Black Power symbols by ethnically, linguistically, and culturally diverse communities through soul indicates that both the genre and the movements transcend the constraints of narrow black cultural nationalism.

1 Theorizing Hemispheric Black Transnationalism

Confronted with diverse patterns of racial exclusion from national projects after emancipation from slavery in the 19th century, various generations of Afrodescendants across the Americas have searched, and found, references and allies beyond the nation. Due to its dominance in world affairs as well as the extraordinarily polarized character of its race relations, the United States have, in many aspects, become the most visible battleground of a global confrontation between the forces of white supremacy and black resistance throughout the 20th century. In view of the extreme levels to which all areas of social life in the United States have remained institutionally and individually racialized since the formal end of slavery, it doesn't come by accident that it was in this context that the most insightful analyses of racism and also some of the most bold and radical ideas for black liberation were articulated. Processes of transnationalization, fueled by the imperialist drive of the United States to become a global power, major waves of migration, decolonization, and globalization, had a a multidirectional impact which shaped the African American freedom struggle as well as creating the conditions for its global spread. The internationalist currents of Afro-diasporic political thought and cultural practice are essential for an understanding of the ways Afrodescendants from the United States, the Caribbean, and Latin America forged dialogues and connections across national, cultural, and linguistic boundaries through soul music in the 1960s and 1970s. The hurdles that had to be overcome in building these hemispheric connections are reflected both in the academic debates and in the gaps that still exist.

This study is grounded in theoretical approaches that are guided by the objective of overcoming the nationalist and essentialist tendencies in research on the African diaspora. Theories that stress the mobile and hybrid character of Afro-diasporic movements and cultures provide useful frameworks for a better understanding of the transnational and translocal flows related to the popularization of soul and Black Power in Afro-Latin American contexts this investigation is concerned with. While the transnational dimensions of the African diaspora with respect to entanglements between the United States, the Anglophone Caribbean, and Europe have been addressed, research on cultural and political exchange between Afrodescendants in the United States and Latin America has been constrained by persistent "methodological nationalisms" (Anthias; Glick Schiller) and different forms of African American and Latin American exceptionalism. Tracing efforts to overcome these limitations in academic debates on the meanings of concepts such as nationalism, internationalism, and cosmopolitanism in the African diaspora, this chapter outlines how a combination of new approaches in the fields

https://doi.org/10.1515/9783110665550-003

of African American, African Diaspora, Afro-Latin American, and Inter-American Studies provides crucial perspectives for theorizing the dissemination of soul across borders as a practice of hemispheric black transnationalism.

1.1 Transnational Turns: From Black Studies to African Diaspora Studies

The last three decades have witnessed a process of transnationalization of African American Studies. In response to the predominance of traditionalist, essentialist, and U.S.-centered tendencies in the field, research on the African American presence in the United States has gone through a significant expansion towards an increased attention for its transnational dimensions. This development was ignited by the critique of an "African American exceptionalism" (Gilroy, *Black Atlantic* 4) that manifested itself in the tendency to universalize the black experience in the United States and to ignore both its transnational entanglements and the different racial dynamics in other diasporic contexts (Hanchard, "Black Transnationalism" 141). While it is hard to overstate the impact of Gilroy's *Black Atlantic* in African American Studies and the emergence of African Diaspora Studies, his proposal to envision black communities, cultures, and movements beyond national boundaries and essentialist ideologies and as a driving force of modernity was not entirely new. Rather, the related controversies on the meanings of race and nation in the field of African American Studies were rooted in the contributions of earlier generations of black radicals who have grappled with questions of national and transnational belonging in the face of exclusionary national projects. The paradigm shifts within these debates help to make sense of the ambiguous character of black nationalism. On the one hand, it was an ideology of liberation that underpinned international movements such as Pan-Africanism and Black Power, which provided a platform for blacks in the diaspora to express their cosmopolitan sensibilities in search of models of identification beyond the nation. On the other hand, the conservative, essentialist, and traditionalist elements in currents of black nationalism, most importantly cultural nationalism and Afrocentrism, dominated African American Studies in ways that constituted a barrier to overcome in research on the global circulation of Afro-diasporic movements and cultures. Both dimensions are relevant for an understanding of how black nationalist discourses travelled through the hemispheric diffusion of soul music.

W.E.B. Du Bois was among the first to contextualize the African American freedom struggle as part of a global movement for emancipation from the intertwined realities of colonialism and white supremacy, thus formulating some of the ideas that shaped black political thought and intellectual discourse in the 20th century.

For Du Bois, overcoming racism in the U.S. was only a "local phase" in a confrontation that concerned "modern civilization" (Edwards 1–2) as a whole. The internationalist vision of Du Bois had a long-lasting influence on black liberation discourses and the study of the black presence in the United States. According to Manning Marable, the interrelated struggles of black activists on various continents expanded Du Bois' "understanding about the common grounds that people of African descent shared throughout the colonial and segregated world" and gave him "a truly global concept of what today would be termed 'Black Studies'" (2). In its promotion of liberating discourses on the African diaspora from the constraints of the nation, Gilroy's proposal to take the *Black Atlantic* as "one, single, complex unit of analysis" (15) draws on Cedric J. Robinson's *Black Marxism: The Making of the Black Radical Tradition* (1983) which emphasizes how different generations of Afro-diasporic activists, artists and writers have been connected not so much by their shared African roots but by their boundary-crossing engagement with modernity, racial capitalism, and white supremacy. Thus, it should be noted that Gilroy did not invent but rather reinterpret transnational approaches that had been a constant, though marginalized, feature of black political and academic discourses.

While the first half of the 20th century was a period of internationalization of debates in the African diaspora, the 1950s witnessed the silencing of black radical advocates of internationalism like W.E.B. Du Bois and Paul Robeson in the context of Cold War anti-Communism. At the same time, the post-Word War II era was defined by the compartmentalization of the U.S. academy in different departments of area studies. Thus, the establishment of sharply delineated fields which took the nation-state as the primary unit of analysis, resulted in the obfuscation of transnational entanglements between black liberation movements in scholarly debates, as Martin and West argue: "Exiled from the mainstream academy, black counternarratives were literally driven underground".

The emergence of Black Studies in the late 1960s and early 1970s was the result of intense struggles of African American student activists who saw education as a means for black liberation. The significance of this achievement was not only academic but also political. As the ever-increasing number of Black Studies departments throughout the United States would become key arenas for intellectual debates on the issues that united and divided the ideologically heterogeneous African American freedom struggle, their hard-fought institutionalization constituted one of the most significant and enduring legacies of the Black Power movement. It was precisely due to its historical origins in the black liberation movement that African American Studies "was often treated as the child of an illicit relationship between social struggle and the conventional disciplines" (139), as Michael Hanchard has pointed out. Given the rootedness of African American Studies in black struggles, it is not surprising that shifts in the political landscape of Black

America have also affected developments in the academic field. In the early-to-mid 1970s, "white backlash", a state-led campaign of repression against Black Power radicals (COINTELPRO), and internal divisions led to the demise of the revolutionary left wing of the Black Power movement as represented most prominently by the Black Panthers and their advocacy for cross-racial alliances, internationalism and Third World Marxism. Against the backdrop of a generalized crisis of the U.S. and global left, this development went hand in hand with the rise of a socially, politically, and culturally conservative brand of black nationalism as dominant force not only within the black movement but also in African American Studies. As Carol Boyle-Davis criticized, this sort of U.S. African American nativism and isolationism mirrored general tendencies in U.S. society and failed to see the crucial international relationships of African American without which "no one can fully study the Black experience" ("Rethinking Black Marxism").

The hegemony of black cultural nationalism and Afrocentrism in the African American public and academic spheres manifested itself in the salience of essentialized notions of blackness based on the invocation of pre-modern African traditions, patriarchal family values as a way to restore black manhood, and a vision exclusively centered on the experiences of descendants of enslaved Africans born on U.S. soil.[1] With his concept of "Afrocentricity" (1987), scholar Molefi Kete Asante intended to reconnect African Americans with their African past by tracing continuities to ancient African civilizations and traditions that had been destroyed by colonialism and the transatlantic slave trade. Interestingly, this approach was very much in line with the search of "Africanisms", "cultural survivals", and "retentions" in religion, language, music and family structures that had been dominant in traditional research on New World black cultures by white anthropologists such as Melville J. Herskovits, author of the pivotal *The Myth of the Negro Past* (1941). Heavily influenced by Franz Boas' cultural relativist school of thought, Herskovits, in close exchange with Latin American anthropologists such as Mario de Andrade, Arthur Ramos, Raymundo Nina Rodrigues, and Fernando Ortiz delineated the "new" field of research, aiming to counteract anti-black racism by celebrating the contributions of what they perceived as authentic African cultures to national projects in the Americas (Yelvington 227–228). Both, cultural relativist continuity theories in anthropology and Afrocentric discourses, treated the various new cultural and social expressions that Afrodescendants created in exchange with other cultural influences and in response to the racist environment

---

1 The ascendency of the separatist, pro-capitalist, antisemitic, and xenophobic Nation of Islam as the most influential organization among African American youth bore witness to the weakness of the black left in the 1980s and 1990s.

they lived in as a "contamination" or "loss" (18) of authentic African identity as Robin D.G. Kelley and Tiffany Patterson and noted in their influential essay on "Unfinished Migrations".

The theories that undergird this study of transnational and translocal exchange between black movements and cultures in the Western hemisphere have been articulated in sharp contrast to these traditional and essentialist approaches. Challenging prevailing concepts of authenticity, purity, tradition, and fixed identities, new directions in the study of the African diaspora have rather been guided by a concern for the agency of Afrodescendants in the historical and social processes that have shaped Western modernity, such as the rise of imperialism and capitalism, international communism, feminism, decolonization, migration, and globalization. Following a pattern in which Caribbean-descended activists and thinkers from Marcus Garvey to Stokely Carmichael gave crucial impulses to the black freedom struggle in the United States, the impact of the Caribbean-British cultural studies pioneers Stuart Hall and Paul Gilroy on developments in African American Studies was equally consequential. Whereas Hall recognized the causes and political-strategic necessities of unifying narratives of blackness in the international struggle against colonialism and racism as manifested in Négritude, Pan-Africanism, and Black Power in his groundbreaking essay "Cultural Identity and Diaspora", he emphasized the need to acknowledge the ruptures and discontinuities that shape diasporic identity formation: "Cultural identities [...], like everything which is historical, [...] undergo constant transformation. Far from being eternally fixed in some essentialised past, they are subject to the continuous 'play' of history, culture, and power" (225). According to Hall, the African diaspora "is defined, not by essence or purity, but by the recognition of a necessary heterogeneity and diversity; by a conception of 'identity', which lives with and through, not despite, difference; by *hybridity*" (235). The concept of hybrid diasporas and the related emphasis on the modern, transnational, and mobile character of black cultural production and identity formation was intended to serve as a sort of antidote to the very ethnic particularism, essentialism, and nationalism that shaped many of these movements and discourses. Hinting at the ambiguous meanings of "African diaspora", Marxist historian Robin D.G. Kelley stated that the term has "served as [...] a political term with which to emphasize unifying experiences of African peoples dispersed by the slave trade, [but also as] an analytical term that enabled scholars to talk about black communities across national boundaries" ("How the West was One" 31).

For its emphasis on border-crossing, intercultural and transversal flows, the concept of African diaspora has been crucial to what has been labelled the "transnational turn" in American Studies. In the last three decades, there have been significant advances in efforts to situate African American movements and cultures within international contexts and historical developments, breaking with cultural nationalist invocations of a fixed African identity. Focusing on black engagements with modernity in the New World instead of constructing romanticized images of a pre-colonial African past, addressing differences and parallels within the experiences of Afrodescendants, and highlighting the often contradictory and multifaceted dimensions of the African diaspora in the Americas have been some of the crucial features of these new approaches and directions (Kelley and Patterson). As Laura Chrisman and her co-editors of *The Black Scholar*'s special issue on "Transcending Traditions" (2000) emphasized, "our global situation demands conceptual and methodological modes of analysis that capture the new processes of cultural convergence and transnational connection that are underway" (2). In the same issue, E. Chukwudi Eze argues that "broad and international perspectives in the study of Africa, African America, Afro-Latin America and the Afro-Caribbean" (19) are crucial to "transcending particularistic traditions" and "counter-balancing the nativistic and nationalistic tendencies that prevent one from realizing the full scale of our modern experiences, helms in one's politics, and thwarts the freedom to construct more relevant Afro identities" (19). Without succumbing to the essentialisms that have dominated related academic fields and political movements, he claims that the main task is to develop "an adequately universal perspective capable of encompassing the hybrid, creolized, and dynamic character of the exilic African and Black cultures" (19). Eze argues for a global vision that requires to take into account the specific local contexts that will reveal that there is not one unifying racial experience of all Afrodescendants. His call to "pay attention to the always changing nature of both racial experiences as well as African and afro-identities" (19) is particularly important for an understanding of the conflicted meanings and implications of racism and anti-racism in the Americas.

While the classical definition of diaspora, as represented by "the Afrocentric model" (Chrisman et al. 3) assumes a timeless, close, and continuous connection of dispersed populations to their region of origin, more recent approaches emphasize the mobile, flexible, and shifting character of Afro-diasporic identity constructions in the context of globalization and mass migration, expressed in concepts as *creolité, mestizaje,* and hybridity. James Clifford's concept of diasporas as "traveling cultures" (17) criticizes the reduction of diasporas to their connections to the country of origin, since this ignores the reorientations and ruptures with traditions and nationalisms, that are produced by the specific local interactions of diasporic groups. The importance of *translocal* flows and politics between different communities and urban centers in the making of black identities has been addressed in many accounts of Afro-diasporic dialogues. Kim D. Butler emphasizes that "[c]ontact between communities of the diaspora, independent of contacts with the homeland, is vital in forging diasporan consciousness, institutions, and networks" (207). This holds especially true for the intra-diasporic dialogues between black movements and cultures in the Americas which depended on the crossing of national, cultural and linguistic barriers. Starting from the observation that most people in the African diaspora are not English native speakers, Brent Hayes Edwards has stressed the importance of *translation* as a diasporic practice that shapes the ways cultures of black internationalism travel in various global contexts where Afro-diasporic subjects from different linguistic backgrounds speak to each other (7). He points out that in the process of translation, instead of erasing differences, discourses and ideas can change their meanings depending on the different contexts of racialization they are articulated in – a point that becomes particularly apparent when taking into consideration how symbols and slogans of Black Power were translated and adapted to suit the local struggles of Afrodescendant activists in Latin America.

Black transnationalism, defined as "an interdisciplinary project of Black transnational border thinking" (209) by Quito Swan, has constituted a key area of research in African Diaspora Studies. Studies of black transnationalism deal with the ways black migrations to the metropolitan centers of former imperial powers have caused "an interplay of peoples, ideas, and cultural and economic practices that do not fit neatly under the disciplinary and regional studies rubrics" ("Black Transnationalism" 143), as Michael Hanchard has pointed out. Transdisciplinary approaches which combine sociological, historical, and literary methods and defy the demarcations between conventional disciplines and national or area studies paradigms have become a key feature of African American Studies in the course of their transnationalization.[2] Critical of "intellectually conservative" approaches, Hanchard holds that research on black transnationalism requires questioning the "easy assumption of population/culture/nation-state/territory intrinsic to the idea of African American studies as the study of African-descended populations born and raised in the territorial dominion of the United States, with certain recognizable cultural, linguistic, political and other patterns to readily identify them" (153). Instead, as Hanchard argues, transnational black studies must address the question how technological innovations in mass media and transportation have enabled African American and Afro diasporic peoples to interact with each other and other peoples of the world in the context of modernity (147, 152). It is this question that motivates Paul Gilroy's *Black Atlantic*, in which he argued that studies of black transnationalism differ from the dominant currents of

---

2 Michael Hanchard's visionary call for the bridging of African American and Latin American Studies towards the development of hemispheric perspectives on the African diaspora is further addressed in Chapter 1.5.

research on black cultures in the 20th century in that they are not interested in the search for common *roots* of Afrodescendants, but in *routes* – the transnational exchange between diverse manifestations of the diaspora that are constantly being recombined and reinvented and deeply intertwined with modernity.

While Gilroy's focus on transnationalism corresponds with the Marxist critique of the nation-state and the need for a global perspective, his *Black Atlantic* has been particularly criticized by Marxist scholars for its aestheticist fixation on black art as "the only [...] category which can contain and articulate black countercultural ethics, politics and knowledge" (Chrisman, "Journeying to Death" 60) at the expense of a consideration of socioeconomic conditions. In the same vein, Kelley notes that Afro-diasporic identities are too frequently thought of as strictly cultural matters, "when in fact some of the most dynamic transnational identities are created in the realm of politics, in the way people of African descent sought alliances and political identifications across oceans and national boundaries" ("How the West was One" 32). In her analysis of West Indian intellectuals in Harlem, Michelle Stephens also noted the different approaches to black transnationalism from researchers in cultural Studies and those in the social sciences who are less concerned about matters of cultural fluidity but rather focus on how immigrants become "transmigrants" with allegiances, loyalties and networks that go beyond their citizenship in one nation-state ("Black Transnationalism and the Politics of National Identity" 592–593). While arguing that an understanding of "race" as one central category of global analyses of twentieth century geopolitics opens up new conceptual space for thinking about black transnationality in the Americas ("Reimagining the Shape and Borders" 170), Stephens also criticizes "the conceptual erasures of gender and sexuality from discourses of race and blackness in diaspora" which, according to her, become "secondary in the formation, construction, and performance of a political discourse on diasporic blackness" ("What Is This Black?" 34). Countering these omissions, Stephens emphasizes that black transnationalism has also been shaped by the engagement of black activists with other international movements and philosophies such as communism or feminism which are not necessarily linked to blackness or Africa: "To see black transnationalism as a symbolic geopolitics means the recognition of moments, throughout the twentieth century, of the construction of a symbolic political language that represented black political struggle along an internationalist rather than a nationalist axis. By this I mean a discourse that sitting at the intersections of various revolutionary internationalisms [...] reimagined political identity, black specifically, in non-national and nonethnocentric terms" ("Reimagining the Shape and Borders" 174). Stephens' assessment that black transnationalism is shaped by an internationalist and "non-ethnocentric" rather than a nationalist orientation problematizes one of the key concerns of this study which holds that black transnationalism also encompasses the diffusion of black nationalist discourses. Across the hemisphere, the popularization of soul music often went hand in hand with a construction of Afro-diasporic identity that was clearly inspired by U.S. discourses of black nationalism in which blackness is ascribed a set of fixed positive, unifying characteristics. In order to come to terms with this apparent contradiction the following sections are dedicated to debates on the contested meanings of black nationalism, internationalism, and cosmopolitanism.

1.2 Beyond Binaries: Black (Inter) Nationalism, Gilroy, and his Critics

Ideologies of black nationalism date back to the 19th century and are based on the assumption that black people in the United States constituted "a nation within a nation" (Woodward) immersed in a struggle for self-determination after centuries of survival under a regime of racial subjugation and exclusion. Black nationalism constitutes a response to the contradiction that W.E.B. Du Bois had described as *double consciousness* in *The Souls of Black Folk* (1903): whereas African American citizens had contributed in significant ways to the rise of the United States as a world power, it was precisely under the rule of this nation that they were subjected to a brutal system of racial exclusion, marginalization, and discrimination. After the demise of Marcus Garvey's UNIA as the first black nationalist mass movement, the 1960s witnessed a renaissance of black nationalist activism with the rise of Black Power. Inspired by the post-World War II anti-colonial movements in the Third World, whose primary goal was national liberation, black activists in the United States faced the challenge that African Americans constituted an ethnic minority without a specific territory in a society dominated by whites, making the question of which nation to liberate infinitely more difficult to answer. Thus, unlike classical European nationalism and Third World liberation nationalism, black nationalism was a nation without a nation— an ideology directed at an "imagined community" (Anderson) whose boundaries are not defined by the nation-state. The absence of a national territory and the widely shared experience of subjugation to all-encompassing systems of dehumanization on the basis of skin-color turned the search for international allies and the forging of border-crossing networks of solidarity into a main feature of the multifaceted strategies for black liberation that have been articulated within and without the framework of black nationalism. The conflicting prioritizations of race, class, culture, and nation are essential for an understanding of the many overlaps and crucial points of contention between black nationalism and black internationalism as the defining currents of Black Power. Whereas ideologies of black nationalism are widely referred to as the common denominators of the Black Power movement, the term might be somewhat misleading because it was precisely the internationalist outlook that distinguished the imaginaries of Black Power from the domestic agenda of the Civil Rights movement. These intersections, fittingly described by Roderick Bush as the "Peculiar Internationalism of Black Nationalism" (35) hint at the fact that some of the black radical discourses that have shaped what has been commonly summarized under the broad umbrella term black nationalism, can be defined more precisely as manifestations of black internationalism, transnationalism, and cosmopolitanism.

The internationalism of black nationalism is evident in how black nationalist discourses that emerged in the United States spread beyond the African American community and were adapted globally. In order to understand these processes of appropriation and translation, it is important not to see this ideology as a fixed and self-contained set of ideological principles, but to consider its heterogeneous, flexible, and permeable character. Thus, black nationalism, while constituting one of the oldest and most enduring ideologies in African American political thought, has proven to be highly adaptable in a wide variety of local, regional, and national contexts because black people across the diaspora have been able to relate to some of its ideological foundations. Jeffrey Ogbar defined black nationalism as the advocacy for "group consciousness among black people and the belief that they, independent of whites, can achieve liberation by the creation and maintenance of black institutions to serve the best interests of black people" (*Black Power* 3). While the political philosophy of black nationalism stands for a wide spectrum of often contradictory goals and strategies towards black liberation – ranging from the Garveyite vision of a physical return to Africa, cultural nationalist currents such as the Black Arts Movement and Afrocentrism to left-wing revolutionary (inter)nationalism as advocated by the Revolutionary Action Movement and the Black Panther Party – the common theme of all these tendencies and organizations is the invocation of black solidarity in the struggle to overcome regimes of white supremacy (Shelby 666). It is this idea of black unity and connectedness, based on the shared experience of slavery and racism, that explains the ambivalences and complexities of U.S. black nationalism.

On the one hand, foundational figures of black nationalism such as Martin Delaney and Marcus Garvey and organizations such as the Nation of Islam pursued a "race first" approach to politics that, according to Tommy Shelby reflected U.S. white supremacy by reifying "the dubious category of race" (665), assuming "the existence of a transhistorical and organic 'black essence'" (665), and asserting the innate superiority of blacks over whites, often promoting separatism as a core principle of an agenda that was exclusively directed at African Americans in the United States. On the other hand, the idea of global black solidarity as a fundamental principle of black nationalism is not bound by the borders of nation-states and, on the contrary, has the potential to foster the forging of transnational alliances and support internationalist and cosmopolitan visions for Afrodescendants in the diaspora. These opposing interpretations undergird the debates about the meaning of black nationalism, which in the eyes of some critics is an obstacle to overcome in the overdue transnationalization of African American Studies and for others instead constitutes an elemental force in the constitution of an Afro-diasporic counterculture and thus also a key topic of research in African Diaspora Studies.

Black radicals from the left wing of the movement have offered insightful critiques of black nationalism. The decline of Black Power in the mid-1970s was not only the result of massive state repression and a white backlash, but also of internal divisions triggered not least by the limitations and contradictions of a conservative brand of black nationalism that has dominated the African American public sphere in the post-Black Power era. Black Marxists, most prominently represented by the Black Panthers, criticized that the black nationalists' dogmas of "race-first" and "black unity" disguised existing class divisions within the African American community and undermined the building of transformative coalitions (Johnson; Reed). Black feminists such as Angela Davis, Barbara Walker, Toni Cade Bambara, and groups such as the Combahee River Collective and the Third World Women's Alliance denounced reactionary forms of black nationalism for its expressions of male chauvinism, sexism, heteronormativity, and homophobia (Collins; Taylor). Both, conservative black nationalism's reproduction of patriarchal gender relations and its rejection of class-based multiethnic alliances with other oppressed groups weakened the radical democratic and transformational character of Black Power significantly.

Due to their relevance for this study, the debates sparked by Paul Gilroy's scathing critique of black nationalism in *Black Atlantic* will be given a closer look here. Gilroy definition of black nationalism as a reactionary form of racial essentialism and ethnic absolutism attacked the core of many ideas that underpinned the African American freedom struggle. He identified "the fatal junction of the concept of nationality with the concept of culture" (2) which mystified "blacks as a national or proto-national group with its own hermeneutically enclosed culture" (33) as one of the main problems of the racial essentialism and "African-American exceptionalism" (4) that according to him dominated black intellectual discourses. He argued that African American studies were shaped by "a nationalistic focus that is antithetical to the rhizomorphic, fractal structure of the transcultural, international formation that I call the black Atlantic" (4). Considering that the political and cultural currents that have defined themselves as black nationalist span the ideological spectrum, from the Nation of Islam's politically and culturally conservative black separatism to radical Marxist organizations with a distinct revolutionary internationalist orientation, Gilroy's blanket delegitimization of black nationalism seems, at the very least, an undue generalization and misleading reduction of this broad and ideologically heterogeneous political philosophy.

Unsurprisingly, Gilroy's anti-nationalist crusade unleashed a storm of criticism among African American scholars and activists. Afrocentrists and cultural nationalists like Molefi Kete Asante accused Gilroy of trying to destroy the timeless bonds between African Americans and their African roots and please whites with his search for an abstract cosmopolitanism ("Review" 848). But Gilroy also received strong rebuttals from researchers unsuspicious of ethnic particularism. In the views of many, Gilroy's abstract theoretical model with its exclusive focus on intellectual discourses was out of touch with the realities of the lived experiences of the non-academic masses in the African diaspora for which race-based mobilizations, and thus, black nationalism, became an important strategy in struggles against racial exclusion. Many critics of Gilroy's advocacy for "color-blind humanism" share his ideal of a society in which race and "racial thinking" lose their importance, but emphasize the practical necessity of calling the factual correlation between racial categories and social inequalities by its name if the goal is to combat racism. Very much like black activists in Latin America, who were accused of racism because of denouncing presumably universalist ideologies of *mestizaje* and *democracia racial* as a myth, Gilroy's critics hinted at the risks of masking existing mechanisms of oppression inherent in color-blindness. As George Lipsitz argues, he repeatedly lapses into inadmissible generalizations: "While devastatingly accurate in his rebuttal of nationalist claims for primordial, trans-cultural, and trans-historical essences uniting diasporic Africans, Gilroy unfortunately defines as 'essentialist' just about any strategy that relies on ethnic solidarity. But people who catch hell just because they are black act logically and reasonably when they use blackness as a means of augmenting group power and solidarity" ("Review" 195). Furthermore, recourse to strategic essentialism in the form of black nationalism would have enabled African Americans to escape, at least temporarily, from their role as an oppressed minority and to see themselves as part of a global majority. References to Africa, as in pan-Africanism, would not necessarily have to be an expression of a limited essentialism, but could also serve to visualize the historical conditionality – and thus the changeable, non-essential character – of their situation.

Of particular importance to an examination of the transnational, hemispheric dimensions of the Black Power movement is Gilroy's classification of black nationalism as antithetical to his transcultural concept of the African diaspora. Several scholars have pointed out how Gilroy's dichotomy between the international dimensions of the African diaspora on the one hand and black nationalism on the

1.2 Beyond Binaries: Black (Inter) Nationalism, Gilroy, and his Critics — **41**

other in no way corresponds to existing realities in the Black Atlantic world. French anthropologist Christine Chivallon argues that black nationalist and Afrocentric ideologies have played an undeniably important role as social and cultural orientations within the broad spectrum of Afro-diasporic articulations. With regard to Gilroy, Chivallon states: "The nationalism that is rejected as a social theory (with which I agree) is also rejected as an ideological reality" (364). She holds that Gilroy's practice of recognizing Afro-diasporic cultural manifestations as legitimate components of the Black Atlantic only after examining them for their hybridity contradicts his own intercultural and inclusive vison of the African diaspora. Rather than highlighting individual cultural or political aspects as characteristic of Afro-Atlantic exchange processes and excluding others, as Gilroy does, Chivallon argues that it would be more purposeful to consider the contradictions and relationships among the heterogeneous manifestations of the African diaspora in all their diversity. Hinting at the historical particularities due to which "race consciousness" has played a very different role in political mobilizations in the United States, the Caribbean, and Latin America, Chivallon calls for greater consideration of local contexts and the multiplicity of Afro-diasporic realities.

Equally critical of the mutually exclusive juxtaposition of black nationalism and the African diaspora, Laura Chrisman highlights the possibility of the interdependence of Gilroy's propagated "outer- or trans-nationalism" with the nationalism of diasporic groups ("Journeying to death"). According to Chrisman, Gilroy, by viewing all manifestations of black nationalism as incompatible with his hybrid conception of diaspora, is unable to recognize the extent to which various instances of this ideological current are also part of the Afro-Atlantic exchange space. By emphasizing how different forms of black nationalism often constituted the starting point for practices of black transnationalism, Chrisman argues for a focus on the interdependencies between black nationalist and internationalist positions in the context of the Black Atlantic.

Accounts of how black radical networks were forged by Afro-Caribbean migrants in the context of the Harlem Renaissance and Garveyism (Guridy; Valdés; Putnam; Stephens), have provided examples from the Americas of how nationalism and internationalism were not mutually exclusive but complementary strategies in the liberation struggles of "denationalized migrants" (Stephens, "Black Transnationalism" 604). These intersections, are intrinsically related to the fact that African Americans, unlike the anti-colonial movements abroad with which they felt connected, had no national territory that they could liberate from white rule in their quest for freedom. Lara Putnam has argued that black nationalism and black internationalism should be understood as different but potentially complementary approaches to black liberation: "Black nationalism holds that within a racist society, black people's primary political allegiance should reflect racial solidarity. [...] Meanwhile, black internationalism analyzes racial subordination as a part of systems that function on a supranational scale. [...], which usually requires communication and alliance across political boundaries, be they national or imperial" (*Radical Moves* 6). As concerns widespread notions of Black Power nationalism as an expression of racial separatism and essentialism that put an end to the universalist ideals of Martin Luther King and the Civil Rights movement, it is worth noting that also in this context black nationalism was a starting point for internationalism, as evidenced by the ideological trajectory of Malcolm X from black separatism to internationalism and the multiracial and border-crossing alliances forged by the Black Panthers and other anti-capitalist left-wing groups like the Revolutionary Action Movement who identified as revolutionary black (inter-)nationalists (Kelley, *Freedom Dreams*).

These findings suggest that black nationalism does not necessarily represent a self-contained value system limited to African Americans and their recollection of African roots, but rather provided a platform for a transnational and intercultural dialogue and the opening of an emancipatory perspective in various situations. From this perspective, black nationalism no longer appears as an antithesis, but in its mobility and flexibility as an immanent component of the transnational exchange processes that characterize Gilroy's *Black Atlantic.* Approaches which deal with these intersections, instead of positing them as binary opposites, are of significant use for a a conceptualization of hemispheric black transnationalism as a practice of dialogues between antiracist movements and popular cultures in the Americas. As I want to demonstrate, it was Black Power's open and heterogeneous character that enabled its global repercussions in the most diverse contexts.

1.3 Black Cosmopolitanism

For a conceptualization of the apparent contradictory relationship between discourses rooted in ideologies of ethnic nationalism and practices of internationalism that defined the hemispheric dissemination of soul, I propose the term *Black Power cosmopolitanism.* Whereas the essentialized and particularist notions of blackness associated with Black Power seem to be at odds with the universalist, anti-essentialist tenets of cosmopolitanism, the concept reveals its utility in the context of hemispheric transculturation and interethnic coalition-building that defined the 1960s and early 1970s. This conceptualization draws on approaches which have grappled with the contested role of Afrodescendants as both, victims of and agents in, world-historical movements, projects, and processes such as Enlightenment, modernity, universalism, capitalism, and globalization, envisioning a "cosmopolitanism from below" (Ingram). Associating cosmopolitanism with black liberation, as done throughout this study, has the potential of provoking indignation by those who view it as a synonym for Western imperialism, paternalism, a notorious disregard for non-white histories and cultures and the complicity of color-blind universalism in the concealment of white supremacy – a Eurocentric elitist project detached from the realities not only of black struggles but of all kinds of social justice movements. As Posnock has correctly observed, "cosmopolitanism has often been attacked by both ends of the spectrum: the Right regards it as unpatriotic and hence suspect; the Left finds its detachment elitist, apolitical, and hence irresponsible. [....] both sides regard cosmopolitanism a betrayal of roots, hence inauthentic" (803). According to Posnock, it was "the dream of deracination as freedom" (804) associated with cosmopolitanism that inspired many black intellectuals and lay at the core of a specific *black cosmopolitanism.*

For an understanding of how cosmopolitan approaches have constituted a constant feature of black liberation struggles in the Western hemisphere, Ifeoma Nwankwo's *Black Cosmopolitanism* is particularly insightful. In her account of the engagement of African American 19th century radical abolitionists and early black nationalists like Frederick Douglass and Martin Delaney with the legacy of the Haitian Revolution, she describes the uprising as the origin of a distinct black cosmopolitanism that challenged both, essentialized notions of blackness which advocate for an inherent unity of black people, regardless of historical and geographical context, and also dominant Eurocentric discourses of universalism which have left the claims of formerly enslaved and colonized peoples for participation in the road to global emancipation unanswered. According to Nwankwo, the Haitian revolution was a "a crucial turning point for Americans of African descent" (6) because for the first time it forced them "to name a relationship [...] to a transnational idea of Black community" and "to decide whether to define themselves as citizens of the world [...] and how to express their connection both to their country of residence and to the world of people of African descent beyond that country" (7). Nwankwo argues that the Haitian Revolution and its legacies are necessary, and too often ignored, points of departure for an understanding of the interactions between Afrodescendants in the Americas and their struggles "to define self and community between multiple local and global affinities" (8).

The exclusion of Afrodescendants from revolutionary ideals of universalism as manifested in the synchronicity of the European Enlightenment project with the dehumanizing systems of slavery, colonialism, and imperialism, or, as Nwankwo phrases it, the "denial of access for people of African descent to cosmopolitan subjectivity" (10), lay at the heart of these struggles. Black cosmopolitanism, thus, is defined by the quest of Afrodescendants not to be reduced to their racial identity as *blacks*, but to be recognized as humans and equal subjects in the project of modernity (9). According to this vision, cosmopolitanism as the ideal of identifying as a "citizen of the world" free from the limitations and particularisms inherent in the concepts of national belonging and nationalism, had a special appeal to people of African origin who were violently excluded from the national projects of their countries of residence. It carried the potential of providing oppressed and marginalized groups with a "substitute national identity [which] may include people in places they have never visited, and with whom they have never had contact, because the connection they imagine is based on the common experiences of slavery and discrimination and African heritage, rather than shared terrain or face to face encounters" (13). While shared experiences with other colonized or enslaved peoples have consistently constituted an important frame of reference, it is the liberating potential of being able to participate in global projects of emancipation beyond nation, race, and heritage that made practices of cosmopolitanism so attractive to many Afrodescendant luminaries and trailblazers of the 19th and 20th centuries.

The complicity of Eurocentric interpretations of cosmopolitanism with nationalist, racist, and patriarchal discourses and large-scale human rights violations partly explains the wide-spread skepticism among anti-racist and feminist theorists. The cosmopolitan ideas of "world citizenship" and universalism were first and most prominently articulated by European thinkers in the context of 19th century Enlightenment – a project, which, while proclaiming the equality of all humans, was paralleled by the subjugation of racialized and colonialized people across the globe, justified as a necessary step towards civilizational progress by many of its masterminds. Critical voices take issue with the fact that cosmopolitanism made in Europe has often equated the interests of hegemonic powers in the North with the universal good, displaying the very particularist world views it proclaims to overcome by judging the world by its own local standards. In the name of global progress, "civilization", and universal values, non-European peoples have been subjected to violence and subjugation. As Kwame Appiah noted, many of the "attacks on Enlightenment humanism' have been attacks not on the universality of Enlightenment pretensions but on the Euro-centrism of their real bases" (249). According to his interpretation, what appears as "anti-universalism" in ideologies and practices of resistance of people of color is often motivated by the rejection of universalism as a "a projection of European values and interests" (249), not a dismissal of Enlightenment as such but a critique of its failure to live up to the ideals it proclaims and a demand for a full realization of its promises for humanity as a whole.

In light of the devastating effects of radical nationalisms and ethnocentrisms that have manifested themselves in slavery, colonialism, imperialism, fascism, the Holocaust, two devastating world wars, and a series of horrific genocides throughout the 20th century, it seems well worth the effort to think about ways to recuperate what is useful, promising, and potentially emancipatory about the widely criticized idea of cosmopolitanism. Whereas current debates on decoloniality, antiracism, and feminism emphasize the value of difference and the strategic potential of identity politics, the cosmopolitan vision of a world liberated from the boundaries and divisiveness imposed by nationalist, essentialist, and ethnocentric discourses and projects appears as relevant as ever, despite all its shortcomings. Karl Marx and Friedrich Engels were among the first 19th century intellectuals to appropriate the idea of cosmopolitanism for a theory of worldwide revolution against the hegemonic capitalist and imperialist powers when they issued the slogan "Workers of the world, unite!" in their Communist Manifesto from 1848. The Marxist vision of an international alliance of oppressed peoples of diverse national, cultural, and ethnic backgrounds, unified by shared experiences of exploitation and deprivation of their most basic rights and the common goal of achieving liberation was powerful and highly attractive, shaping the struggles of various generations of activists, freedom fighters, and intellectuals across the globe throughout the 20th century. Nevertheless, the corruption of the Communist ideals of emancipation under Josef Stalin which went hand in hand with a decisive turn towards nationalism, and the failure of the Communist International to address race- and gender-based inequalities as any other than side contradictions, led to the disenchantment of many Afro-diasporic intellectuals and activists with Moscow-dominated Communist orthodoxy and authoritarianism in the era of decolonization. Still, a reinterpretation of Marxism from a black perspective, as outlined in Cedric Robinson's *Black Marxism – The Making of the Black Radical Tradition* – remained a salient feature of black liberation movements throughout the 20th century, as the trajectories and contributions of Afro-diasporic intellectuals such as W.E.B. Du Bois, Paul Robeson, Claudia Jones, Richard Wright, C.L.R. James, George Padmore, Frantz Fanon, Walter Rodney, Angela Davis, and revolutionary internationalist groups such as the Revolutionary Action Movement, DRUM, and the Black Panther Party demonstrated.

A common critique of cosmopolitanism takes issue with the elitism inherent in the premise of thinking and behaving as a world citizen, which often manifests itself in a condescending delegitimization of local experiences and struggles. Fuyuki Kurasawa criticizes the "'class consciousness of frequent travellers' [...], that fawns at its own deterritorialized sophistication while cringing at the 'provincialism' of anything it perceives to be the more rooted experiences and lifeworlds within which most human beings actually live" (237). It is this "cosmopolitanism from above" (240) which is often rightly criticized for its failure to articulate an agenda which speaks to the needs of poor and working-class peoples whose involuntary exposure to intersecting race-, class-, and gender-based systems of marginalization restricts their access to the mobility and their ability to detach themselves from surrounding realities, that is often taken for granted in cosmopolitan discourses. For example, by sweepingly disqualifying as essentialist all struggles that address racist exclusion and injustice by organizing the affected communities on the basis of racial solidarity, this "anaemic version of cosmopolitanism" (237) which only approves of the association of "individuals on the basis of their standing as abstract bearers of universal rights and freedoms" (ibid.) refuses to take into account the specific socio-cultural realities and dynamics of social movements. By universalizing the world views of socially upward mobile and mostly white elites and presupposing the freedom to desist from local rootedness or ethnic identifications as a given – without acknowledging the privileges that are necessary for developing such a universal perspective – this brand of cosmopolitanism contributes to the camouflage of the interrelatedness between power relations, social inequalities and processes of racialization (239).

Taking into account the critiques of "cosmopolitanism from above" by feminists, social and racial justice advocates, theorists such as Kurusawa and James D. Ingram propose to rethink the concept and advocate for a "cosmopolitanism from below". Instead of abandoning the ideas of cosmopolitan egalitarianism and universalism, they argue for using cosmopolitanism as a program for political action which addresses its complicity with domination (Ingram 73). "Cosmopolitanism from below", thus, differentiates itself from the bottom-down approach of preceding global discourses by centering the perspectives of those who have been excluded from failed universalist projects of past and present, and emphasizing their struggles for equality and recognition as quintessential element of a revised cosmopolitanism. Ingram claims that "in order not to violate its central values in ways that countless universalisms have done before, cosmopolitanism must be contestatory" (67–68). According to him, "a contestatory cosmopolitanism would consist of a politics by which particular forms of exclusion, domination, exploitation and marginalization are challenged by those who suffer them. From this viewpoint, universal values or principles become actual when they are taken up against a false universal by those whose oppression that false universal justifies" (73). This approach allows for the re-appropriation of a concept which has its strength in providing a strong ideological foundation against the pitfalls of the diverse currents of nationalism and racial essentialism that have shaped many of the counter-hegemonic movements of colonized and racialized peoples throughout the 20th century as described by Frantz Fanon, Gilroy and many others. Following this line of thought, instead of a priori condemning specific local or identity-based struggles and movements for their particularisms their agendas should be examined for their potential to further the universal causes of emancipation, freedom and justice. Instead of submitting all kinds of political and sociocultural projects to a purity test by checking them for possible deviations from "real cosmopolitanism" this could mean to have a closer look: unapologetically criticizing the celebration of difference and identity politics where they degenerate into an end of itself, a cause for division and an obstacle to coalition-building; and at the same time acknowledging the particularities of certain localities and historical and cultural contexts, and maintaining the possibility of finding common ground through transnational, translocal, and cross-cultural dialogues – a practice of non-hierarchical multi-directional border-crossing exchange that Walter Mignolo has defined as transversality (73).

What is promoted here is an understanding of cosmopolitanism which doesn't automatically exclude the vast majority of non-white articulations because of their "particularities" (mostly shaped by violence, subjugation, and class-, race-, and gender-based marginalization in the name of universal progress), but rather intents to develop a cosmopolitan vision that is not centered in Europe but composed of the diverse experiences, visions, and struggles of peoples and groups in different local contexts across the planet. What at first appears contradictory, to acknowledge the local character of cosmopolitanism, actually makes a lot of sense "because the agents of the cosmopolitan cause of universal freedom and equality, of democracy and human rights, will most often be particular groups in particular struggles for particular stakes", as Ingram has it (76). Through this lens, even groups which organize around a shared experience of race-based exclusion, particularistic in the sense that they only include people of color and often explicitly exclude whites, can ultimately be considered to be part of the cosmopolitan project to the extent that their struggles contribute to the larger goal of emancipation on the basis of a shared vision of universal values and under the condition that they promote the building of worldwide coalitions across national, cultural, and ethnic affiliations. In this sense, it is argued here that organizing resistance on the basis of shared experiences of oppression, such as racism, certainly can be but is not necessarily an expression of narrow essentialism and reactionary ethnic nationalism as it also carries the potential of liberating communities from the devastating effects of their dehumanization. This inclusive approach enlists a much broader range of people for the cosmopolitan project, as it takes into account the transnational identifications of people who might lack the mobility of others, and, importantly, it encourages the forging of global alliances and networks of solidarity. Its premises – decentering Europe in accounts of cosmopolitanism and modernity, emphasizing the pivotal role of colonialized and racialized peoples in the struggles for humanist and universalist goals – lay at the core of various related concepts such as Appiah's "rooted cosmopolitanism" (213–272) and "minor cosmopolitanism" as investigated by the Potsdam University-based Research and Training Group which share the objective of recuperating the idea of cosmopolitanism for the emancipatory project.

The salience of cosmopolitanism as a term to conceptualize global freedom struggles in the 20th century is also evidenced in several studies which deal with practices of black internationalism that shaped liberation movements across the Atlantic world. Focusing on the transnational activism of W.E.B. Du Bois in the early 20th century, Nico Slate has proposed "colored cosmopolitanism" as a way to define his "inclusive humanism that defied narrow, chauvinist definitions of race, religion, or nation while simultaneously defending the unity of 'colored' peoples" (66). In her account of Black Panther leader Eldridge Cleaver's efforts to strengthen the ties between the Black Power movement and African decolonization during his visit to the Democratic Republic of Congo, Sarah Fila-Bakabadio discerns practices of "insurgent cosmopolitanism" (146–160). Stressing the sense of empowerment and agency that is forged through translocal interactions between marginalized diasporic groups, David Featherstone proposes "subaltern cosmopolitanism" as a constitutive feature of black internationalism and a way to refer "to forms of worldliness, mobility, and geographies of connection" that are not taken into account by nation-based analyses of international politics (1409). References to cosmopolitanism are also to be found throughout Paul Gilroy's account of the Black Atlantic as a counter-culture of modernity, in which he posits the globalizing force of black popular culture as an antidote to ethnic particularism.

For an analysis of processes of hemispheric black transnationalism in Afro-diasporic migrant communities Nina Glick Schiller's concept of "diasporic cosmopolitanism" is equally insightful. Glick Schiller proposes to challenge the dominant understanding of the cosmopolitan by linking "the term cosmopolitanism with a modifier that implies its opposite – vernacular, rooted, ghetto and diasporic" ("Diasporic Cosmopolitanism" 103). Focusing on the displaced urban poor in metropolitan migrant communities, she defines diasporic cosmopolitanism "as the sociabilities formed around shared practices, outlooks, aspirations and sensibilities – however partial, temporary, or inconclusive – that emerge from and link people simultaneously to those similarly displaced and to locally and transnationally emplaced social relationships" (105). According to Glick Schiller, shared aspirations for equality and social justice "can link those who are socially displaced not only to each other but also with those similarly positioned around the world" (113). Through this lens, the experience of mobility and the related familiarity with diverse and contradicting visions of the world turn migrants into facilitators of urban cosmopolitanism with "a unique set of analytic, emotional, creative/imaginative and behavioral competencies and skills that distinguishes them from those who have not traveled" (114). Following this approach, it is possible to get an understanding of how cities like New York and Colón became breeding grounds of cosmopolitanism in which migrants and natives from diverse ethnic and national backgrounds converge and in which common experiences of marginalization spark the building of cross-cultural and interethnic alliances in contestations of urban spaces. The cohabitation of diverse diasporic communities in urban contexts not only becomes the setting but the very precondition for the emergence of cosmopolitanism among migrants in multiethnic neighborhoods.

With her concept of "sonic cosmopolitanism", Daphne Brooks has offered another take on cosmopolitanism that is very useful for this study. In an article on Nina Simone and Eartha Kitt's role as sonic cosmopolites who "use their musical performances to question global power, geographical, and racial boundaries and who struggle with belonging in ways that open up their expressive repertoire" (117), Brooks defines "sonic cosmopolitanism" as marked by "contradictory, complex, heterogenous, cultural solidarity, fearless spontaneity" (112). Tracing the routes of Eartha Kitt, she argues that her cosmopolitanism stretches, revises, and ironizes dominant perceptions of race, gender and sexuality in circum-Atlantic popular culture, drawing from a rich repertoire of Afro-Caribbean and Latin American aesthetics" (112). Brooks argues that sonic cosmopolitanism in the African diaspora is a kind of self-reinvention, encouraged by marginalization, rooted in "fugitive vocalities that referenced and remixed notions of the 'global', drawing from the sounds of the 'local' and vernacular" and shaped by the making of "global geographies of irreverent, culturally heterogenous 'blackness'" (113). Importantly, her concept is based on an understanding in which cosmopolitanism and hybridity are not inherently opposed to manifestations of black nationalism (117).

1.4 Overcoming Invisibility: Afro-Latin America in Transnational Perspectives

Transnational influences have played a significant role in the shaping of Afro-Latin-American mobilizations, cultural productions and identity constructions throughout the 20th century. The participation of Afro-Puerto Rican activist Arturo Schomburg in the Harlem Renaissance, the influence of Garveyism in different sites of the Hispanic Caribbean, the emergence of radical alliances between Afro-Latin American immigrants and African Americans in 1960s New York, the impact of négritude, Rastafarianism, Black Power, soul, funk, salsa, reggae, and hip-hop throughout the region – all of these examples bear witness to the ways Afro-Latin Americans engaged in practices of black transnationalism (Guridy and Hooker). Despite of the magnitude of these phenomena and the fact that most Afrodescendants in the Americas are Spanish or Portuguese native speakers, Afro-Latin America was not even mentioned in Gilroy's *Black Atlantic* and has until recently been conspicuously absent from research on transnational flows in the African diaspora. The reasons for this relative underrepresentation, described as "doble subalternación" ("Hilos descoloniales" 61) by Agustín Laó-Montes, are two-fold. On the one hand, research on exchange in the African diaspora has long focused on the United States and the Anglophone Caribbean. On the other, Latin American Studies have been shaped by historical patterns of invisibilization, marginalization, and folklorization of Afro-Latin cultures. In academic circles, the dominant ideologies of *mestizaje* and *democracia racial* have manifested themselves in strong nationalist defense reflexes against approaches that relate the Afro-Latin American populations and their cultural and political manifestations to the African diaspora in general and to the United States in particular. Latin American scholars and intellectuals perceived foreign influences on local black communities as a threat to national unity and the related ideologies of *mestizaje* and *democracia racial.* According to Dulitzky, there has been an "incredible effort at containing the internationalization of their Afro-populations as a form of preemptive deface against threats from the outside to national unity with an unstated implication that Afro groups were best protected, for their own good from outside contagion" (56–57). The following section outlines how these mechanisms have played out and how recent developments in the field of Afro-Latin American Studies have contributed to overcoming them.

A look at how scholarship on black transnationalism in Latin America has been constrained by nationalism and essentialism provides important insights into the ways inter-American relationships have shaped academic discourses on race. Latin American racial exceptionalism has been based on the claim, that racism is a problem of the United States whereas Latin American societies have achieved the universalist ideal of color-blindness. Related identity discourses like *mestizaje* and *democracia racial* drew significantly on negative references to polarized race relations in the United States (Alberto and Hoffnung-Garskof). Jim Crow laws and racial violence against African Americans were used as a deterrence to highlight the exemplary advances concerning the inclusion of black Latin Americans. Hence, there was also a racial dimension to the widespread hostility against influences from the North that had become a defining feature of Latin American academia in light of 20th century U.S. imperialism. New discourses on blackness that evolved in African American Studies departments in the wake of the Civil Rights and Black Power movements were rejected as typical manifestations of an obsession with race specific to the U.S. context, alien to Latin American egalitarianism. The negative reception of critical race theories that originated in Anglophone academia found its logical continuation in the dismissal of African diaspora as a new framework which also addressed hemispheric exchange between Afrodescendants in North and Latin America as these approaches allegedly reproduced neocolonial and cultural imperialist power mechanisms in which Latin America's autonomy is negated and dependence on the USA is maintained through the imposition of paradigms (Stam and Shohat 113–117, 181–183).

Mass migration from the Caribbean and Latin America to the United States complicated the prevalent binary race models. The appearance of transnational Afro-Latino identity constructions and the consequent emergence of new research fields was intrinsically linked to the large-scale arrival of Afrodescendants from the Hispanic Caribbean in the course of several migration waves to the United States. In their pioneering contributions to the field, scholars Juan Flores and Miriam Jiménez have analyzed how the presence of Afro-Latin American migrants in the United States and their encounters with African Americans in urban centers like New York complicated homogenizing notions of race and ethnicity prevalent in the United States and Latin America. In the context of U.S. racial classifications which divided people into "Blacks" and "Latinos", Afro-Latinos, who were both, occupied a contested intermediary space which, according to Flores and Jiménez, challenged "the African American and English-language monopoly over Blackness in the US context, with obvious implications at a hemispheric level" (320). The dialogues with African Americans that led black immigrants from Spanish-speaking countries in the Caribbean and Latin America to identify as Afro-Latinos in the US context (for which soul was a platform as I will show) also had the effect of revealing that constructions of homogenous "Latino" or "hispanic" identities, rooted in legacies of Latin American racial exceptionalism and color-blind racism, were "decidedly *non*-Black – and in significant ways discursively *anti*-Black" (325), as the authors emphasize. Addressing these multilayered processes of racialization and identification, Flores and Jiménez, drawing on Du Bois, propose the concept of "triple consciousness" – black, Latino, American (327) – which has shaped the salience of *afrolatinidad* as a crucial trope in recent scholarship on black Latino identity constructions, mobilizations, and cultural productions in the Americas.

Due to its emphasis on transnational, translocal, and hemispheric flows in the making of black identities between Latin America, the Caribbean, and the United States, the concept of *afrolatinidad* has provided a useful framework in efforts to overcome methodological nationalisms and exceptionalisms in research on the Black Americas. By drawing points of intersection between Black and Latino studies, and putting Latin America and the Hispanic Caribbean on the map of formerly Anglo-centered studies of the African diaspora, *afrolatinidad* as a historical category can "reveal and recognize hidden histories and subalternized knowledges, while unsettling and challenging dominant, essentialist, nationalist, imperial, patriarchal) notions of African-ness, American-ness, and Latinidad," as Agustín Laó-Montes has argued ("Afro-Latinidades" 118).

In the introduction to *Afro-Latin@s in Movimiento*, Petra Rivera-Rideau, Jennifer A. Jones, and Tianna S. Paschel make the case that a transnational and hemispheric approach to *afrolatinidad* is necessary for a better understanding of the "dynamic and continual circulation of people, cultural representations, and politics" and "the shared articulations of blackness across the Americas" (4). These studies on the mobile and changing characteristics of *afrolatinidades* in different historical and geographical contexts of dislocation and displacement demonstrate the uselessness of static and essentializing concepts that assume a fixed black identity independent of political and social conditions. The diasporic frameworks conceptualized in *afrolatinidad* speak to the ways practices of black transnationalism have served Afro-Latinos as a means of resistance to exclusionary and homogenizing nationalist discourses in Latin America and the Caribbean and after migration to the United States. In addition to these emphatically hemispheric perspectives, it is the key role of interactions between Afro-Latinos and African Americans in the formation of *afrolatinidades*, highlighted in several contributions to the field, that makes approaches from this area so relevant to this study (De la Fuente and Andrews; García Peña; Richardson).

1.5 Towards Hemispheric Black Studies

Exploring the flows of U.S. Black Power discourses through the diffusion of soul in different Afro-Latin American contexts across the hemisphere requires the adoption of multiple transregional, transnational and translocal perspectives and a fusion of approaches and concepts from different research fields that have been outlined above. Due to its unconventional and inherent openness to transdisciplinarity and studies that transcend regional, national and linguistic demarcations between research areas and disciplines, Inter-American Studies has provided a compelling framework for this project. Wilfried Raussert holds that "Inter-American studies has challenged the ways of thinking about the Americas beyond South American and North American 'Creole Nationalisms'" and conceptualizes "the Americas as transversally related, chronotopically entagled, and multiply interconnected" ("Mobilizing 'America/América'" 62). One of its key features constitutes in problematizing one-dimensional narratives of dependency and unidirectional homogenization on a North-South axis by conceiving the Americas as a space of multiple entanglements shaped not only by U.S. imperialism but also by the transversal mobility of people, ideas, and cultural products. What distinguishes Inter-American Studies is that it not only proposes to reinvent area studies through concepts such as mobility, flows, and geopolitical imaginaries but that it also draws on a variety of dialogical and horizontal methodologies from disciplines as diverse as cultural and literary studies, history, sociology, and political science (Kaltmeier). These conceptual and methodological approaches are of particular use to this study, which not only examines soul music as a cultural product, but also analyzes the movements and ideologies that inspired its creation and how they were transnationalized through its dissemination from a sociohistorical perspective.

Drawing on insights from scholars of African American, African Diaspora, and Afro-Latin American Studies and their conceptualizations of discourses and practices such as black nationalism, internationalism, transnationalism, cosmopolitanism and *afrolatinidades*, I propose to insert *the Black Americas* as a research perspective more firmly in the field of Inter-American Studies towards the articulation of a Hemispheric Black Studies. This is not a new approach by any means. Rather, this book is to be understood as a contribution to manifold efforts which hint precisely in this direction and also as a response to a growing number of calls of scholars who, like Ifeoma Nwankwo, have noted the "dearth of critical scholarship on the relations between US African Americans and the rest of the Americas" ("Promises and Perils" 188). With his concept of "Nuestra Afroamérica", Agustín Laó-Montes has only recently provided a useful framework for the analysis of hemispheric entanglements between Afrodescendant movements and cultures across the region (*Contrapunteos diaspóricos*). In his paradigmatic essay "Black Transnationalism, Africana Studies, and the 21st Century", Michael Hanchard already outlined some essential thoughts on the conceptualization of Hemispheric Black Studies as early as 2004. Emphasizing the interrelatedness of processes that have shaped the Black Americas, Hanchard questions the categorical demarcations of traditional area studies because "literatures, peoples, territories, languages, influences, and ideologies rarely line up in the way that area studies paradigms do" (150). As he pointed out, inter-American perspectives on the African diaspora allow for insights into how immigration from Latin America and the Caribbean has challenged U.S.-centered racial categorizations, leading many "African-descended immigrants to acknowledge, often for the first time in their lives, anti-Black racism" (148). Hinting at the often-neglected overlaps in the realities of Afro-descendants in the Western Hemisphere related to shared experiences of slavery, colonialism, racism, capitalism, imperialism, and migration, Hanchard questions the established presumptions of national and regional difference that undergird the distinctions between African American and Latin American Studies. As Peter Wade emphasized: "Both societies were slave societies, built on racially ranked stratification; they developed in different ways, but they also share a good deal in terms of the hierarchisation of racial identities" (51).

Hemispheric perspectives on the African diaspora not only reveal the common features of white supremacy and black resistance throughout the Americas, but also shed light on the differences in black experiences, providing a useful tool against essentialist and homogenizing notions of blackness. Referring to Stuart

Hall's concept of race as "floating signifier", Silvio Torres-Saillant argues that blackness can

> [...] signify differently in Haiti, Jamaica, Costa Rica, the Dominican Republic, Cuba, Puerto Rico, or Brazil, compared with the structures of racialization and configurations of blackness when members of these Caribbean and Latin American territories relocate to the United States, or Canada, or Britain, for example, and move back and forth between and among these territories (4).

Arguing for an understanding of racial experiences "that accords with the distinctness of the sites, genealogies, and histories in which race occurs" Torres-Saillant hints at the centrality of specific local conditions in the heterogenous processes of racialization that shape the realities of black people in the Americas, insisting "on the need to speak of blackness as many things, not one, and as a phenomenon worthy of historical scrutiny in each of the differentiated sites and moments in which it occurs" (8).

Bridging research traditions delineated by region, nation, or language such as African American, Latin American, or Caribbean Studies by paying more attention to often silenced or ignored practical and symbolical dialogues between Afrodescendants from different contexts, thus, represents a main objective of Hemispheric Black Studies. Referring to Afro-Latin Americans of British Caribbean descent in Central America, Nwankwo has advocated for more attention to those communities that "blur the lines" between distinct ethnic groups because "an "understanding of the hemisphere can truly be advanced only if we are more attentive to the nuances and complexities of interaction (whether collaboration, conflict, or some combination)" ("Making Sense" 225–226). Studies on how the convergence of black migrations from the U.S. Deep South, the Caribbean, and Latin America in the urban centers of the North and the circum-Caribbean created contact zones such as Panama and New York where a sense of "hemispheric blackness" (Winant) was forged have contributed significantly to the envisioned crossing of research areas. Contributions on the trajectories of Caribbean-descended New Yorkers such as Arturo Schomburg, Marcus Garvey and Felipe Luciano embody the often-neglected intersections and dialogues between African Americans and Afrodescendants from other New World contexts as manifested in the inter-American dimensions of the Harlem Renaissance, *New Negro* radicalism, Négritude, Pan-Africanism, and Black Power (Haas; Valdés; Meehan; D. Brown; Raussert and Steinitz).

In a special special issue of *The Black Scholar* on "Post-Soul and Afro-Latinidades" (2022), guest editors Regina Mills and Trent Masiki addressed "the increasing interest in and need for critical discussions of Afro-Latino and African American interculturalism in the post-segregation era" (1) and called for a bridging of existing demarcations between Latin American and African American Studies by putting concepts from both disciplines into dialogue with each other. These hemispheric and comparative perspectives on the Black Americas allow us to discern not only the legacies of "divergent racialization" (34) but also "patterns of convergence" between diverse Afro-diasporic movements and cultures as a "significant (...) feature of inter-American life" (51), as Kevin Meehan has argued in his analysis of African American and Caribbean cultural exchange.

Building on these approaches which are guided by the objective of overcoming Latin American and African American forms of nationalism and exceptionalism, the adoption of *the Black Americas* as a hemispheric research perspective promises insights into parallels, overlaps, and differences in the experiences of Afro-diasporic communities and the processes of exchange that have shaped their daily lives and world views. First and foremost, this perspective requires a bridging of the demarcation lines between Latin American Studies and African American Studies, as these divisions obscure the mutual influences and interactions. The distinction between the two disciplines is based on the assumption of national and regional differences, with a tendency to neglect overlaps: Many Latin Americanists have until recently neglected the realities of racism dismissing the topic as an obsession of the ethnically polarized United States. At the same time, African American Studies have long reproduced dominant patterns by not taking into account the perspectives of Afro-Latin Americans, as criticized by García Peña, who made a call to decenter "hegemonic blackness" made in the USA. Although the central position of U.S. race discourses in the scholarly diaspora debate has in part led to the marginalization of Afro-diasporic perspectives from the non-Anglophone world, the discourse around race in Latin America has been able to contribute to the identification of previously hidden racist mechanisms. Revisiting studies of black populations in specific national contexts may provide an important correction to historiographies in which the contributions and presence of the African diaspora have been minimized or glossed over. Through a transnational, hemispheric and comparative analytical framework, however, such studies can assist in the identification and analysis of the multidirectional flow of ideas, people and cultural products that have shaped the realities of Afrodescendants in the region and relate them to each other. Hemispheric Black Studies, thus, proposes a comparative look at diverse expressions of black transnationalism which reveals that these practices have often displayed an emancipatory potential in the freedom struggles of Afrodescendants across the region.

2 "It's a New Day" – Black Liberation and the Politics of Soul

In August 1972, the Memphis-based label Stax organized a festival in Los Angeles commemorating the seventh anniversary of the Watts Rebellion, an urban uprising which heralded the shift from Civil Rights to Black Power in 1965. The Wattstax Festival featured soul stars like Isaac Hayes, Eddie Floyd and the Staple Singers and was opened with a speech by Black Power organizer Rev. Jesse Jackson. In his "black litany", he exclaimed:

> This is a beautiful day…It's a new day…it is a day of black awareness, it is a day of black people taking care of black people's business…We are together, we are unified… and all in accord… Because when we are together we got power… and we can make decisions… Today on this program you will hear gospel, and rhythm and blues, and jazz. All those are just labels. We know that music is music… All of our people have got a soul, our experience determines the texture, the tastes and the sounds of our soul. We may be in the slum but the slum is not in us. We may be in the prison, but the prison is not in us. […] That is why we've gathered today, to celebrate our homecoming and our own sense of somebodyness. That is why I challenge you now to stand together, raise your first together, and engage in our famous black litany. Do it with courage and determination:
> I am… somebody! I may be poor, but I am… somebody! I may be on welfare, but I am somebody! I may be unskilled, but I am… somebody! I am… black…beautiful… proud! And must be respected! …. (J. Jackson, 1972).

Before Kim Weston started off the musical part of the show with the song "Lift Every Voice and Sing" (declared the black national anthem by the NAACP in 1919), Jackson concluded his speech asking the all-black audience of about 100.000 Los Angeles residents "What time is it?", to which the crowd answered: "It's nation time!". The slogan had been introduced by Newark-based Black Arts Movement founder Amiri Baraka (LeRoi Jones) and had become a rallying cry among a new generation of black militants, who had lost their belief in the prospects of integrationism when Civil Rights leader Martin Luther King Jr. was assassinated in April 1968. Wattstax epitomized the close relationship between soul music and the rise of black nationalism as the dominant current in the African American political, social and cultural life of the Black Power era. Thus, tracing the meanings of soul for black liberation struggles beyond U.S. borders not only requires a closer look at the discourses of black nationalism that travelled with the genre but also at the debates surrounding its emancipatory potential.

When Ben E. King released the song "What Is Soul?" in 1966 he not only landed a major hit for Atlantic Records, but also raised a question that has been controversially debated among activists, intellectuals, and scholars of black popular cul-

https://doi.org/10.1515/9783110665550-004

ture in the United States. At the core of these conversations lays a concern which is also of relevance to this study: In how far can soul, understood as a musical genre, a culture, a style, and a theoretical concept, be interpreted as the "purest and most powerful expression of the black experience in America" (qtd. in Hanson 347), as Black Arts Movement poet Larry Neal phrased it? If "soul" was a signifier of "blackness", was "Soul Power" synonymous with "Black Power", as the conflation of both terms in many accounts suggest? And, of particular importance to this examination of the ways in which ideologies travelled hemispherically through soul, if Black Power was a movement fueled by black nationalism, was soul a black nationalist genre? The multilayered and contradictory answers given by activists and scholars point at least to some significant parallels between soul and Black Power. Both the movement and the genre were ideologically diverse and multifaceted in their messages in a way that prohibit one-dimensional narratives which reduce them to their character as revolutionary, emancipatory, essentialist, masculinist, or nationalist. Addressing a variety of issues that encompassed all spheres of life in urban Black America, both coincided in capturing the dreams, aspirations and frustrations of many American Americans between the mid-1960s and mid- 1970s. Soul singers and Black Power activists spoke about issues related not only to race but also class, gender, love, sex, oppression, and freedom in bold and unprecedented terms. The transnational and interethnic appeal of soul, like Black Power, suggests that both, while grounded in the specific experiences of black Americans in the United States, conveyed universal messages that resonated in a variety of contexts, which speaks to their potential as platforms for the expression of cosmopolitan sensibilities abroad.

2.1 Soul Music, Cultural Nationalism and the Black Arts Movement

The controversies on the role of soul music in the African American freedom struggle among various factions of the Black Power movement provide some insights into the contested relationship between black popular music and social movements. Following the teachings of Malcolm X, revolutionary nationalists, cultural nationalists, and Afrocentrists alike agreed on the necessity of liberating African Americans from the degrading psychological effects of white racism, but they disagreed on the meaning of black culture in this struggle (Ward, "Jazz and Soul" 161). As Amiri Baraka, then LeRoi Jones, had pointed out in his influential book *Blues People* (1963), there has always been a close relationship between the developments in black music and the historical trajectory of African American social and political activism. This became especially apparent with the shift from blues to soul as the most popular black music genre in the 1960s, a development that coincided with the rise of Black Power, as Nelson George noted: "To younger blacks – the soul children of the sixties – the blues just wasn't [...] 'relevant' in a world of dashikis, Afro picks, and bell bottoms.... Black music is in constant flight from the status quo. Young blacks at the time abandoned the blues because it was 'depressing', 'backward', or 'accommodating' to white values" (108). Black cultural nationalists like Ron Karenga and his US. organization dismissed contemporary expressions of black American culture such as blues and soul altogether. According to Karenga's Afrocentric philosophy, these forms were devalued by its contact with white society and thus represented "an aesthetic of political self-defeat that impeded black revolutionary praxis" (Hanson 354). Rather, blacks in the United States should return to authentic African culture in their quest for psychological liberation from white supremacy. In the propagation of an imagined mythological Africa as the only valid source for African American culture, Karenga's stance reflected the uneasy relationship of black nationalists with soul as a hybrid, modern, and secular genre.

The Black Arts Movement (BAM), "the aesthetic and spiritual sister of the Black Power concept" (L. Neal), represented a different brand of black cultural nationalism. BAM activists initially embraced free jazz as "the blackest of the arts" (Ward, "Jazz and Soul" 170) in their search for a "Black Aesthetic", that was defined by efforts to isolate "authentic" non-Western African elements in black music. Deeply skeptical of the white-owned music industry and hybrid commercialized forms of black popular music like soul, they considered avant-garde musicians like John Coltrane, Max Roach, Ornette Coleman, and Archie Shepp to be heroes of black liberation from white aesthetic values. According to the principles of the "Black Aesthetic", cultural producers had the political obligation "to make relevant and consumable aesthetic expressions that spoke to black experience" (Hanson 345). However, there was a major problem: the allegedly revolutionary jazz music was consumed primarily by white intellectuals and did not have any considerable impact in the black community among which the popularity of soul music was unmatched by any other black music genre during this period (Street 128). Eventually acknowledging that "jazz moved too far away from its most meaningful sources and ... becomes, little by little, just the music of another emerging middle class", Amiri Baraka urged his readers to listen to "The Supremes, Dionne Warwick, Martha and The Vandellas, The Impressions, Mary Wells, James Brown, Major Lance, Marvin Gaye, Four Tops, Bobby Bland, etc. [...] all the really nasty ideas are right there, and these young players are still connected with that reality, whether they understand it or not" (*Black Music* 125). In his influential text "The Changing Same (R&B and New Black Music)", Baraka argues that with their often encoded messages several soul songs "provided a core of legitimate social feeling, though mainly metaphorical and allegorical for Black People" (125). BAM leaders like Larry Neal recognized the ability of soul to reach urban black youth on a scale that had been out of their reach and hoped to leverage the popularity of soul singers as "the poets and philosophers of black America" (qtd. in Hanson 347) for their struggle to foster black consciousness and a sense of nationhood.

BAM's black nationalist reinterpretation of soul as "the voice and spirit of the people" (Smethurst 108) was fueled by the way the growing self-confidence of African Americans was reflected in soul music. Arguing that soul music rather reacted to shifts in black public opinion than acting as a vanguard of the movement, Brian Ward points out:

> Until the later 1960s, soul artists and their management largely eschewed public comment or agitation on the civil rights issue, fearing that such racial militancy might undermine their chances of reaching a lucrative white mass market....Thus, soul's popularity with African Americans initially depended less on its occasional forays into social activism or commentary than on its distinctively black vernacular lyrics, its adoption of certain musical devices and performance practices drawn from a gospel tradition to which blacks had an intensely proprietorial relationship. (*Just My Soul* 163)

Nina Simone had been one of the very few black entertainers in the early years of the movement to show with songs like "Missisippi Goddam" (1963) that she didn't let the fear of alienating white audiences stop her from speaking out about the ongoing struggles. Songs like Sam Cooke's "A Change is Gonna Come" (1964), "Keep On Pushing" (1964) and "People Get Ready" (1965) by The Impressions signaled the beginning of a new era. As the first of a series of anthemic black uplift songs performed by Curtis Mayfield, "Keep on Pushing" contains these lines: "I'll reach that higher goal/ I know I can make it / With just a little bit of soul / 'Cause I've got my strength / And it don't make sense / Not to keep on pushing." In "Keep On Pushin': Rhythm and Blues as a Weapon" (1965), a pamphlet by Askia Touré (then Roland Snellings), founder of the Black Artists Repertory Theatre and School, the song is referenced: "This social voice of Rhythm and Blues is only the beginning of the end. Somewhere along the line, the 'Keep on Pushin'' in song [...] is merging with the revolutionary dynamism [...] of Brother Malcolm of Young Black Guerril las striking deep into the heartland of the Western empire" (qtd. in Vincent 142–143). Although the efforts to enlist soul stars for the support of BAM's cultural nationalism remained quite ineffective, the emergence of radical spoken word artists like Gil Scott-Heron, The Last Poets, and The Watts Prophets and their role as important influences in the making of hip-hop bore witness to this movement's intervention in black popular music.

Due to the scarcity of explicit message songs in soul recordings prior to 1968, activists like Touré and Baraka engaged in practices of creative consumption as a central feature of black music under the conditions of white supremacy. This meant appropriating popular unpolitical songs and giving them new meanings, as in the case of Martha Reeves and the Vandellas' "Dancing in the Streets" (1964). According to Reeves, who was under contract with Motown, a label that was extremely politically restrained at the time, it was nothing but a party song and the lyrics seem to confirm that: "Calling out around the world/ are you ready for a brand new beat?/ Summer's here and the time is right/ for dancing in the street/ They're dancing in Chicago, Dancing in the streets!/ Down in New Orleans, Dancing in the streets! / In New York City, Dancing in the streets! ..." Nevertheless, it captured the imagination of young black militants who reinterpreted "dancing in the streets" as a celebration of riots, often referred to as "long, hot summers" which had become a common feature of urban life in Black America with regular large-scale confrontations between police and black youth in Watts (1965), Detroit (1967) and other major US cities. According to Michael Hanson, these "urban rebellions of the mid- to late 1960s inserted [...] a new black political subject: the self-determined, militant ghetto brother" (350). When Amiri Baraka wrote about how he was arrested during the Newark riot of 1967, he called the summer violence "the magic dance in the street" (Kurlansky 166). Showing that activists would make use of the sounds of soul on their own terms, Baraka replied when journalists told him that Martha Reeves insisted in the unpolitical nature of the song:

> No matter what she might think. At that particular time it coincides with people who were dancing in the street. They were the only people I knew who were dancing in the street. It doesn't matter to me what they meant. If you take the words in the context they came in, that's what it came to mean. It was used at rallies by Black Panthers and other groups. (qtd. in Kurlansky 189)

After replacing Stokely Carmichael as the new chairman of SNCC in 1967, H. Rap Brown used to play "Dancing in the Streets" when speaking from the roof of a car, as Kurlansky describes in his account of how the song became an anthem for the movement that defined the era (181–182, 187) To many, "calling out around the world" conveyed the spirit of the black revolution and its global appeal as demonstrated in Touré's manifesto for an internationalization of the black freedom struggle:

> [A]ll over this sullen planet, the multi-colored 'hordes' of undernourished millions are on the move like never before in human history. They are moving to the rhythm of a New Song, a New Sound; dancing in the streets to a Universal dream that haunts their wretched nights. They dream of Freedom! From the steaming jungles of Viet Nam to the drought-ridden plains of India: Dancing in the streets! From the great African savannahs to the peasant-ridden mountains of Guatemala: Dancing in the streets! (Touré 1965)

2.2 James Brown, Soul Brother No. 1

There was arguably no black artist of the era who symbolized the fusion of soul with Black Power more than James Brown. Evidencing the interrelatedness between changes in the black freedom struggle and soul music, the release of James Brown's "Papa's Got a Brand New Bag" in February 1965 signaled the beginning of a new era for the genre and the movement. The song revolutionized soul music: for the first time, rhythm instead of melody was emphasized, a characteristic which later gained "Papa's Got a Brand New Bag" the reputation of giving birth to funk as a "rhythm-based extension of soul" (Vincent 96), which was also interpreted as a way of "blackening" soul music (Ward, *Just My Soul* 350). In this context, James Brown's "new bag" also represented the new mood of black pride and assertiveness that was taking hold of urban black youth at this time. The influence of Malcolm X and his ideas on black self-determination and freedom "by any means necessary" would only grow stronger after his assassination on February 19, 1965 (three weeks after the recording of "Papa's Got a Brand New Bag"), gaining support in significant portions of the black community who were frustrated by the persistence of white supremacy in the United States. Tellingly, it was only a week after the passing of the Voting Rights Act in August 1965, one of the major achievements of the Civil Rights movement, when the Watts rebellion as one of the largest riots in U.S. history erupted in a black neighborhood of Los Angeles. The Watts uprising was a turning point in the black freedom struggle. Whereas many integrationists and white liberals saw Watts as a symbol for the "declension" (Joseph 751) of the heroic and peaceful Civil Rights era into the nihilistic and violent Black Power phase, black radicals welcomed it as a source of community pride, a manifestation of the anti-assimilationist sentiment and grown militancy among African American youth and an act of resistance linked to anti-colonial struggles in Africa, Asia, and Latin America (Murch 37–38). Evidently, the black youth of Watts and other ghettos in the United States were into something new. Instead of singing "We Shall Overcome," they shouted, "Long live Malcolm X" and "Burn Baby Burn" – a slogan popularized by soul DJ Magnificent Montague (Hanson 349). Watts and James Brown's "brand new bag" heralded the age of Black Power.

James Brown's status as "Soul Brother Number One" and the voice of Black America was reinforced during the watershed year 1968. When the assassination of Martin Luther King on April 4, 1968, accelerated the rise of black nationalism, it was Brown's new aggressive and funky grooves which captured young African Americans' mood more than Motown's polished "Sound of Young America" which was designed to cross over to white audiences. Vincent argues that "in a symbolic fashion, in much the same way that the direct talk of Malcolm X served to bring about a direct dialogue about race and equality in society, Brown's late 1960s music pushed against the traditional modes of music making to become something explicit, articulate, and assertive in ways never heard before in popular music" (92).

Although James Brown's new funk sounds were musically in line with Black Power's increased militancy, his relation to the movement had been ambiguous in many ways. By 1968, many black radicals despised him as "Uncle Tom" for releasing the patriotic "America is My Home" at the height of the Vietnam War and paying a visit to the GIs in order to show support for the troops. Black nationalists criticized Brown for his patriotism and failure to speak out in favor of the movement. Larry Neal recalls how he and other poets of the Black Arts Movement were envious of James Brown's ability to reach the very black masses on which their dreams of liberation were based: "We all thought that James Brown was a magnificent poet, and we all envied him and wished that we could do what he did. If poets could do that, we would just take over America. Suppose James Brown had consciousness. We used to have arguments like that. It was like saying, 'Suppose James Brown read Fanon'" (qtd. in Hanson 358–359). Questioned for his credibility and allegedly under pressure by black militants, it was in the very same year that James Brown seems to have taken the decision to follow Black America's shift toward nationalism and embrace the movement (Vincent 104). Released in August 1968, two months before fast-track athletes Tommie Smith and John Carlos created one of the most iconic images of the Black Power era with their raised fist protest at the Mexico Summer Olympics, James Brown's "Say It Loud – I'm Black and I'm Proud" provided the movement with its quintessential anthem:

> Say it loud: I'm Black and I'm proud!
> Some people say we got a lot of malice
> Some say it's a lotta nerve
> But I say we won't quit moving
> Until we get what we deserve
> We've been 'buked and we've been scorned
> We've been treated bad, talked about
> As sure as you're born
> But just as sure as it take two eyes to make a pair, huh
> Brother, we can't quit until we get our share
>
> Say it loud: I'm Black and I'm proud!
>
> I've worked on jobs with my feet and my hands
> But all the work I did was for the other man
> Now we demands a chance
> To do things for ourselves

We're tired of beating our heads against the wall
And working for someone else

Look here, there's one thing more I got to say right here
Now, we're people, we like the birds and the bees
And we'd rather die on our feet than keep living on our knees

Say it loud (I'm Black and I'm proud)
Say it loud (I'm Black and I'm proud)
Say it loud (I'm Black and I'm proud)

(James Brown, 1968)

While soul music had typically followed developments in black consciousness, it seems that this particular song reversed the usual sequence: the bold move of Black America's superstar to unapologetically embrace the movement with this song had an immense impact on a generation of politicized African Americans with implications throughout the African diaspora. As an immediate consequence, "Say It Loud" ensured that one of Malcolm X's central demands, that African Americans begin to refer to themselves as blacks rather than *negroes* became a reality. An advertisement stated: "We know the Negro deejay won't play this record. We know the coloured deejay won't play this record, but every BLACK deejay will play this record!" (Hanson 357) As Reverend Al Sharpton noted, there were other black entertainers who had become mainstream, but James Brown made the mainstream go black (Vincent 124). He stated: "There were many in the movement who wanted to raise the consciousness of black America from Negro to black. James Brown did it with one song. He could reach the masses much quicker than a lot of the leaders" (qtd. in Vincent 107). While "Say It Loud" led to a significant loss of James Brown's white audiences (he wouldn't reach the pop top ten charts for 17 years after its release), it was precisely his economic success that gave him the control and the artistic freedom to release controversial songs, turning him into a symbol for black self-determination. While never affiliating himself with a black nationalist organization and guarding a cautionary distance to the militancy of Black Power advocates, James Brown continued to position himself as the "most prominent popular entertainer to openly promote and celebrate black pride" (Vincent 91). As Michael Hanson put it, James Brown was a "conduit of black nationalist desires that could represent both the political and quotidian practices of the black masses" (357).

2.3 Soul Style: "Black is beautiful"

It was not only James Brown's musical productions that revolutionized Black America but also his styles. When he first appeared with an Afro it was celebrated as a significant act of liberation by Black Power advocates and gave a huge boost to the popularization of the hairstyle, nationally and internationally (Munro 194). James Brown's new style was applauded as a meaningful step by activists across the spectrum of the Black Power movement. An editorial in the *Soul* magazine commented: "The King's been a slave for years .... James Brown's been putting up with painful and time-consuming process hair do for as long as anyone can remember... until last month that is. Now the King's got a natural. Everyone, including the Black Panthers and SNCC, think it's fine, just fine" (qtd. in Munro 194). Promoting the new look, James Brown produced the song "How You Gonna Get Respect (When You Haven't Cut Your Process Yet)" (1968) for his sideman Hank Ballard, in which black audiences were urged to abandon the practice of straightening their hair ("process"):

> You're black and you're beautiful, yes I know,
> just being your natural self
> It's a new day now, time has changed,
> and I wanna be identified
> Everywhere I go, I see brothers getting in the natural bag
> And I feel so proud to see this pride, something that we've never had
> Now I'm gonna do what I gotta do and put my process down
> I got the message from a friend of mine, his name is James Brown
> Together we stand, divided we fall, that's what history say
> Now can't you see brothers, the coming of a brand new day?
> How you gonna get respect,
> When you haven't cut your process yet?
> (Hank Ballard, "How You Gonna Get Respect (When You Haven't Cut Your Process Yet)", 1968)

By encouraging blacks to take pride in their natural self and connecting aesthetic issues such as a hairdo with hopes for a "brand new day" for Black America, the song expressed some of the core messages of the Black Power movement: African Americans would only be respected by wider society when they would develop a positive attitude toward their own identity. Ballard also references "Black is Beautiful", a slogan coined by a Harlem-based Garveyite modeling agency named Grandassa Models, to which blacks in the United States and globally showed allegiance by starting to wear natural hairdos instead of straightening their hair.

Defying Eurocentric beauty standards that were dominant in different colonial and post-colonial contexts, the Afro was, according to Jeffrey Ogbar, a bold "statement of black pride, a metaphorical exclamation point, affirming the beauty of black people and their hair" ("The Looks" 128). As Tanisha Ford has shown in *Liberated Threads*, black female singers like Nina Simone and Miriam Makeba had started to popularize the Afro as one of the most visible symbol of a transnationally disseminated "soul style" years before James Brown positioned himself at the front of the movement. According to Ford, "soul style comprises African American and African-inspired hairstyles and modes of dress such as Afros, cornrows, denim overalls, platform shoes, beaded jewelry, and dashikis and other garments with African prints" (4). Based on the the collective consumption of soul music, "soul style" was connected to a range of symbolic representations of blackness which conveyed in-group messages through distinct forms of dancing, talking, clothing, and complex "soul handshakes" (Van Deburg 202–204).

The success of James Brown brought to the surface a trend that had long been apparent in the releases of soul singers on countless small local labels, which had not made it to national and international prominence: by forging a sense of unity and community pride among black people, soul music converged with the goals of black nationalism in the late 1960s and early 1970s. As "Say It Loud" demonstrated that songs with messages aimed specifically at African American audiences could also generate profit, many labels, formerly driven by fears to alienate white audiences, responded to the growing demand for conscious lyrics among black consumers which made political commitment by their artists a question of political credibility and economic necessity (Ward 361).

In the wake of "Say It Loud", Motown's director Berry Gordy, always anxious about losing white audiences, was pressured by black activists and his own musicians like Stevie Wonder, who was "not interested in 'baby, baby' songs any more" (Ramsey 2), to produce politically committed music. Worried about Motown's standing in an increasingly politicized black community, the new marketing strategy materialized in the release of politically conscious songs like "War" (1970) by Edwin Starr, The Temptations' "Message from a Black Man" (1970) and Marvin Gaye's influential protest song "What's Going On?" (1971). When it became clear that consciousness sells too, Motown as Black America's most successful company and symbol of black capitalism did not hesitate to jump on the Black Power train.

In the same period, Memphis-based Stax Records, Motown's strongest rival with a reputation of an unpolished and somewhat "blacker" southern soul sound and home to stars like Otis Redding, Carla Thomas, Sam and Dave, and Isaac Hayes, also gave up on its abstinence from the struggle. By the end of the 1960s, the white-owned company decisively embraced the Black Power movement by hiring the black DJ Al Bell as marketing executive (Werner, *Change Is Gonna Come* 170). Bell, who eventually became co-owner, directed the label's appeal explicitly toward mobilized black audiences, authorized sponsorship of SNCC activities, and established a close relationship between Stax and Reverend Jesse Jackson

(George 139). Bell was also a key figure in the organization of the Wattstax festival in 1972 which would become known as "black Woodstock" (Werner, *A Change Is Gonna Come* 165). *Wattstax*, a documentary of the event, provided national and transnational audiences with powerful images of this symbiotic moment in the relationship between soul music and black nationalism: Kim Weston singing the black national anthem "Lift Ev'ry Voice and Sing" accompanied by 100,000 enthused black spectators, Isaac Hayes posturing as "Black Moses" while performing his legendary "Theme from Shaft," Al Bell and Jesse Jackson greeting the audience with fists raised for a Black Power salute, and reciting his "black litany" (referenced at the beginning of the chapter).

Previously completely absent from black popular music, direct references to blackness became more common in the immediate post-"Say It Loud" period as demonstrated in releases like The Main Ingredients' "Black Seeds", Grady Tate's "Be Black", Syl Johnson's "Is It Because I'm Black", Curtis Mayfield's "Miss Black America", Nina Simone's "To Be Young, Gifted and Black" (and Aretha Franklin's interpretation of the song), The J.B.'s "Blessed Blackness", and Hank Ballard's "Blackenized." In line with these developments, pictures of artists with Afro hairdos and African-inspired clothing became commonplace on soul records. In this context, the term "soul" became a marker for a new notion of assertive urban blackness. In songs like "I Know You Got Soul" (Bobby Byrd), "We Got Soul" (Bad & Good Boys), "We Got More Soul" (Dyke & The Blazers), "Can't Buy Soul" (Hebrew Rogers), "Soul Revolution" (Desciples Of Soul) and "Soul Power" (James Brown), to have "soul" was invoked as a source of pride as it was celebrated as something that distinguished African Americans from white people. In constructing a collective black identity based on the shared ownership of soul, allusions to "soul brothers" and "soul sisters" as in "The Message from the Soul Sisters" by Vickie Anderson, "Brothers and Sisters (Get Together)" by Kim Weston and "Soul Brothers Testify" by The Soul Senders were highly significant. The term "soul brother" was used to signal black identity as became apparent during several urban riots when shop-owners displayed signs that read "soul brother" in order to signal to rioting African American youth that their shops were black-owned businesses (Maultsby 278).

The use of a "we" perspective as in optimistic and uplifting songs like "We Can Do It" by The Hesitations or songs which posited the shared experiences of racial and social exclusion of African Americans as a source of pride like "We The People From The Ghetto" by Vernon Garret and "We The People Who Are Darker Than Blue" by Curtis Mayfield, and the ever recurring call to "keep on keeping on" hint at the ways soul celebrated collective black resilience under white supremacy. In her definition of the meaning of soul, Emily Lordi argues: "To have soul was to have developed a kind of virtuosic survivorship specific to black people as a group.

And soul musicians, through a series of practices drawn from the black church, modeled virtuosic black resilience on a national stage" (5). When Syl Johnson sang about "different strokes for different folks" this was interpreted as a way of saying that soul was something only black people would understand. Inspired by a radicalizing ghetto youth and fueled by a record industry which had discovered unapologetic blackness as a marketing strategy, these shifts in soul music signaled a declaration of independence from white sensitivities and listening habits. Thus, in creating a distinct language to articulate black consciousness and the recuperation of black manhood as symbolized by James Brown's aggressive masculinity, these changes in soul music made many of the dreams come true that small and sectarian circles of cultural nationalists had pursued for years.

2.4 "Right on!" Black Panthers, Soul, and the Universal Dream of Freedom

Whereas these linkages seem to confirm the assumption of soul as a quintessentially black nationalist sound, the views of other currents within the ideologically heterogeneous Black Power movement problematize reductive and often essentializing interpretations of the genre. The Black Panther Party as the most visible Black Power organization held a radically different position on the meaning of soul for the struggle. As revolutionary Marxists, they were diametrically opposed to the racial separatism of cultural nationalists as Ron Karenga and Amiri Baraka and their stance that forging, or returning to, an authentic black culture, uncontaminated by Western influences, was the most pressing issue in the struggle for black liberation. As Bobby Seale, one of the founders of the Black Panthers put it "power for the people will not grow out of the sleeve of a dashiki" (256). Since they saw racism in the United States as interrelated with global capitalism and imperialism, they considered a revolution to be reactionary if limited to the concerns of African Americans, advocating for a politics of cross racial coalition building and revolutionary internationalism instead. While the Black Panthers were more successful than any other Black Power group in mobilizing the militant ghetto youth who made up the core constituency of soul music, they criticized the cultural nationalist and essentialist meaning of "Say It Loud – I'm Black and I'm Proud" for its alleged lack of emancipatory political message. According to their view, the song illustrated the futility of an apolitical fetishization of blackness. Besides the rejection of the ethnocentric orientation of the song, James Brown's promotion of black capitalism was antithetical to their anti-capitalist convictions. At the height of Brown's popularity as a movement icon, Emory Douglas, the party's minister of culture, denounced the Godfather of Soul for exploiting blackness for commercial means: "You hear James Brown talking about Black and Proud, then you hear him on the radio saying, 'Why don't you buy this beer?'" (qtd. in Ward, "Jazz and Soul" 182). James Brown's overt advocacy of black capitalism as a liberation strategy, expressed in songs such as "I Don't Want Nobody to Give Me Nothing (Open Up The Door I'll Get It Myself)" (1969) and his support for Richard Nixon in his 1972 presidential campaign, was, according to this critique, an example of a larger problem in which black capitalists used the ideology of Black Power and claims for black unity to disguise class hierarchies and exploitation within the African American community.

However, Black Panthers did see the political potential of soul as music of the proletarian masses in the ghettos they wanted to enlist for the movement. In the Black Panthers' class-based analysis, soul constituted an urban street culture which addressed the social conditions of Black America much more directly than the artificial Africanisms promoted by Karenga's US organization (Ward, "Jazz and Soul" 181–183.). The defiant ghetto chic of soul fit perfectly with the Panther ideology; there were even analogies between soul's "collective imperative" (the frequent use of "we" instead of "I") and the party's socialist visions of brotherhood and community (188). Although critical of most prominent soul musicians' lack of commitment to the struggle and the commodification of soul, the party also tried to use the music as a medium for their revolutionary propaganda. In the tradition of Robert Williams (along with Malcolm X one of the most important inspirations for the Black Panthers), a revolutionary black internationalist who, in Cuban exile, played Curtis Mayfield's "Keep on Pushing," Nina Simone's "Mississippi Goddamn," and Sam Cooke's "A Change is Gonna Come" on his Radio Free Dixie, which was broadcast to the southern United States (Tyson 286), soul music played an important role at Black Panther mobilizations. In his efforts to forge "rainbow coalitions" with other oppressed communities, Fred Hampton, chairman of the Chicago chapter of the Black Panther Party who was assassinated by the police in 1969, regularly played "Someday We'll Be Together" by The Supremes on political rallies (Sullivan 71).

Emory Douglas, the BPP's minister of culture, criticized the elitist positions of Afrocentrists like Karenga, who had scoffed at the high value blacks placed on music by saying "the 'Negro' has more records than books and dances his life away" (Ward, "Jazz and Soul" 181). Douglas criticized this stance as detached from the reality of African Americans and argued that "revolutionary art is art that comes from the people" (181). In order to come to terms with the contradiction that Black Panthers were critical of most soul songs' lack of revolutionary consciousness but admired the ways it mobilized the urban poor, Emory Douglas recruited rank-and-file members to form The Lumpen (referring to Marx' *lumpenproletariat*), the party's own revolutionary agitprop soul band. In his text "The

2.4 "Right on!" Black Panthers, Soul, and the Universal Dream of Freedom — **69**

Lumpen – Music as a Tool for Liberation", Douglas wrote: "We like the Beat of James Brown, we say the Temptations sound great, but if we try to relate to what they are saying to our conditions we'd end up in a ball of confusion. [...] The Lumpen sing not to make profit or stimulate emotions, but to make revolution and stimulate action" (qtd. in Ward, "Jazz and Soul" 194–195). The Lumpen started to play regularly at party rallies where they performed songs like "Revolution is the only solution" and "Free Bobby Now" for the imprisoned Black Panther leader Bobby Seale (Vincent). In May 1971, The Lumpen played alongside Curtis Mayfield and guest speaker Muhammad Ali at a "Malcolm X Day" organized by George Jackson's chapter of the BPP in the San Quentin prison. Elaine Brown was another member of the BPP who performed soul music and released the album "Seize the Time" on the Motown sublabel Black Forum. The elusiveness of their success, however, suggests that The Lumpen and Elaine Brown, "in elevating the political message over the artistic statement, [...] fell into the agitprop trap, where their music could not transcend the political message" (158), as Joe Street argues.

The Black Panthers' soul politics speak to the fact that the genre was much broader and flexible than narrow nationalist interpretations of soul as an exclusive manifestation of the U.S. black experience suggest. Though supremely important in the making of a counterhegemonic black group identity, soul also conveyed a range of universal messages that, by transcending race, could also serve the ends of a distinctly non-ethnocentric liberation movement like the Black Panthers. Sly and The Family Stone, a multiethnic and mixed-gender band that fused soul and funk with psychedelic rock, embodied many of the Black Panthers' ideals, according to which alliances with the hippie and student movements and the broader 1960s protest culture were an essential part of the agenda. In line with the Black Panthers' universalist aspirations for liberation, the trope of freedom as a dream or as a concrete demand is a concurrent theme in a number of soul songs such as Nina Simone's "I Wish I Knew How It Would Feel to be Free", The Hesitations' "Born Free", Mary Queenie Lyons' "I Want My Freedom", The Young Rascals' "People Got to Be Free", Syl Johnson's "Talking about Freedom", and The Staple Singers' "Freedom Highway". In the "Freedom Song", The Congenial Four claim "We want freedom, we'll do whatever it takes ...we gonna protest, we gonna demonstrate, 'cause our freedom just won't wait.. don't just discuss, make up a fuss, let freedom ring! Right on, keep on pushin'!" There were also several bands who made explicit reference to the Black Panthers' ideas and slogans such as The Chi-Lites with "Give More Power To The People" or The Voices of East Harlem's "Right On Be Free". In 1970, Barbara and Gwen released "Right On", a song whose lyrics evoke the Black Panthers' call to collective action:

> It's an invitation to the nation,
> chances for the people to meet
> Let's get as tight as a hand in a glove
> Right on everybody, to the street corner!
> Everywhere we live and everywhere we go,
> there should be love, unity, and peace...
> Together we stand, and divided we fall
> Right on everybody, to the street corner!
> With trouble all over this land...
> All you need is love for humanity
> 'cause that's the way it oughta be...
> Right on everybody, to the street corner!
> (Barbara and Gwen, "Right on", 1970)

In the song, Barbara and Gwen's references to the Black Panthers are not limited to the party's slogan "Right on". They can also be found in "the streetcorner" as the place where their mobilizations of the ghetto youth take place, the glove as symbol of Black Power, and their universalist appeal to unity, peace and "love for humanity" which is very much in line with the BPP's politics of radical humanism as opposed to the cultural nationalists' black separatism. In the liner notes of the album *Laugh To Keep From Crying*, a band named The Nat Turner Rebellion cites Malcolm X, Martin Luther King and Huey P. Newton as their main influences. Ending the Vietnam War with its devastating effects on thousands of African American youths was not only a global issue of the 1960s youth revolt and a major demand of the Black Panthers in their joint activities with the student movement but also the topic of soul songs such as Edwin Starr's "War" and Freda Payne's "Bring the boys back home". Social issues which spoke directly to the interrelatedness of class and race-based forms of oppression that shaped life in the inner cities of the United States and elsewhere are referenced in Marvin Gaye's "Inner City Blues (Make Me Wanna Holler)", The Barons' "Society Don't let us down", The Unemployed' "They Won't Let Me", Curtis Mayfield's "Mr Welfare Man" and "On the other side of town", Warren Lee's "Direct from the Ghetto", and Marlena Shaw's "Women of the Ghetto."

Even the dominant trope of love, often cited as a proof of the apolitical nature of soul, has political and universalist connotations when contextualized as an expression of longing for humanity under the most inhumane conditions. As Amiri Baraka observed, "this missed love that runs through these songs is exactly reflect of what is the term of love and loving in the Black world of America Twentieth Century" (*Black Music* 190). The power of love and appeals to togetherness, invoked in many soul songs, in this sense become a redeeming source of strength and resilience which makes survival possible against all odds. Love politics were also a

2.5 "Message from the Soul Sisters": Black Feminist Perspectives

Black feminists have articulated insightful critiques of black nationalism as "a vehicle to push black patriarchal values" (hooks 5). The same holds true for soul music which has been criticized for its masculinist and sexist tendencies. While painfully accurate in the observation that soul often expressed mysoginistic and chauvinistic views of women as sexual objects of male desires, these classifications often overlook that soul, like the Black Power movement, also provided a platform for sexual liberation and black female empowerment. In fact, I would argue that in the 1960s and 1970s there was no other popular music genre, globally, in which women played such an outstanding role as in soul music. The influential contributions of female soul singers like Nina Simone, Aretha Franklin, Roberta Flack, Carla Thomas, Tina Turner, Diana Ross, Lyn Collins, Vickie Anderson, Marva Whitney, Minnie Ripperton, Betty Davis and many others question narratives of soul as a male-centered genre. Indeed, the history of political commentary in 1960s black popular music begins with Nina Simone, according to Stokely Carmichael the "true singer of the civil rights movement" (Redmond 191), who wore an Afro look and used her voice to support the struggle long before it became fashionable and marketable to do so. In the tradition of earlier black female blues singers such as Bessie Smith and Billie Holiday, Nina Simone's pioneering acts of "musical maroonage" (Brooks, "Nina Simone" 177), established black female soul singing as a form of black feminist dissent, as Daphne Brooks has argued. With recordings such as "Four Women" (1966) which addresses the intersections of gender and race-based discrimination, her internationalist activism, and her promotion of Afro-centered styles, Nina Simone "offered black cultural nationalism within and outside the United States that insisted on female power well before the apparent ascendance of black power or second-wave feminism in the late 1960s and 1970s," as Ruth Feldstein claims (1352).

For a deeper understanding of the role of women in male-dominated soul, it is useful, as in an analysis of the relationship of black feminists to black nationalism, not to see them as oppressed and marginalized victims of male objectification but as self-determined participants in a controversial debate on gender that took place *within* the Black Power movement and soul music simultaneously. Few songs mirrored the intersections and frictions between black and women's liberation more clearly than "Respect" by Aretha Franklin. While the original version of the song by Otis Redding contained a husband's request to his wife to submit to his patriarchal demands, the meaning changed radically in Aretha Franklin's version. Released in June 1967, three weeks after the Black Panthers made their highly mediatized armed intervention at the California state capitol in Sacramento, "Respect" came to be perceived as a musical manifesto of the black freedom movement, expressing one of its fundamental demands in a critical moment of transition from Civil Rights to Black Power. Addressing the ways "Respect" spoke to a state of insurgency in light of the ongoing urban rebellions, the *Ebony* magazine announced a summer of "'Retha, Rap, and Revolt" (Vincent 154). A black woman demanding respect in 1960s America, also represented a bold statement of black female empowerment, as it was read as a comment on the intersection of white racism and widespread misogyny and sexism within the male-dominated African American movement, as Patricia Hill-Collins argues: "Even though the lyrics can be sung by anyone, they take on a special meaning when sung by Aretha in the way that she sings them. On one level the song functions as a metaphor for the conditions of African Americans in a racist society. But Aretha's being a Black woman enables the song to tap a deeper meaning" (108). Aretha Franklin, whose father Reverend C.L. Franklin was a friend to Martin Luther King, used her distinct gospel-derived singing style in songs on secular affairs in ways that reflected the roots of soul in the black church. According to Nelson George, Franklin's singing "[c]ompared to Motown, made few concessions to 'white' sensibilities" (106), gaining her enormous popularity especially among black women as radical poet Nikki Giovanni, who, in her "Poem for Aretha" claimed that she "pushed every Black singer into Blackness … Aretha was the riot was the leader if she had said 'come let's do it' it would have been done" (qtd. in Martin 67). While Emily Lordi interpreted the song as "an anthem of Black Power, more specifically of black female power" (199), Franklin did not not associate herself explicitly with Black Power or black nationalism in the years after "Respect". Following the general shift towards politically and socially committed songs in soul music, Franklin embraced the movement publicly with the release of the album *To Be Young, Gifted, and Black* in 1970, on which she appears with an African-styled turban. In the same year, she offered to post the bail for Angela Davis, who had just been arrested, challenging state authorities who had vilified Davis as a dangerous extremist. In an interview to *Jet* magazine, she explained her bold move which also spoke to her newly gained economic independence and self-determination:

> Angela Davis must go free. Black people will be free. I've been locked up (for disturbing the peace in Detroit) and I know you got to disturb the peace when you can't get no peace. Jail is hell to be in. I'm going to see her free if there is any justice in our courts, not because I believe in communism, but because she's a Black woman and she wants freedom for Black people. I

2.5 "Message from the Soul Sisters": Black Feminist Perspectives — **73**

> have the money; I got it from Black people – they've made me financially able to have it – and I want to use it in ways that will help our people. (qtd. in Okosun 233)

As Mark Anthony Neal has pointed out, the sonic and political interventions of Aretha Franklin, Nina Simone, and many other female soul singers "created musical counter narratives to the heroic black male soul singer" (69), which was most prominently represented by James Brown. With his dismissive and abusive attitude toward women and the lyrics of songs like "It's A Man's World", "Get Up (I Feel Like Being a Sex machine)", and "Hot Pants" he gave voice to a male-centered chauvinistic vision of black nationalism which was based on the assumption that black liberation was based on the recuperation of black manhood through the subjugation of black women. According to this view, both, white supremacy and feminism were aimed at the emasculation of the black male. In "It's a New Day (Let a Man Come In)", Brown opens with a complaint: "Fellas, things done got too far gone! We got to let the girls know what they got to do for us! It's done got to be a drag, man, a man can't do nothin' no more!" As E. Taylor Atkins has argued, these words "characterize Brown's response to the Women's Liberation Movement of the 1960s and 1970s as a misogynistic backlash, an effort to re-establish a male-dominated order in which women were primarily and fundamentally objects for male titillation and sexual conquest" (238).

While James Brown's self-positioning as the leading voice of aggressive black masculinity is unambiguous, his simultaneous promotion of a number of female soul singers like Vickie Anderson, Marva Whitney, and Lyn Collins whose work provided self-conscious responses to their employer's sexist attitudes further proves that the gender politics of soul are more complex than they first appear. In their songs, often conceived as explicit "back-talk" to James Brown's own releases, the female singers expressed messages about the dignity of black womanhood, self-respect and female autonomy that, according to Atkins, were "as clear and unyielding an articulation of feminist empowerment as any found in popular music of the time" (339). As he argues, the female soul singers of the James Brown enterprise encouraged black women's emotional and economic self-sufficiency by projecting "images of strong black womanhood that were persuasive and appealing in the contexts of second-wave feminism and Black Power. They spoke to and for black women who were increasingly disaffected with both the 'mainstream' feminist and black pride movements, because the former ignored racism and the latter downplayed sexism" (344). Sexual agency is a recurrent theme in these songs, which were all recorded by James Brown and his band The J.B.'s and released on his People label. In "Women's Lib" (1972), Lyn Collins claims, "the time is here at last for sisters to take a stand," and "you can't love me if you don't respect me." In "The Message from the Soul Sisters" (1970), Vickie Anderson announces that "we're gonna use what we got to get what we want". Marva Whitney's "It's my thing, I can do what I wanna do/You can't tell me who to sock it to" is a clear statement of female self-determination and sexual agency. In the same vein, Lyn Collins claims "if you don't give me what I want I got to get it some other place" in "Think (About It)".

Assertions of sexual agency, claims for respect, and defiance of male authority were not limited to Collins, Whitney and Anderson. Rather, they became a defining feature of late 1960s and early 1970's female soul productions, sparking a conversation on sex and gender between male and female soul singers that was often held through answer-and-response songs, a practice that had its roots in early blues recordings and would also become common in hip-hop. Few songs sparked male outrage, and multiple response songs, like the feminist anthem "Mr. Big Stuff" by Jean Knight:

> Mr. Big Stuff, who do you think you are?
> You never gonna get my love /
> Now because you wear all those fancy clothes,
> And have a big fine car /
> Do you think I can afford to give you my love?
> Do you think you're higher than every star above? /
> I'd rather give my love to a poor guy that has love /
> Than to be fooled around and get hurt by you /
> 'Cause when I give my love, I want love in return /
> I know this is a lesson Mr Big Stuff you haven't learned
> (Jean Knight, "Mr. Big Stuff", 1971)

"Mr. Big Stuff" provoked a series of male response songs such as "(That's Who I Think I Am) I'm Mr Big Stuff" by Wardell Quezerque Band, interestingly composed of the very same musicians who had backed Jean Knight for her hit. These dialogues sparked by the bold interventions of black women in the male-dominated music industry revolutionized the ways gender was addressed in black popular music, laying the groundwork for the emergence of hip-hop as a site of gender contestations in the late 20th and early 21st century in the United States and globally.

2.6 "What happened to soul?" Debates in the Post-Soul Era

While the perspectives and dialogues between the different currents of the black liberation movement presented above illustrate that there are no simple answers to the question of the complex relationship between soul and Black Power, it can be stated with certainty that the temporal synchronicity of the rise of the movement and the genre was maintained until its end. Against the backdrop of deteriorating conditions in the urban America and the commodification of blackness, the demise of Black Power due to internal cleavages and fierce government repression went hand in hand with the advent of the disco era which put an end to the golden age of soul. Asking "What happened to soul?", Rickey Vincent holds: "A case can be made that soul music survived as long as there was a movement in place to give the music social meaning" (163).

Interrogating the relationship between music and social movements, one of the central questions remains whether sounds are able to inspire changes in political attitudes or whether they just reflect these transformations. Historical scrutiny supports the position that the social changes brought about by the black liberation movement preceded the changes in music: The increased mobility and self-confidence of soul musicians facilitated by the rise of the black freedom struggle in the Civil Rights era were preconditions for the changes that would take place in soul music in the late 1960s and early 1970s. As Munro states, it is possible to detect a "lapse between the progress the movement was making and the translation of that progress into the form of overtly political lyrics and extra-musical activities for the cause" (210). So on the one hand, the history of political comment in soul music is a history of increasing self-consciousness and growing social awareness in Black America. However, it is also a history of "mass commodification of the black protest tradition" (Neal 62). As Amiri Baraka had predicted in "The Changing Same (R&B and New Black Music)" (1966), the white-controlled music industry recognized the profit perspectives of political content in black music. Labels, formerly driven by fears to alienate white audiences, finally encouraged soul musicians to celebrate their blackness and show support for the movement when it became convenient in terms of popularity and commercial success. As depicted in Gil Scott-Heron's famous "The Revolution Will Not Be Televised" (1971), during the Black Power era, black nationalist discourse and symbolic representations of black pride in soul music had become fetishized objects of massification and very successful marketing resources for the popular music industry (Hanson 354). However, when soul music and Black Power had already lost momentum in the U.S. context, they would exhibit significant emancipatory potential when exported to different hemispheric contexts.

The question of what soul is and what it isn't has been at the center of US-centered debates on the concept of a "Post-Soul Aesthetic". While Mark Anthony Neal (2002) and Nelson George (1988) draw a connection between the commodification of soul and the loss of its emancipatory potential as a defining feature of post-soul, critics like Trey Ellis, Greg Tate and Bertram D. Ashe celebrate the end of the soul era as the liberating beginning of something new. They use "soul" as a metaphor for the "call for a fixed, iron-clad Black aesthetic" (Ashe 615) that has shaped the diverse currents of black cultural nationalism which emerged at the height of the Black Power movement in the late 1960s and early 1970s. Tired of "deny[ing] or suppress[ing] any part of our complicated and sometimes contradictory cultural baggage to please either white people or Black" (Ellis 235), advocates of the "Post-Soul Aesthetic" like Ashe promote "a hybrid [...] sense of Black identity" (614) and propose to explore "a set of *non*traditional Black expectations" (617).

Whereas Emily J. Lordi welcomes this anti-essentialist approach in discussions on black popular culture in her groundbreaking book *The Meaning of Soul – Black Music and Resilience since the 1960s*, she rejects the impulse of post-soul theorists to "conflate [soul] with the worst impulses of the Black Arts and Black Power movements – for instance, with the masculinism, misogyny, and binary vision of race [...]" and frame "soul as post-soul's vague yet racially essentialist, masculinist, heterosexist other" (13). She emphasizes that there was much more gender parity and inclusiveness in soul than admitted by its critics and that the often-neglected importance of soul as a platform for female and queer articulations "exceeds the logic of heteronormative patriarchy so often associated with black nationalism" (32). According to Lordi, "[s]oul was not [...] an inherited essence black people held in in common. Nor was it a simply a genre of music. It was a logic constituted through a network of strategic performances – musical, literary, journalistic – meant to promote black thriving, if not liberation" (5). While proposing an understanding of soul which disentangles the genre from the black cultural nationalists' efforts to discern a timeless black identity, Lordi acknowledges the intrinsic relationship between soul and the ways, African Americans dealt with the historic and social conditions they faced in the United States: "...struggle yields black resistance. This is the logic of soul" (3). Through this lens, which underscores that "soul was fundamentally linked to black solidarity, to the kind of togetherness forged under siege" (6), it is possible to discern the overlaps between soul and race-based solidarity as one of the core principles of black nationalism. Following Lordi's argument, soul as a concept and a philosophy forged a sense of belonging among African Americans that was based on the shared experience of suffering, survival, and overcoming: "What the discourse of soul gave people ... was an assurance that even their most chilling experiences of grief did not isolate them but rather connected them" (8). The significance of soul for the African American freedom struggle, thus, can be explained by the way it organized "a community's redefinition around the concept of stylized survivorship" (9), conveying "a more generalized ethos of readiness and resilience... a belief that black people, having already overcome, were spiritually fortified for the necessity of doing so again". As Lordi shows, soul "gave people a beloved 'I' and a complex 'we'- a sense of individual and collective mattering – that was the necessary starting point for political mobilization" (37). Coinciding with Robin Kelley who held that the "concept of soul was an assertion that there are 'black ways' of doing things, even if those ways are contested and the boundaries around what is 'black' are fluid" (quoted in Lordi 44), Lordi's interpretation of soul "not as black essence but as a 'discourse' through which black Americans reimagined the contours of their community in the late 1960s" (44) helps to explain its complex nature as both, an important tool for activists in their efforts to forge black unity, but also a genre in which blackness was not rigidly defined (14). To grasp the ambiguities that thwart the unilinear and essentialist notions of soul, Michael Hanson's concept of "aural blackness" is equally helpful:

> Aural blackness denotes the conjuncture of culture, history, and racial performance in musical practices. As a way of hearing and sounding, it refers specifically to style, or, the historically developed and culturally conditioned constellation of practice, orientation and sensibility that coheres in musical experience. Racial distinctions in musical style are non-static, shifting delineators of difference that appear as intensities rather than indices of discrete practices. The term aural blackness departs from the premise of mutable musical meanings and differences by raced subjects formed in the context of nonetheless discernable differences in terms of social, cultural and structural location and outcome historically. It is in this way that audible structures of race can circulate without falling into the essentialisms of inherent, innate biologistic explanations of their emergence. [...] Aural blackness registered the dispersions of black difference within the social collective during the civil rights transition to black power. As a site of symbolic contest across various axes of black social difference, black music signifies intra-racial difference as much as it marks black-non-black difference. Yet black music *speaks* blackness, as a shared, abstract sense of collective experience, while also shaping how one can hear the multiplicity of black positions, diasporic layers, and historical traces of the local or the individual [...] Aural blackness thus opens the terrain of an understanding of musical difference that is both racially specific – *black music* – yet also historically conditioned outcomes of shifting structural and cultural circumstances including the condition of racial marginality and the imaginary sphere of racial collectivity. With the non-institutional informal public sphere as the realm of necessity for excluded black masses in this period, the knitting function of black popular music in particular, performed the strategic alliance across and within a Manichean black public culture, articulating with the unities that cohered around soul, funk, 'black is beautiful', or racial nationalism. Black sound possessed a fluidity and hybridity that mirrored intrablack differences during the civil rights and black power periods, yet it also functioned as a unified notion under the sign of aural blackness. And thus musical mediations over the social and political meanings of blackness in this historical moment capture an *audible* structure of feeling, indeed an aural poetic, that ultimately eluded the intensively praxeological efforts of Black Arts nationalism. (343–344)

Lordi's "logic of soul" and Hanson's "aural blackness" both advocate for a non-essentialist reading of the genre which does not reduce the sounds, discourses, and protagonists of soul in their complexities. Both approaches are meritorious and insightful, as they contribute to an understanding of why and how soul could become an open platform for the articulation of solidarities and identifications to diverse constituencies beyond the African African community. Some arguments in Lordi's analysis reveal, however, how much discourses on soul are still shaped by a certain African American exceptionalism, as she defines soul as the "inappropriable result of oppression" (9) and an "enviable style that nonblack people could not learn or claim" (23) – an assertion that is challenged by the appropriation and popularization of soul among non-black Latin Americans in New York and Panama (see chapters 3 and 4).

It is precisely the transnational, hemispheric and interethnic dimension of soul that has neither been addressed thoroughly by its defenders nor by its critics. While the rise of African Diaspora Studies during the three decades since the publication of Paul Gilroy's *Black Atlantic* has been part of wide-ranging efforts at deconstructing African American exceptionalism and decentering U.S. "hegemonic blackness", the appeal of soul beyond the African American community, among black and non-black Latin Americans and Caribbean immigrants for instance, has not been taken into account in the Post-Soul debates sufficiently. As it was the Post-Soul critics' goal to complicate and de-essentialize the U.S. black experience it might be promising to follow Malin Pereira's call for a "Post-Soul Cosmopolitanism" and include other Afro-diasporic perspectives on soul into their critiques of homogenizing narratives of blackness: within and without U.S. borders the circulation of soul provoked diverse forms of reception and rejection that exposed the fluidity and heterogeneity of soul-related Blackness constructions. When Neal and George criticize the devastating effects of commodification on the capability of soul to transmit progressive messages, their perspectives seem to be limited to the U.S. context. As George Lipsitz emphasizes in his analysis of diasporic transculturations in popular music, "commercial culture can provide an effective means of receiving and sending messages," (13) shedding light on the "emancipatory possibilities of new technologies and the readiness of marginalized and oppressed populations to employ them for humane ends" (37). In other words, it was the commodification of black pride and protest critique that enabled the global circulation of these messages in contexts where their consumption by racialized and marginalized groups became a way to express dissent with a repressive status quo. In this sense, another dimension of the emancipatory potential of soul becomes apparent when we take a look at its reception in diverse Latin American contexts, where it was often met with outright hostility by ruling elites who perceived soul as a foreign attack on dominant *mestizaje* and *democracia racial* discourse or as a manifestation of US cultural imperialism, while to Afro-Latin American youth it became a method of rebellion that enabled them to particpate in transnational liberation struggles. The following chapters address these dynamics.

3 Spanish Harlem: Latin Boogaloo and Black-Nuyorican Coalition-Building

In 1971, the *New York Magazine* published an article titled "The song of Joe B", written by Felipe Luciano. In the article, Luciano, who had spent several years in Coxsackie prison, paid tribute to the man who had jumped to his side after he was threatened by other inmates: Joe Bataan, by then a feared leader of the Spanish Harlem-based street gang The Dragons. After their release from prison in the mid-1960s, Luciano became a leading figure in the forging of radical black-Nuyorican coalitions while Bataan gained a reputation as the "king of Latin Soul" (Fig. 6). In the article, Luciano wrote:

> Latin and soul music have been the traditional musical forms in Spanish Harlem: Latin music because it represents our own unique life-force, and soul because for better or worse our destinies are inextricably tied to that of the black nation insofar as we live, work, and die with it. (49)

The text continues with Luciano's account of how Joe Bataan became Spanish Harlem's "street singer, our own troubadour", singing about "cops, riots, unwed mothers, prayers to God, and the names of streets in El Barrio we all know" (50). His article gives an impression of how music became a key site of articulation for Spanish Harlem's Nuyorican and black youth in an urban environment shaped by crime, poverty, gang wars, and racism. In their post-prison careers, both, Luciano and Bataan, became important bridge-builders between African American and Latin American communities, not only in El Barrio, but across the United States and beyond. Bataan's debut single "Gypsy Woman" (1967), a Latin cover version of a soul song by The Impressions originally recorded in 1961, became an instant hit among New York's Nuyorican and black youth, marking the beginning of his trajectory as pioneer of Latin soul. Luciano, the son of Afro-Puerto Rican migrants, would become the only non-African African member of the Last Poets, a black nationalist spoken-word group that had emerged in the context of the Black Arts Movement (Fig. 7). In 1969, he joined other young Nuyorican and African American radicals and became one of the founders of the New York Young Lords to improve living conditions in Spanish Harlem and infuse its mostly Puerto Rican residents with the spirit of rebellion that had already taken hold of large parts of Black America. Another founding member of the organization was Pablo 'Yoruba' Guzmán, like Luciano also a second-generation New Yorker whose parents were

https://doi.org/10.1515/9783110665550-005

Afro-Puerto Rican and Cuban migrants. In his text "Before People Called Me A Spic, They Called me a Nigger"[3], Guzmán remembers coming of age in the 1960s:

> In New York, Puerto Ricans were growing up alongside African-Americans in the same barrios, and only the fools among us [...] could not see that we had a heck of a lot in common. And it began, of course, with rhythm and dance. [...] After the conga, the rest followed pretty quickly: 'Chitlins,' 'Cuchifritos.' 'Soul.' 'Salsa.' At least half the Puerto Rican family had to pick up on having the same nappy hair as their African American cousins. (240)

Concluding his thoughts on the close relations between African Americans and Puerto Ricans and the significance of the black freedom struggle for the emergence of the Young Lords in the late 1960s, Guzmán recalls: "We did this while we danced at parties after a day of fighting the police, just to get basic rights, with the Panthers. Blasting James Brown and Tito Puente" (243).

Guzman's evocation of rhythm and dance, soul *and* salsa, as starting points for cross-cultural dialogues between African Americans and Nuyoricans in the 1960s, as well as his memories of Young Lords dancing with Black Panthers to the sounds of James Brown *and* Tito Puente, the kings of black and Latin music respectively, speaks for the outstanding role of popular music in the forging of inter-ethnic alliances between two marginalized communities who struggled for empowerment in the streets of New York. Along these lines, there's some logic to the fact that the foundation of the Young Lords– an organization modeled after the Black Panther Party – was preceded by the emergence of Latin boogaloo three years earlier. The Young Lords' perspectives reveal the meaning of the "New York Afro-Latin Soul Sound" (Joe Panama) for black-Nuyorican coalition-building in the Black Power era.

3.1 "Alliance of Survival": The Making of Spanish Harlem

The transformation of East Harlem into Spanish Harlem, and the consequent emergence of a contact zone between Puerto Rican and African American communities that gave birth to hybrid sounds and interethnic movements, was the result of imperialism, migration, and racism. Between the 1920s and the 1950s, New York became the main destination of parallel waves of African American and Caribbean migrations. Thousands of black rural workers from the Deep South, striving for a new life without Jim Crow and extreme poverty, and immigrants from the Caribbean islands converged in Harlem and other deprived neighborhoods of

---

3 "Spic" is a derogatory term for Puerto Ricans in the U.S. context

the city. A large portion of the newcomers hailed from Puerto Rico, which was a U.S.-controlled colony and strategically important naval base since the Spanish-American War of 1898. The first wave of Puerto Rican immigration took off after the Jones-Shafroth Act of 1917, which granted Puerto Ricans limited U.S. citizenship. Against the backdrop of the First World War, "the U.S. made Puerto Ricans American citizens in order to draft them for the military" second-generation migrant and as former Young Lord member Carlos Aponte, points out. Many migrants from Puerto Rico had also followed specific recruitment measures by the U.S. Labor Department that tried to compensate the labor scarcity that was caused by a sharp decrease in European immigration after the enactment of more restrictive immigration laws. After the Second World War, a second wave of migration followed, turning Puerto Ricans alongside African Americans into the city's second-largest non-white community with almost one million living in New York in the mid-1960s (González 90).

Upon arrival in New York, Puerto Ricans were confronted with a heavily segregated urban geography in which the opportunities to find housing were rigidly determined by class, skin color and ethnicity. As "the only place where they would let us live was closer to the blacks" (Aponte), many oft he first Puerto Rican immigrants started to settle in the eastern section of Harlem, following a pattern in which Puerto Rican neighborhoods emerged as "buffer zones between blacks and whites" (González 92). Carlos Aponte described the demarcations of the neighborhood that would become home to his parents as follows:

> Spanish Harlem is the space between 5th Avenue and 3rd Avenue [on a west-east axis] and between the 120th and 96th [on a north-south axis]. It's like a rectangular part. On the western side you have the Harlem blacks, on the eastern side you had Italians. They were all Italians. On the southern side you had Irish and Jewish. And the middle was this mish-mash area that was always transy. So we began to pour in there and it was called East Harlem. And then we changed it to Spanish Harlem. And then we changed it, eventually, over the decades to El Barrio.

Navigating these sharply drawn inner-city borderlines, in which crossing the wrong street could mean entering a territory where one could be exposed to racist attacks, would become a central feature of Puerto Ricans' daily life in New York. As Latin jazz percussionist Bobby Sanabria remembers when he was a kid, Italian youth would yell at him when he stepped their turf on his way to the next deli: "Hey, you fucking *spic*. What you doing? What you fucking doing here?" When the numbers of Puerto Ricans in East Harlem increased in the post-WWII period, Italian Americans expressed their concern regarding the "dangerous influx" (L. Thomas 201). Although their mixed-race composition did not fit into the prevailing racial black-white dichotomy in the United States, Puerto Ricans as the first large non-white immigrant group, experienced a process of racialization that defined their positioning within New York's stratified social geography. Hailing from an island where the existence of racism was neglected and the prevalent stigmatization of blackness disguised behind the veils of multiethnic *mestizaje* discourse, Puerto Rican migrants who arrived in New York City were confronted with the U.S. "one-drop rule" binary racial discourse, which often classified them as black for the first time in their lives (Zentella 27). This meant that the boundaries between Puerto Ricans and African Americans were much more porous than those that delineated them from Irish, Italian, and Jewish neighborhoods. Puerto Ricans and African Americans could move and live on both sides of the imagined demarcation lines and, in the process, despite undeniable tensions, developed an "alliance of survival" (Torres 3).

Tito Ramos, who would become an acclaimed Latin soul singer with Johnny Colón and the TNT Band in the late 1960s and early 1970s, recalls how language played a key role in the marginalization of immigrants from Latin America and the Caribbean: "I remember when I went to school they would say to me: "You don't speak Spanish here. This is America! Speak English!" (*We Like It Like That,* 00:11:38) As their status as immigrants and foreign language speakers added to the race-based discrimination, Puerto Ricans faced multilayered disadvantages in income, employment and education, and, according to widely held views among community activists there was "no group so completely voiceless" (Thomas 217) in New York City politics. During the 1960s, Puerto Ricans in New York were disproportionately affected by a social crisis with family earnings dropping from 71 percent of the national average in 1959 to 59 percent by 1974 (215). The overlapping, though not identical, features of marginalization they shared with African Americans brought about collaborations in struggles to improve education and other issues of concern to both communities. Relegated to the bottom of New York's social hierarchies as "a submerged, exploited, and very possibly permanent proletariat" (Torres 61), living in the same neighborhoods under extremely precarious conditions with high rates of poverty and unemployment, both communities shared experiences of race- and class-based exclusion from the white world on a daily basis. Hinting at African Americans' and Puerto Ricans' common status as New York's racialized and most exploited labor force, Grosfoguel and Georas state that both communities shared "their respective long historical relationships as colonial/racial subjects within the U.S. empire and their subordinated location in the reproduction of those hierarchies today" (104). As they were exposed to African American language, music, customs, and culture, "Puerto Ricans in New York City became African Americanized" (106).

While new interethnic alliances were forged, these processes of racialization did, however, also spur ethnic, economic and generational divisions, bringing to the surface and reinforcing existing hierarchizations within the Puerto Rican community. This showed in the post-WWII period, when mostly light-skinned and upwardly mobile Puerto Ricans – civil service workers, subway engineers, doctors, teachers, bus drivers, taxi drivers – eager to leave behind the misery and insecurity of Spanish Harlem, started to move to the South Bronx. In neighborhoods already inhabited by Irish and Italian communities they found larger apartments and better schools and created a prosperous social and cultural life in an integrated, "whiter" environment. As a consequence of this inner-city Puerto Rican version of "white flight", those who stayed behind tended to be lower-class and darker-skinned. "El Barrio became more black" (Aponte), leading to even further increased neglect by the city authorities.

Such were the conditions in Spanish Harlem when a new generation of New York-born Puerto Ricans grew up in the 1950s, the first Nuyoricans: "smart, urban, English-dominant – [...] acutely aware that the broader Anglo society still regarded Puerto Ricans as less than full American" (91), as former Young Lords organizer Juan González writes. In many ways, this experience overlapped with that of the African American youths with whom they shared their daily lives. These interactions had the effect that Nuyorican youth started to adapt many of the habits of their African American peers, as Carlos Aponte recalls:

> We went to school with them, lived the same building. So we began to talk like blacks. We developed a combination of Spanish and black accents, what you now call a Nuyorican accent. I had African American friends and we were intermingled in community and there was no conflict between us, unlike other parts of the country. They were just who they were, they were neighbors.

One activity that brought the youth from both communities together was stickball, a type of street baseball that was played extensively at that time when there were not so many cars blocking the sidewalks (Sanabria). These stickball teams gave rise to some of the gangs that fought for turf on the streets of Spanish Harlem in the 1950s and 1960s: the Viceroys, the Dragons, and the Devils, composed primarily of black and Nuyorican youth. As job opportunities were scarce and social conditions were tough, street culture became another unifying factor, as Felipe Luciano stresses: "We were working together on the streets, we were selling drugs together. And we started going to jail together." While poverty, violence and conflicts with neighboring communities were rampant, many of those interviewed remember their childhood and youth in Spanish Harlem with nostalgic pleasure. Benny Bonilla (Fig. 4), whose Puerto Rican parents had arrived in New York in the 1920s and who would become a *timbalero* in the Pete Rodríguez Orchestra in the 1960s, says:

> I loved growing up in Spanish Harlem. Just the smell alone was great. You smell rice and beans. All that Latin type of food in the air the whole time. And you heard music... all day long, everywhere. Because, they all have their radios on. Walking through the streets, you could hear all kinds of Latin music but also R'n'B which had a tremendous influence on whatever is out there. Dances, the way you dress. The way to talk also, we picked that up in school or in the neighborhood. If you're living in a neighborhood that's mixed like ours, you're not gonna speak like an Irish man. I went to an all-black school and almost all of my friends were black. Some races I know and lived among, they just don't want to live next to black people. For me, I hang out with black people all my life. I don't care who my neighbor is. When my father, who was working for the Navy, moved us to the Bronx I thought it was a disaster, I thought I'm gonna die because I moved out of Harlem. I was so accustomed to Harlem.

When the kids grew up, dating became another site of interaction between blacks and Nuyoricans, as Felipe Luciano points out: "Going out with a black girl changes your perspective. You begin to see other things. We ate in each other's homes. We were listening to each other's arguments. [...]. Yeah, that affects a whole different way of looking at life. And out of that came a different politic, too." While these accounts confirm that a special form of interethnic conviviality between two excluded communities emerged in the setting of Spanish Harlem, the close interactions with African Americans and the related "blackening" of Nuyorican youth caused increasing tensions with their parents. Many first-generation immigrants held deeply rooted anti-black prejudices that were reinforced in a society in which blackness was a social stigma. As Juan González states, "gradually, almost imperceptibly, I watched my aunts and uncles begin to adopt antiblack attitudes, as if this were some rite of passage to becoming authentic Americans" (92). The ways in which their children adopted African American habits of language and style challenged their sense of self, which defined Puerto Rican identity in sharp distinction to blackness and was marked by a denial of Puerto Rico's role as an important site of the African diaspora. Bobby Sanabria remembers how Nuyorican teenagers had to navigate between the two worlds they were living in: "When we were on the streets, we walked, we talked, just everything like the blacks. But when we got home, we were speaking Spanish. You do code-switch." Although most of the Puerto Rican families had also African roots, "many Puerto Ricans had attitudinal perceptions about blacks that were horrible", as Felipe Luciano points out: "They didn't want to be black and African Americans were called names like *moyeto* or *cocolo*." Carlos Aponte stresses the contradictions he faced when his father, the son of an Afro-Puerto Rican, used to tell him when he was in high school: "Don't bring any black girls home. You're not gonna marry a black girl." As the teenagers wouldn't refrain from intermingling with African Americans, they were warned by their parents, "if you have a kid, your kid will end up being dark and your kid will end up being ugly because you married a black person." Puerto Rican girls "were being beaten viciously by their fathers for going out with black guys" (Aponte).

Hence, the racialized environment of the United States in general and New York particularly spurred controversies on Afro-Puerto Rican identity and racism that had been formerly silenced, as prominently discussed in Piri Thomas' autobiography *Down These Mean Streets* (1967). Many Afro-Puerto Ricans found themselves caught between conflicting modes of racialization: Not only did their identities as black *and* Hispanic jeopardize dominant U.S. racial categorizations and delineations according to which the label "Hispanic" was constructed in sharp contrast to "Black." In addition, by identifying with African Americans and affirming their black identity, some of them challenged the homogenizing identity discourses that shaped the views of their parents. Inspired by the anti-authoritarian impulses and the burgeoning Civil Rights movement that shaped the late 1950s and early 1960s in the United States, Nuyorican youth rebelled against the outdated views and prohibitions of their parents. Music would become the main tool in their drive to overcome traditions and embrace modernity.

3.2 The Roots of Afro-Latin Soul

The emergence of the "New York Afro-Latin Soul Sound" was preceded by decades of sonic dialogues between African Americans and immigrants from the Hispanic Caribbean which started to take place since the first migration waves in the 1920s. While the protagonists of New York's vibrant Latin music scene in the 1950s and 1960s were mostly Puerto Ricans, the foundations of the new sounds that emerged in this period were laid by Afro-Cubans. Although always infinitely smaller in numbers than Puerto Rican immigration, an exodus of Afro-Cuban musicians who were escaping rampant racial discrimination in Cuba in search for new opportunities, brought luminaries such as band leader and trumpet player Mario Bauzá, singer Frank "Machito" Grillo and conga player Chano Pozo to New York in the 1930s and 1940s. With the foundation of Machito and the Afro-Cubans, led by Mario Bauzá, in 1940, they revolutionized popular music in more than one way. When the band came up with "Tangá" in 1943, they were the first to fuse Afro-Cuban rhythms with jazz elements and arrangements for a big band, inspiring African American musicians such as Dizzy Gillespie and Max Roach in the creation of Latin jazz and bebop. Boldly calling themselves "Afro-Cubans", they also challenged the deeply entrenched racism that reigned in New York's music scene and the United States at a time when nobody even used the word "Afro."

The addition of Spanish Harlem-born and raised Puerto Rican timbales player Tito Puente to Machito and Bauzá's band in 1943 had a lasting impact on the development of New York's Latin sound. Blending the Afro-Cuban, jazz and big band influences into an even more danceable genre, Puente was the driving force behind the creation of the mambo, which became a nationwide dance craze in the 1950s by also reaching broad non-Latino audiences. While criticized by many for its "black American vulgarity" (qtd. in Raussert, "Ethnic Identity Politics" 10), Puente's mambo turned him into the first national celebrity from Spanish Harlem, endearing him to Nuyoricans across generations. Next to Machito and fellow Nuyorican Tito Rodriguez, Tito Puente was one of the three big band leaders who reigned New York's Latin music in the 1940s and 1950s, their orchestras alternating at the famous Palladium in downtown Manhattan. Puente established a feature that defined New York's Latin music scene until the rise of salsa: Afro-Cuban styles mixed with African American influences and played by mostly Puerto Rican musicians.

While mambo, *cha-cha-cha* and traditional *jíbaro* music from Puerto Rico were the sounds the youth of Spanish Harlem grew up with when at home with their parents, there was a new thing going around on the streets: doo-wop, a subgenre of rhythm and blues and precursor to soul that featured African American vocal groups and gained the peak of its popularity with the release of "Why Do Fools Fall In Love" by a band from Washington Heights called Frankie Lymon and The Teenagers. Released in 1955, the hit resonated heavily in El Barrio, not least because next to the three African American vocalists the band also included two Puerto Rican singers, Herman Santiago and Joe Negroni. The success of the song heralded the dawning of a new era in which Nuyorican youth started to embrace the sounds of Black America, departing from the listening habits of their parents. As Bobby Sanabria put it:

> When you're a teenager growing up, you always rebel. You always have your own music We embraced black music because it was infectious and it was for dancing. The main thing in NYC that broke down racial barriers was music. Because when you go to the dance at a high school gym or at a catering hall, and the music moves you, then that breaks down everything.

Confirming the decisive role of doo-wop in the alignment of second-generation Puerto Ricans with African Americans, Felipe Luciano holds:

> We were hanging with black Americans every day in the projects, in the schools, in the jails, in the hospitals, on the subway. We were listening. And that which was being promoted was black music. It was called race music then. Before soul, doo-wop was the one integrating factor. Blacks and Puerto Ricans singing together, and making it big like Frankie Lymon and The Teenagers had a huge impact on us. And that began the unification of the groups in a real way, in an umbilical way. We weren't into rock and roll. We were into black music, of course. We gravitated more to this new music that was in English, by the way, and that had a differ-

ent beat. Now, when we went to our house parties, we understood that mambo and such was the music of our parents. The kids were not as interested in the esoteric sounds of jazz either. But R&B was the music we could understand.

The popularization of doo-wop among the youth of Spanish Harlem was by no means limited to its consumption. Rather, street singing in groups of four or five in stairwells, subway stations, the large hallway entrances of the projects, or bathrooms, where the acoustics made the harmonic melodies sound better, became, along with stickball, one of the most important joint activities of African American and Nuyorican youth in the second half of the 1950s. The success of the mixed-race vocal group of Frankie Lymon was part of a larger development in which many young Nuyorican musicians collaborated with African American musicians, fusing the sounds that circulated between Black and Spanish Harlem. While R&B and doo-wop had an enormous impact, this didn't mean that Latin elements were erased from the repertoire of local groups. Quite to the contrary, the Afro-Cuban patterns served as a base for new sonic experiments which were shaped significantly by the cosmopolitan mix of cultures and influences but also the racial divisions that defined the New York scene in the 1950s and 1960s. One decisive factor for the emergence of mutually influencing African American – Afro-Latino sounds was the fact that, with the exception of Machito and some highly acclaimed jazz musicians, only white bands could play lucrative gigs in downtown Manhattan, bringing together black musicians from the Caribbean and the United States in the clubs and dancehalls of Upper Manhattan and the Bronx. Benny Bonilla provides insights, into how racial divisions shaped his formation as a musician:

> Racism in New York was very, very bad and all Latino bands, Puerto Rican bands primarily, they could only work downtown beyond 86th street if they were white. From there up to 116th, the Latino bands, the Puerto Rican bands, they were the dark-skinned, black musicians. People like my friends Willie Bobo and Jimmy Sabater, who brought me to the place where I bought my first drum. They introduced me to their mentor: a gentleman named Santos Miranda, a black Puerto Rican man and a very talented drummer who played with African American rhythm and blues bands on the Westside of Manhattan. Yeah, he had to, because he couldn't work with no Latino band. Although he was one of the best, bandleaders wouldn't hire him because with him they couldn't play gigs in downtown, because he was black. So, as he knew from experience, he taught Jimmy Sabater and Willie Bobo black American drumming. So when Willie Bobo and Jimmy Sabater started to play Latin soul and funk, it was also because they were influenced by that guy, Santos Miranda. That was their teacher. So we would go to see him play with these r'n'b bands. That's how we picked up both. Picked up the Latin rhythm and the American stuff, man. When you listen to that kind of music and

hang out with blacks all the time, you catch the thing. And that's what helped me doing 'I Like It Like that'[4] later on. It came to me straight away.

Thus, the cross-cultural ventures that led to the creation of a distinct Afro-Latin New York sound were fueled by the racial divisions that forced black musicians from different backgrounds to collaborate. The path that led to the emergence of Latin soul in the mid-1960s was neither unidirectional nor one-dimensional, in the sense that second-generation Puerto Rican immigrants simply adapted, or copied, African American styles, as several accounts suggest. Rather, it was intrinsically linked to the visionary ideas and contributions of musicians from different locales of the circum-Caribbean migratory sphere and Black America. The Afro-Cuban conga player Mongo Santamaría was one such visionary. After starting his career as a conga player at Havana's prestigious Tropicana club, he moved to New York in 1950 where he joined the Tito Puente orchestra and became a member of Cal Tjader's band in 1957. His solo career took off with the release of "Watermelon Man" in 1963, an adaption of a jazz classic by Herbie Hancock that competes with Ray Barretto's "El Watusi", released the same year, for recognition as the first Latin soul song. The role of the black Panamanian immigrant David Preudhomme aka Joe Panama and his band as a laboratory and a bridge between Caribbean, Afro-Latin, and African American musicians who would revolutionize Latin music in the 1960s has already been mentioned in the introduction. It hints at the often ignored importance of Panama, as an afro-hemispheric crossroads and an integral part of the trans-Caribbean circuits that connected New York with Cuba, Puerto Rico and Colón (see Chapter 4).

The Joe Panama Sextet also was the point of departure for the career of Henry "Pucho" Brown which illustrated that the flows between African American and Nuyorican communities were a two-way street. Many African American musicians of the era were heavily influenced by Latin music, as evidenced by the impact of different Afro-Latin rhythms in jazz, rhythm and blues, and other US black popular music genres, defined as the "Latin Tinge" by John Storm Roberts. Brown was born and raised in Black Harlem and decided to become a Latin music percussionist when he was a teenager:

> I've got around to hear a record by Tito Puente, called 'Babarabatiri'. And when I heard that, that blew me away. I fell in love with Tito Puente. The whole black community fell in love with the mambo. From 1951 maybe all the way to about 1959, every dance that you went to, you had

---

4 The Pete Rodríguez Orchestra released "I Like it Like That" in 1966. It was composed by Benny Bonilla and would become one of the major hits of the Latin boogaloo era. It was sampled in Cardi B's "I Like It" featuring Bad Bunny and J Balvin in 2018.

an American band and you had a Latin band in the black community. Even in the Apollo, every two weeks, three weeks there was a Latin band.

Determined to to follow in the footsteps of his idol Tito Puente, Brown bought himself a set of *timbales* and started to call himself by the Latin-sounding name "Pucho", inspired by a poster for a concert by Machito and Pucho Marquez that was hanging in his room. Pucho's musical career started when he joined Joe Panama's band after the the breakup with Joe Cuba and Jimmy Sabater. Remembering the Panamanian bandleader, Pucho says: "He was more black than he was Latin and he had a lotta' black guys in the band. Only two Latin guys. He was also from the black side, playing this Latin music." After his time in the Joe Panama Sextet, Pucho took over the African American band members and began performing in Harlem under the name Cha-Cha Boys, including several gigs with Chick Corea, who, like many of his band members, was eventually recruited by Mongo Santamaría: "I always had first-class musicians in my band. So Willie Bobo and Mongo Santamaría, who were the only ones who were able to combine Latin, funk and jazz the way I did, but were much more famous at the time, came and took my musicians after I had trained them." In the first half of the 1960s, Pucho befriended Malcolm X, "a good, good guy," who, despite his unsuccessful attempts to recruit him to the Nation of Islam and the organization's dismissive attitude toward black popular music, hired him to play with his band at a Black Muslim rally at their 116th Street Harlem mosque. Revealing the increased tendency of labels to respond to the growing demand for productions that were in tune with the rise of a movement that rallied around "soul" as a source of black pride, Pucho remembers how his producer proposed a new band name when he was about to record his first album *Tough!* in 1966:

> "Why don't we call the group 'The Latin Soul Brothers'?" So that's how we got the name Pucho and The Latin Soul Brothers. I guess because at that time everything was soul, you know. Soul power, soul food, everything was soul. Also Black Power, afros, power to the people. When you hear soul that means it was black. So I was just part of the movement. And then I put a soul singer in my band. A guy named Jackie Soul.

Whereas Pucho's band rose to prominence with what he defined as "cha-cha with a backbeat" and albums such as *Saffron & Soul* and *Shuckin' And Jivin'* in the 1960s, proving that "there was a lotta' black musicians that played that shit just like a Puerto Rican", their bookings were almost exclusively limited to concerts for African American audiences, because "a lot of Latins didn't like blacks playing that music". He would, however, become the sole African American who would receive significant recognition as a *timbalero* by his idol Tito Puente and other greats in the highly demanding Latin music scene. Jeopardizing widely held adscriptions of which music could be played by whom, Pucho confused the audiences, as he recalls:

> When I became successful as a bandleader and started to play with the big shots of Latin music, people were really surprised when they learned that I was a black guy from Harlem who didn't speak a word of Spanish. Pucho was just a name I picked from a poster in my room.

The Joe Panama Sextet was an incubator in more than one way as it also was the site from which the single-most important band in the making of Latin boogaloo emerged. It was here where the Spanish Harlem-born Jimmy Sabater and Gilberto Miguel "Sunny" Calderón, who had become friends during a 1950 El Barrio stickball championship match between the Viceroys and the Devils, first played music together (Salazar 228). During his youth, Calderón, a light-skinned Puerto Rican who attended the all-black Cooper Junior High School and whose friends were mostly African Americans, was into Nat King Cole, Louis Jordan and other R&B stars: "Latin music meant nothing to me" (228). When Calderón adopted the artist name Joe Cuba and formed the Joe Cuba Sextet with himself on the congas, Nick Jiménez on piano, Jules Cordero on bass, Tommy Berrios with his distinct vibraphone inputs, Jimmy Sabater on timbales, Willie Torres and eventually Cheo Feliciano as a vocalist, their new innovative sound became very popular among the Puerto Rican youth, as Nuyorican poet Victor Hernández Cruz remembers: "Joe Cuba had a special flavor that was Caribbean but brewed in New York. It was tropical urbanity" (Cabanillas 39). The release of the soul ballad "To Be With You" in 1962 would become a watershed movement in the music of El Barrio as it was the first time an all-Latin band would use English lyrics (as lead singer Cheo Feliciano's English had a strong Spanish accent, Jimmy Sabater did the vocals). Whereas the other songs on the *Steppin' Out* album were in Spanish, this bilingualism spoke to the realities of the migrant youth who were used to switching between both languages as they moved between their homes and the streets. The album *We Must Be Doing Something Right* (1966) featured the fast Latin track "El Pito" in which a chorus repeats the refrain "I'll never go back to Georgia" – a citation of the words spoken by Dizzy Gillespie at the beginning of his 1950s Latin jazz recording "Manteca" –, easily interpretable as an allusion to the mindset of thousands of black Harlemites who had changed Jim Crow in the Deep South for the big city. Victor Hernández Crúz emphasizes in which way the song reflected the sense of connectedness Nuyoricans felt towards their African American neighbors: "So here were these New York City Puerto Ricans talking about 'I'll never go to back to Georgia' and perhaps none of them had been south of the Jersey turnpike, but in a spiritual relation we certainly have our 'Georgias' and that made a very important connection" (Cabanillas 39). According to Felipe Luciano, Joe Cuba was someone who "unified blacks and Puerto Ricans, to the consternation of a lot of our parents. He was able to take the language, the idiomatic expressions, the accents of black Southerners and applied it to live music. We the people loved it." In the second half of the 1960s, Joe Cuba and his band would continue to set trends that turned New York's racialized music scene upside down.

3.3 The Latin Boogaloo Era (1966 – 1969)

1966 was a year of radical change. On June 16, during a civil rights march in Greenwood, Mississippi, SNCC leader Stokely Carmichael announced the beginning of a new era in the African American freedom struggle: "We've been saying 'Freedom' for six years and we ain't got nothin'. What we gonna start saying now is Black Power." Four months later, Huey P. Newton and Bobby Seale founded the Black Panther Party for Self-Defense in Oakland, California. Billboard soul hits of the year like "Get Ready" by The Temptations, "Hold On! I'm Coming!" by Sam and Dave, and "Reach Out I'll be There" by The Four Tops conveyed a dynamic sense of expectation that was in synch with the overall spirit of new beginnings that had taken hold of the black movement in that year. Continuing the history of Nuyorican engagement with new black popular music forms, soul also became the sound of the hour in Spanish Harlem: "Everybody was into soul music. Everybody, white, black, everybody. Soul music is like jazz. It's the country's music" (Aponte). Informed by daily news of protests, demonstrations, urban riots, and anticolonial movements in the Third World, many Nuyoricans, like their African American peers, came to perceive the uplifting and optimistic sounds of soul as a source of encouragement in the face of racial and social exclusion. Although soul was promoted as a unique expression of U.S. blackness by black cultural nationalists, Puerto Rican youth embraced the genre wholeheartedly, as Felipe Luciano confirms:

> "There's a rose in Spanish Harlem" by Aretha Franklin obviously was big hit in El Barrio. But also the music of Smokey Robinson, The Dells, Marvin Gaye, Tammi Terrell, Etta James, Sam Cooke, Otis Redding, and many others. All of these guys were important to us because they were articulating our problems with urban America. There were no protest songs then, but we felt what they were feeling. And you'd be surprised how many Puerto Ricans identified with it. That music roused our spirits and it actually had themes that we could relate to: love, betrayal, romance, all that stuff. And we we were into that because we were in America.

In September 1966, the Joe Cuba Sextet released the single "Bang, Bang". The refrain of the song went "Cornbread, hogmaw, and chitterlings," referencing some typical elements of African American "soul food" from the Deep South. "Comiendo cuchifritos", exclaimed by a voice in Spanish alludes to a classic of Puerto Rican street food in New York City. The song celebrated the fusion of African American and Puerto Rican cultures, not only in terms of lyrical allusions to food but also by combining rhythms and sonic elements from both traditions. "Bang, Bang" was born out of on stage-improvisations during their gigs at the regular "black dances" at the Palm Gardens Ballroom which attracted predominantly African American audiences to Latin music. Jimmy Sabater recalls: "The place was packed, but when we were playing all those mambos and cha-chas, nobody was dancing. So at the end of the first set, I went over to Joe Cuba and said, 'Look, Sonny, I have an idea for a tune that I think might get them up" (qtd. in Flores, *From Bomba to Hip-Hop* 79). According to Sabater, the African American listeners instantly began to dance when the band added a funky backbeat to their usual Latin repertoire. As for the lyrics, Tommy Berrios recalls they were also inspired by interactions with black concertgoers: "No matter what we played, a few brothers sang 'bang, bang' to every tune. Jimmy and Nicky started it with a piano vamp, then all of us contributed to its creation. Someone added 'beep beep', another 'uh-uh.' ... another 'umgawa, black power.'... At a rehearsal we worked it all out in less than a half hour" (qtd. in Salazar 236).

As accounts of the era confirm "Beep beep! Bang Bang! Umgawa! Black Power"[5] had become a slogan in which African American activists combined Stokely Carmichael's call for Black Power, voiced only three months before the release of "Bang! Bang!", with the Suaheli word *umgawa* which is translated as meaning "united", "together", "entangled".[6] The musicians had picked up the slogan from the chants of their audience who welcomed the statement of the musicians, as Joe Cuba recalls: "When we started to play the tune and sang 'black power'!' we began to notice the black clenched fists above heads" (Salazar 236). When they wanted to record the song, they presented it to controversial New York music business mogul and Tico Records owner Morris Levy, who, according to Cuba, was not

---

5 In the autobiography of Seattle Black Panther Aaron Dixon he tells how he and his comrades from the local Black Students Union chanted "Beep beep! Bang bang! Ungawa! Black Power!" (12) during a protest march for the inclusion of black and Asian staff in Franklin High School. In a video posted on Twitter by Kyra E. Azore in 2018, it can be seen how this slogan is still used by black students in the 21st century and how its intonation matches with the rhythm of Joe Cuba's "Bang Bang" (https://twitter.com/KyraAzore/status/9823542418503 63904?lang=de, June 26, 2024).

6 According to Azizi Powell, "umgawa" is a word from the East African Suaheli language which means "entangled": (http://pancocojams.blogspot.com/2015/08/the-real-origins-of-word-ungawa-vari ous.html, June 26, 2024)

amused: "When Morris Levy heard it for the first time, he jumped out of his chair and said, 'What's that?' He didn't like the words, so we changed them" (Salazar 236). As a result of Levy's intervention, the original "umgawa" and "Black Power" of the slogan were replaced by the chorus singing "haah" on the recording ("Beep beep, haah, Bang bang, haah"). The genesis of "Bang! Bang!" suggests that a song whose title seemed to embody the widespread perception of Latino boogaloo as a completely apolitical party music is actually the result of a show of solidarity by Nuyorican musicians with the Black Power slogans of their African American audience. That the Joe Cuba Sextet's reference to the increasing spirit of black pride was not accidental is demonstrated by the song "Alafia", which, like "Bang! Bang!", was also released on the *Wanted Dead or Alive* album. It contained the line "me siento afortunado porque nací chocolate" ["I feel lucky because I was born of chocolate color"]. Remarkably, a year after "Bang! Bang!", the band record-ed "Hey Joe" (1967) in which the slogan was taken up once again and this time only slightly modified by the one word, which would probably have provoked the cen-sorship of the label owner again. The refrain of the song now went: "Beep beep, bang bang, umgawa, *that's* power!"

With the instant cross-over success of Joe Cuba's "Bang! Bang!" (over one million copies sold) and the end of the glamorous era of Latin big bands marked by the closing of the Palladium Ballroom a few months earlier, 1966 became a turning point in the history of the New York Latin music scene (Leymarie 222). In the wake of "Bang! Bang!", the Pete Rodriguez Orchestra followed suit with "I Like It Like That" and Johnny Colón released "Boogaloo Blues", both similarly success-ful, reinforcing the overall sense that something new was in the air. On the sleeve notes of Pete Rodriguez' second album *Latin Boogaloo*, Pancho Cristal, the produc-er of Alegre and Tico Records where, next to Fania and Cotique, most of the re-cords of the era were released, diagnosed the arrival of the "new sound" freneti-cally:

> A combination of Rhythm & Blues Soul Music, together with the exciting sound of Latin tem-pos ... have caused quite a stir among all the listening and dancing audiences. Everywhere fingers are snapping and heads are bobbing in rhythm to this different and stimulating new beat. Thus the latest sound and dancing craze has been born. ... Is everybody ready? Latin Boogaloo is here!

The term "boogaloo" with which labels such as Tico and Cotique started to promote the new genre was originally the name of an African American dance style that was brought to national attention by soul songs such as "(Papa Chew) Do the Boo-Ga-Loo" by Tom & Jerrio, "Boogaloo #3" by Roy Lee Johnson and J.J. Jackson's "Do the Boogaloo", all released in the months before the advent of Latin boogaloo in the autumn of 1966. Ricardo "Richie" Ray, who would become one of the main artists of the era with albums such *Se Soltó – Introducing the Bugaloo* and *Jala Jala y Boogaloo* and is credited to be the first to use the term, claims that it was inspired by African American youth:

> We noticed that when we would play like a *guajira* that there were some soul brothers doing some steps that we hadn't seen before. So one day we went over to talk to these folks and said, "Man, you're dancing something when we we play the *guajira* that we haven't ever quite seen before. What's going on with that? And they said it was called the *boogaloo* and it kinda goes with the *guajira* thing, you know. The only thing is that it has some more funky notes in it, so it's kind of like a funky guajira. And I was fascinated by that. (*We like it like that!* 00:21:05–3)

The emergence of Latin boogaloo represented the compelling answer to increasing demands among Puerto Rican and African American audiences and promoters "to add a little soul to [Latin] music", as songwriter and Pete Rodriguez' trumpet player and singer Tony Pabón recalls (Salazar 223). While rooted in the black-Nuyorican collaborations of the preceding doo-wop era, the Latin boogaloo did not just imitate African American forms but represented an innovation that Nuyoricans could claim as their own. Initially extremely successful in opening up new sales markets, Latin boogaloo experienced a steep rise and an abrupt fall in the period between 1966 and 1969. While the boogaloo craze was short-lived, the genre was the initial spark of the much broader phenomenon Latin soul, understood as the fusion of Hispanic Caribbean styles with African American soul and funk. As Benny Bonilla had it: "It's not that music from Havana, Cuba, that was pure. It ain't pure no more. We here!" (*We Like It Like That*, 00:01:58–7). Like its pioneers Joe Cuba, Pete Rodriguez and Johnny Colón, other protagonists of the boogaloo era such as Joe Bataan, Héctor Rivera, Bobby "Mr. Soul" Valentin, Joey Pastrana, Ray Terrace, Richie Ray, Johnny Zamot, George Guzman, and Ralph Robles had grown up in Spanish Harlem and translated the mixture of African American and Latin music that shaped their daily life experiences into a new sound. The absence of women in this enumeration is no coincidence but reflects the quasi-complete dominance of male artists in Latin boogaloo. Promoted as the "Queen of Latin Soul", Afro-Cuban singer La Lupe was a notable exception with songs like "Fever" and "Que Bueno Boogaloo" but most of her recordings with Tito Puente from that time did not fall under this category. Even by the anything but progressive standards of the U.S. popular music industry in the 1960s and 1970s, it is striking how much the patriarchal structures of Latin American societies were reflected in the extreme scarcity of female performers in New York's Latin music scene with La Lupe and Celia Cruz virtually the only Latina performers to get some kind of recognition in the 1960s and 70s era (Aparicio).

To the boogaloo generation, the "swingin' combination" (Orquesta Olivieri) of Latin and soul music represented the possibility of creating a sound that combined their Caribbean heritage and the influences they drew from their day-to-day interactions with African Americans more than any previous style. According to Bobby Sanabria, the advent of boogaloo was "inevitable":

> Latin boogaloo fulfilled the need that came from the unique experience of young Puerto Ricans, people from the mambo generation, interacting with African Americans. Even though most Latin boogaloo recording did not contain explicit political messages, my philosophy is that all music is a socio-political statement. So even though the musicians making this music weren't thinking of that, it did make a socio-political statement. The statement is that Nuyorican identity is shaped by our contact with the African-American experience. It's part of the New York City identity. Just like hip-hop is. When you're growing up in this city, you're looking at things and you wanna emulate people that you admire. So we admired James Brown, we admired Gladys Knight, we admired Smokey Robinson. We admired the pimps and the hustlers in the streets. So we wanted to be bad, too. But we were also influenced from the stuff we heard from our parents. Because the Afro-Cuban rhythm in itself is just hip. So Latin boogaloo is Puerto Ricans, using Cuban rhythms, with African-American R&B, mixing it all together.

By appropriating R&B and soul and departing from sophisticated Latin jazz-inspired traditions, boogaloo musicians created a style whose popularity transcended the Nuyorican community, reaching out to African American audiences and showing "the greatest potential that we had to really cross over in terms of music" (qtd. in Flores 89), as Latin music promoter Izzy Sanabria put it. Due to the cross-cultural success of the new sound, Latin boogaloo musicians were signed to perform and tour with soul music superstars as James Brown, The Drifters and The Temptations (83). Inspired by Latin soul, many African American soul and funk bands of the era started to include Latino-oriented percussion in their repertoires. For a musical classification of the Latin boogalo, Juan Flores has offered a definition that draws its benefit precisely from the fact that it does the most justice to the heterogeneous character of the genre in its breadth and flexibility:

> The boogaloo repertoire actually ranges along a continuum from basically Latin sounds and rhythms with the trappings of African American styles on one end, to what are R&B, funk, and soul songs with a touch of Latin percussion, instrumentals, Spanish-language lyrics or inflections. The only proviso for it to be part of the world of boogaloo is that both musical idioms be present, and that both the Latino and the African American publics find something of their own to relate to. (*From Bomba*, 88)

Taking into account that Latin boogaloo was made first and foremost by second generation immigrants, Juan Flores defined the genre as "first Nuyorican music", which was "both a bridge and a break, for with all the continuities and influences in terms of musical style, the Boogaloo diverged from the prevailing models of Latin music in significant ways" (80). Several elements distinguished the boogaloo from previous Latin forms. Importantly, the genre reflected the conflicted identities of its protagonists as it was bilingual. Many boogaloo tracks were sung in English or switched easily between both languages, often combining African American expressions common in soul songs like "sock it to me", "shucks", "good god", "out of sight", "get down" with words and phrases from the Hispanic Caribbean lexicon such as "sabroso", "echale candela," "a gozar." Most albums included sleeve notes in both, English and Spanish. Other than the established big band leaders of the mambo era, most boogaloo musicians were young, often still in their teenage years, and not as sophisticated in their musical skills displaying a less elitist and more horizontal approach to musical production. As Bobby Sanabria points out, most boogaloo musicians were "teenagers, that didn't have that much musical training, they would be the equivalent to a garage band."

The male-dominated boogaloo youth proudly auto-identified as *pollos*, the Nuyorican version of the hip and defiant urban soul brother. Very much a phenomenon of the broader 1960s counterculture, the boogaloo generation rejoiced in challenging established norms and breaking taboos by the provocative and explicit ways they talked about sex and drug use as in songs like "Let's Get Stoned" by the Lebrón Brothers, "Hierba Buena (Good Grass)" by George Guzmán, or in the line "LSD got a hold on me" in Johnny Colón's "Boogaloo Blues". The psychedelic cover art by Izzy Sanabria, featured on many boogaloo albums such as *El Exigente* (1967) by the Orchestra Harlow openly reflect the changing attitudes of the Spanish Harlem youth. In "Be Free", released on the same album, singer Ismael Miranda gives voice to the antiauthoritarian spirit of Latin boogaloo: "Who cares what they say? I'm gonna do it anyway! Gonna live my life my way, Do just what I please, I gotta be free!"

Because of these liberatory elements, Nuyorican activist and poets who came of age in the 1960s embraced the new sound. Critical of the ways previous generation of Puerto Rican musicians had, according to poet Victor Hernández Cruz, simply reproduced "old Cuban tunes, *son montunos, guajiras*", he celebrated "the sway", "the cadence" and "nervous rhythmic energy" of Latin boogaloo in his anthology *Snaps:* "it was choppy, fast images, jolts, jittery, young, arrogant, foul-mouthed, naked, uneven raw exhibition like a volcanic eruption in the middle of urbanity" (Cabanillas 37). To many musicians of the era, it was precisely these disruptive elements which made boogaloo attractive, as Harvey Averne stresses: "Every generation wants their own music. They don't want their parents' music. In fact, if their parents hate the music they even like it better" (*We like it like that,* 00:04:02).

Breaking with traditions and patterns of anti-black racism, Latin boogaloo functioned as a platform for celebrating black-Nuyorican connectedness and the very forms of adaptation of African American soul culture and new hybrid and diasporic Afro identities that older generations despised. In 1969, Jimmy Sabater recorded the Latin soul song "Times Are Changin'" which gave voice to the increasing sense of identification with the African American freedom struggle among many Nuyoricans:

> I've got ambition, no inhibitions;
> I got my pride, and the guts on my side
> I got my goal, I'm black as coal;
> The times are changin' in the USA
> It's time for freedom, it's time for rights;
> Things still ain't right, baby, no, no, not yet
> But nowadays, we'll have our way;
> The times are changin' in the USA
> (Jimmy Sabater, "Times Are Changing", 1969)

With "Times Are Changing", Sabater expressed the growing sense of urgency that shaped the rise of Black Power in the late 1960s. The phrase "I got my goal, I'm black as coal" spoke to the widespread tendency among young Puerto Ricans to assume a black identity as a form of rebellion against Puerto Rican anti-black racism and neglect of the island's African heritage. Master *conguero* Ray Barretto, although deeply critical of the lack of sophistication of Latin boogaloo in later interviews, provided some of the most explicit anti-racist and humanist Latin soul songs that emerged during the era (Fig. 5). In "Together", Barretto, phenotypically a light-skinned Nuyorican, claims "I'm black, I'm white, I'm red", expressing the hybrid and multiple identifications the genre gave a voice to and calls on "black and white" to "get together before it is too late". The album *Barretto Power* features the song "Right On" which evokes a slogan of the Black Power movement and includes the line "Got some Afro, some Latin too, how you do it, it's up to you", asserting pride in the flexible mix of racial identities that gave birth to the new sound. The repeated references to "soul" in several Barretto releases of the era hint at the strong sense of connectedness with African Americans among Nuyoricans of all colors. In his single "New York Soul", Barretto celebrates the interethnic fusions that result from joint street culture experiences and offers a definition of the new sound: "This is the New York soul, the New York kind of soul, it has a funky beat, right from the New York streets, let's take the Afro thing and add a Latin swing, it's more than rock 'n' roll, this is the New York soul!" The practice of translating blackness to a Latino context via the invocation of "soul" also can be found on Barretto's album *Latino Con Soul,* his recordings "Soul Drummers", and "Deeper Shade of Soul".

The sleeve-notes of Latin boogaloo albums suggest that many labels initially shied away from using the term "soul", which was closely associated with blackness, and promoted the new style as "Latin rock" or "barrio rock", even though electric guitars or other rock elements are completely absent from boogaloo. While the Joe Cuba Sextet lived up to their status as cross-over pioneers and released an album titled *El Alma del Barrio – The Soul of Spanish Harlem* as early as 1964, references to "soul" and the promotion of boogaloo as "Latin Soul" increased in the late 1960s, reflecting the commercial success of ethnic identity affirmation in soul music by singers like James Brown and the impact of Black Power on popular culture. In this period, "soul" beame a recurrent theme in Latin muic productions such as "Soul Gritty" by Ralph Robles or the TNT Boys' "Música del Alma" (a Latinized cover version of the soul hit "Tighten Up" by Archie Bell and the Drells). The children of immigrants from the Caribbean claiming "to have soul" in an era, when "soul" was not only a genre but also a concept related to blackness, hints at the overall sense of affinity and identification that many Nuyoricans had developed with respect to African American identity. When Mongo Santamaría released "We Got Latin Soul" (1969), a cover version of Dyke and the Blazers' black pride funk song "We Got More Soul" in 1969 he gave voice to this form of appropriation which asserted a new U.S.-black-inspired Latin identity that distinguished itself by its heterogeneity. In "Puerto Rican Soul", Pete Bonet sings: "I'm Puerto Rican, I got a thing going on, I can do the mambo, I can do the cha-cha, I can do the boogaloo, I got Puerto Rican soul!" In Pete Rodríguez' "I Like it Like That", co-composed by Benny Bonilla, singer Tony Pabón claims: "Here and now baby, let's get this straight, boogaloo baby, I made it great, 'cause I gave it the Latin beat, boogaloo baby, I'm kind of hard to beat ...I've got the soul, I've got the feeling, I like it like that". In "Creation", The Latinaires, a band led by Louis Small from the Virgin Islands and Carlos Grossman Jr from Panama[7] and integrated by Puerto Rican and African American musicians from the Bronx hint at how boogaloo met the demands of New York's interethnic audiences ("boogaloo was made especially for you"). "Creation" encourages participation in the new movement, referencing the flows that brought it into being: "Do the boogaloo everybody, Latin boogaloo; started out as a Motown sound, now it's here, Puerto Rico-bound."

In "Afro-Shingaling", The Latinaires also evidence how a distinct Afro-Latin New York mix of identitifications, cultures, and languages was negotiated in Latin boogaloo: "Come on, let's do the shingaling, baby, the Afro-Shingaling that

---

7 The Panamanian background of Crossman Jr. is addressed in the song "Panama" (1970)

is, I just come from Africa...Este boogaloo en Puerto Rico está de moda ya, en Nueva York lo gozan de verdad, I like it like that!" The African-ness of the new sound is also asserted in Joey Pastrana's "Afro Azul" in which he claims that the "boogaloo is the African blues". Songs like Eddie Palmieri's "African Twist" and Tito Puente's "Black Brothers" demonstrate that the new tendency toward the affirmation of black Nuyorican identity and the articulation of solidarity with African Americans propelled by boogaloo even had an impact on those established musicians who were not part of the scene or explicitly opposed to it. In 1971, Eddie Palmieri and his brother Charlie launched Harlem River Drive, a band project which incorporated Latin and African American musicians (who had played with Aretha Franklin) releasing the album *Harlem River Drive*, which was a socially conscious and pioneering piece of Latin funk-soul-jazz fusion that symbolized the persistent relevance of black-Nuyorican dialogues, even after the end of the Latin boogaloo era.[8]

The rise of Latin boogaloo had completely transformed the New York Latino music scene in a very short time. Whereas until 1966 a small group of big-band leaders ruled New York's Latin music scene, the rapid commercial success of a young, unabashed and, for the most part, non-classically trained generation of boogaloo musicians put them abruptly out of business. The sudden appearance of a large number of small bands who gratefully accepted every opportunity to play, also meant that it was suddenly possible to organize concert evenings with many bands and lower fees, instead of hiring the established and expansive big bands. Accordingly, between 1966 and 1969, many Latin musicians had problems being signed on for gigs. This caused envy, resentment and fear, as expressed by Bobby Rodríguez during that time: "If the current trend continues in today's swinging social set, we will soon have nothing but our old 78s and LPs to hear and remember the original, or 'típico' Latin rhythms. [...] mambo and cha-cha is being completely overwhelmed by today's Boogaloo" (Leymarie 222).

In addition to the fact that they had problems to get bookings, Latin boogaloo was held in disdain by New York's established bandleaders for its lack of sophistication. The older musicians felt relegated to the sidelines by a couple of "kids [who] were off clave" (Flores, *From Bomba* 109), and "didn't even know what side of the instrument to play out of" (95), as Eddie Palmieri put it. Latin soul singer Joe Bataan (whose contributions to the genre will be discussed in the next section) claims: "We young guys came into their territory. They controlled this business for years. To now hear some young kids, changing something and doing

---

8 In "Justicia" (1969), in which Palmieri claims "justicia para boricuas y niches" ["justice for Puerto Ricans and blacks"] had already expressed his advocacy for cross-ethnic solidarity.

things they couldn't, made them feel threatened." While older generations of established Latin musicians despised Latin boogaloo for musical and commercial reasons, there were also racial implications regarding its rejection on behalf of nationalist Puerto Rican elites from the island who spoke out against the genre, condemning it as a betrayal of the community (Lipsitz 79). As Felipe Luciano points out, Puerto Rican nationalists denounced the ways Nuyoricans embraced African American culture and style:

> They couldn't stand it. When we went to Puerto Rico, they said that we were becoming blacks. They said, 'you come with your Afros and you come with your Latin boogaloo, you guys are acting too black.' They were against boogaloo because they wanted to keep it pure. The ways they wanted to keep us separated from African Americans resembled the plantation politics that was initially fostered by the slave master who wanted to keep the light skinned guys from the dark skinned guys. 'We don't want you to be too black, because if you're too black, we can't handle it.' And boogaloo was definitely black, so they wanted to keep that away. Interestingly, many of the established Latin musicians like Machito and Tito Puente made it clear that they were doing African music. But still, many Puerto Ricans did not want to identify with black Americans. This is the the distinction: identifying with Africa was accepted, identifying with black Americans was not.

The rejection of the new style among established musicians who were put out business, as well as among purists and traditionalists who rejected the "contamination" of "authentic" Latin music through the appropriation of soul and R&B styles, ultimately led to the abrupt cancellation of the Latin boogaloo era in 1969. Fania Records, an upcoming label founded by Dominican musician Johnny Pacheco and businessman Jerry Masucci in 1964, was a key player in the events that ended the reign of Latin boogaloo. Allegedly following a concerted move by old bandleaders, promoters, radio DJs, music entrepreneur Morris Levy and Fania, New York's concert halls stopped hiring boogaloo musicians for gigs and radio stations stopped playing their records (Flores, *From Bomba* 107). Many versions circulate about whether there was actually a conspiracy to cut off Latin boogaloo. However, it is undisputed that the move happened after boogaloo musicians started to protest against the ways they were exploited and forced by the promoters to play several gigs in different clubs in one evening for very low fees. Latin soul singer Joe Bataan – who was one of the most booked artists of the period and whose debut single "Gypsy Woman" (1967) was one of the first major successes and crossover hits of Fania, was a driving force in the attempts to fight back:

> I tried to organize the bands. I called them in. I said, 'Look, it is your time/ 'We gotta organize.' 'Let's form a union.' They went back to Fania Records and they said, 'You know what, Joe Bataan is organizing. He's starting trouble.' So the promoters got together with the record companies and decided to boycott 'Boogaloo'. Especially because of me, they felt that I was a rebel.

They took all of my records off the radio and cut off the boogaloo altogether. Let's bring back the old masters, they said. And that's what they did. And then they launched salsa as the new thing and the 'Fania All-Stars' became big.

It was probably no coincidence that Joe Bataan, as a musician who was not of Hispanic Caribbean descent and whose contributions embodied the transgression of the boundaries between soul and Latin music, played a decisive role in the conflict between the boogaloo generation and New York's Latin music establishment. The label stopped producing boogaloo recordings and devoted itself fully to the promotion of *salsa* – a term that was conceived by Johnny Pacheco as part of Fania's marketing strategy which paved the way for the success of the label's aggressive push to monopolize New York's Latin music scene. Combining a variety of genres from the Hispanic Caribbean such as *son montuno, guaracha, bomba* and *plena*, salsa acquired an unrivaled status as the ultimate trans-Latino sound in the 1970s, turning Fania into the hemisphere's most important and influential Latin music label, "the Latin Motown."

The advent of salsa also reflected the calls for a return to "authentic" Latin music, and the widespread unease with the bilingual crossover experiments that boogaloo represented. Obviously, the framing of salsa as "pure" Latin music neglected its origins in the fusion between Afro-Cuban rhythms and African American jazz that had given birth to Latin jazz and mambo in the previous decades, as Bobby Sanabria emphasizes: "That's the irony of this purity claim, because if you listen to Machito, Tito Puente, Tito Rodriguez, the forerunners of salsa, what are they influenced by? Jazz harmony and arranging, which comes from the African American community." In the same vein, the use of "funky" horn riffs, the increasing references to African roots in the lyrics, and the ways in which many of salsa's Afro-descendant protagonists such as Roberto Roena, Cheo Feliciano, Pete "Conde" Rodríguez and Celia Cruz, contributed to the popularization of the Afro and other elements of African American soul style in Caribbean, Central and South American contexts, suggest that salsa, rather than representing a clear-cut break was a continuation of the cross-cultural dialogues featured in Latin soul and boogaloo. Salsa did, however, put an end to the short-lived careers of many boogaloo musicians.

While established musicians like Mongo Santamaría, Tito Puente, Eddie Palmieri, Ray Barretto, Cheo Feliciano, Larry Harlow and Celia Cruz, who were all members of the Fania All-Stars, benefitted heavily from salsa's triumphal march to world success, most protagonists of the boogaloo generation were not part of the show, many of them leaving the music business. This was not the case for Joe Bataan, who founded his own Ghetto Records label at the margins of the dominant Fania in the 1970s and whose long-lasting impulses and contributions proved the accuracy of his conviction that "Latin soul was much broader than the booga-loo."

3.4 Joe Bataan: "Young, Gifted, and Brown"

> On a rainy sunday morning in 1942,
> a mother was blessed with a son who grew up, too
> He was Young, Gifted, and Brown,
> with the strength to tear a mountain down
> And when he grew up, and learned his ABC
> He found out very quick he was destined to be
> Young, Gifted, and Brown
> With the chance to change the world around
> (Joe Bataan, "Young, Gifted, and Brown", 1969)

Joe Bataan's autobiographical "Young, Gifted, and Brown" was released on his album *Singin' Some Soul* in 1969 – the only record featuring an African American studio band and strictly non-Latin soul numbers ever recorded by Fania. Whereas label manager Masucci had intended to further expand the label's markets beyond the Latin immigrant community, the experiment failed, as it confounded the established marketing strategies: "Fania ended up with an album alienated from their Latin base .... Its poor sales translated to low circulation numbers" (Wang). Despite the commercial failure of the album, "Young, Gifted, and Brown", became an anthem to Latin American immigrants living in the United States, epitomizing the appeal of soul beyond the African American community by adapting Nina Simone's "Young, Gifted, and Black". As Bataan remembers, even Chicano activists of the organization La Raza from the west coast loved the song and started to play it at their rallies.[9]

Joe Bataan's personal trajectory, referenced in the lyrics of "Young, Gifted, and Brown", and his role as a rebel against the established forces in the Latin music business, represented the meaning of Latin soul as a bridge between diverse ethnic communities, movements and sounds like few others. His non-Latin ethnic background and his pioneering contributions to the genre reveal its non-essentialist and socially conscious dimensions. Joe Bataan was born as Peter Nitollano jr. on November 15, 1942, at Harlem Hospital. His mother was African American. His fa-

---

[9] The Smithsonian Institute paid tribute to Bataan's legacy as bridge-builder between African Americans, Latino and Asian migrant communities with the video *A Fusion Between Culture and Identity: Joe Bataan's Latin Boogaloo Music:* https://oursharedfuture.si.edu/stories/a-fusion-of-culture-and-identities-joe-bataans-latin-boogaloo-music.

ther was an immigrant from the Philippines who had moved from San Francisco to New York in the 1930s. Following the Spanish-American War of 1898, the Philippines had, very much like Puerto Rico, fallen under U.S. control and did not gain formal independence until the end of World War II in 1946. Like many Puerto Ricans at the same time, Bataan's father had accepted a deal offered by the U.S. government that would reward residents of the colonies with citizenship if they joined the military service. Hence, Nitollano Sr. joined the U.S. Navy. As a native Spanish speaker, he settled where most of his Puerto Rican peers did after arriving in New York, in Spanish Harlem. Reflecting on his personal positioning in the environment he grew up in, Bataan says: "My father is Filipino. My mother is Afro-American. But my heart is Latin. I grew up in the Barrio where I was surrounded by a community that is Spanish speaking. As my father didn't speak Spanish at home, I had to learn Spanish by myself. There were some blacks and whites also but most of my neighbors were Puerto Rican". Immersed in the Spanish Harlem community as a black child, Bataan learned some lessons on the mechanisms of Puerto Rican colorism that he would not forget: "They had that dividing line, where they separated you by color. The darker you were the less rights you had. A lot of the older Puerto Ricans didn't like the 'dark'. They thought they were better". At the same time, Bataan experienced how solidarity between different ethnic groups was forged:

> The poverty brought blacks and Puerto Ricans together. And the environment, where they lived. They had to survive. Some of the same things, that the Puerto Ricans went through, the blacks went through too. They had to go on the same line to get cheese or welfare. The same low-paid jobs were offered to blacks and Puerto Ricans, so they had to intermingle.

Like most of his friends, Bataan didn't get the opportunity to go to college. After high school, there were few options: "You can become an entertainer. I tried to be a baseball player. Didn't make it. Or you go in the street, you hustle for a dollar. So I became a hustler." As outlined in the first sections of this chapter, street life, while often conflictive and violent, was a key factor in the emergence of interethnic alliances. Such was the case for Bataan, who as a black Filipino teenager, became the leader of the mostly Puerto Rican leader of the Dragons street gang, feared throughout Spanish Harlem for his reputation as a "tough guy" and skilled street fighter. In 1959, he got arrested driving a stolen car and was sentenced to five years in Coxsackie prison. He was released after three years but after violating his parole was put back in prison in 1964. Determined to change his life, he started to study music during the last year he spent in jail.

Eager to start a career as a musician, Bataan taught himself to play the piano after he was released in 1965. He remembers going to a rehearsal of upcoming musician Johnny Colón, with whom he had grown up and gone to school, hoping to get a chance but his bad reputation as a troublemaker got into his way: "I sat there, proud that my life had changed and I hear Johnny Colón whispering: 'We don't want him here.' So they came to me and said: "Joe, I'm sorry..." Bataan was angry and wanted to punch him, as he used to do but instead said to Colón: "I just wanted to hear what you're doing because I know nothing about Latin music. I'm gonna leave but I'm gonna make a band and kick your ass". After that encounter, he tried desperately to find a band which he finally did after catching some teenagers rehearsing in a studio that he oversaw. As they hadn't asked for his permission, he had an idea when he saw they didn't have a piano player: "I took my knife out of my pocket and I stabbed it into the grand piano. I said, 'I'm gonna be the leader of this band!' Nobody said nothing. They were scared of me. You stay with me. I'm gonna put you into heights that you never heard before! So they said, Ok agreed." The parents of the musicians, who were all Puerto Rican teenagers and most of whom still went to school, knew about Bataan's reputation. "They didn't want them to be with me. 'Not with that guy!' So I had to go. I had to take them home and beg the parents. 'Look, I'm a changed guy. I'm not the same. Trust me I'll bring them home every day So they trusted me". This is how the Joe Bataan Band was born.

In 1967, when the Latin boogaloo craze was at its peak, Fania Records was trying to assert its place in New York's highly competitive Latin music scene, dominated by the labels Cotique, Tico, and Alegre and producers such as George Goldner, Pancho Cristal, and Adalberto Santiago. Aware that Latin soul fusions were generating large profit margins at that particular time, label managers Masucci and Pacheco decided to give the newcomer Bataan a chance and recorded "Gypsy Woman", a cover version of a 1961 recording by The Impressions featuring Curtis Mayfield. It became an instant hit, conquering dancefloors in both, Black and Spanish Harlem. What followed was a meteoric rise from gang boss and ex-convict to one of the most booked artists in the boogaloo era, Bataan's very own "Cinderella story", as he put it:

> It was a dream come true because you dream of getting the attention and when they first played that record on the radio all of the Barrio lit up. Everybody had their radio on and now we became celebrities in our own neighborhood. We were recognized. And then it became like a new style and then I was on the same stage as James Brown. The same stage as Gladys Knight and The Pips. I mean it was like a whole new world opening up and it was exciting. Maybe it was too exciting because it was ahead of us growing. So that took us everywhere. A young kid from El Barrio that grew up like a gangster, that didn't have nothing and then taught himself music.

Joe Bataan hit a nerve. While his rival Johnny Colón, Joe Cuba, Pete Rodriguez, and many other bandleaders succeeded in gaining immense popularity among Nuyoricans and were already about to release their second boogaloo albums by 1967, Bataan appealed to even broader audiences. He approached Latin soul from the soul side rather than from the Latin side. His unique singing style, his unmatched street credibility earned through his first-hand knowledge as a gang leader and a convict, and his upbringing as a navigator between languages, cultures, and ethnicities who was neither strictly African American nor Puerto Rican, endeared him to New York's ghetto youth across ethnic lines. As Bataan recalls, "Puerto Ricans identified me as being Puerto Rican. Blacks identified me as being black. So the argument in the street was: 'He's Puerto Rican!' 'No, no! He's black.' And me: 'It doesn't matter, as long as you like my music!'" Importantly, Bataan's songs addressed the realities and daily hardships of young black and Puerto Rican New Yorkers explicitly in ways that most other boogaloo releases didn't. The rise of Bataan also showed to many young people that they could do it without prior knowledge: "We played the way we thought we had to play from the way we grew up. A lot of us were self-taught musicians. We were just like in a rush. We wanted to get things out there. We wanted to create excitement" (*We Like it Like That* 00:02:32–8). After his debut smash hit, Pacheco and Masucci didn't hesitate to sign him for the recording of an album, also released under the title *Gypsy Woman* in 1967. The album also featured the song "Ordinary Guy", which contrasted sharply with the content of most Latin boogaloo releases of the era.

> I can't move a mountain top
> Everything's ordinary on my block
>
> I don't drive a beautiful car
> And I don't own an elegant home
> 'Cause I don't have thousands to spend
> Or a seaside cottage for the weekend
>
> I'm just an ordinary guy you left behind
> Ordinary guy you left behind
>
> Exclusive nightclubs are out of style with me
> 'Cause I don't associate with high society
> I don't hang around playboy millionaires
>
> I'm just an ordinary guy you left behind
> Ordinary guy you left behind
>
> (Joe Bataan, "Ordianry Guy", 1967)

By distancing himself critically from "playboy millionaires" and "high society", Bataan, an "ordinary guy" who doesn't have neither a "beautiful car" nor an "elegant home" positions himself as someone working-class people can relate to. While soul stars of the era like James Brown or Wilson Pickett celebrated their wealth expressively in ways that put them in spheres that were unreachable to their fan bases, Joe Bataan's popularity as a black man from the ghetto rested precisely in that people could relate to the realities he addressed because it were their own. Bataan's songs also reflected the turbulent times during which his career was launched. When he was released from prison in 1965, important changes were taking place in the United States and abroad: "It' was like waking up. It was about consciousness. These movements influenced me, definitely". When he heard that Martin Luther King was killed in April 1968, "it was like, something was robbed from us. You know, third world people. To have a man in the forefront preaching things about equal rights, that you wanted to say yourself for so long and then they kill him was like, 'Wow, we can never have nothing.' Anytime we get something they kill it all."

After King's assassination, major urban uprisings erupted across the ghettos of Black America. In the same year, Bataan released the song "It's a Good Feeling (Riot)", which starts with the sound of police sirens, and Bataan's voice stating "everybody's doing it, that's alright", and then, evolves into a joyful and fast rhythm, accompanied by the chorus "it's a good good feeling, much too good to hide", evoking comparisons with how ghetto rebellions were celebrated to the sounds of Martha Vandella's "Dancing in the Streets" a year earlier. His 1969 album *Poor Boy* featured a picture of Bataan standing in the still smoking ruins of a building, a clear hint at the devastating housing situation that affected inner-city residents and found its most devastating manifestation in the fire crisis in the South Bronx, during which, starting in 1968, thousands of buildings inhabited by black and Puerto Rican families were burned to the ground. The second song of the album is "Freedom" which evokes the universalist dream of a world without racism:

> Freedom! How long must it take?
> Freedom! How long must we wait?
> I saw a bridge out of candy, in a dream I had last night
> I saw myself dangling from the rainbow
> And I was talking to my son, And then suddenly I heard a voice
> From the clouds up above
> And the voice whispered a story, About a black and white love
> And then I saw black and white children, Walking hand in hand,
> And it seemed that our children, had found the promised land
> Than the heavens above opened, And I fell from the sky
> And I joined hands with the children, Who were walking by
> As I walk past the birds and the trees, I knew how wonderful life could be,
> For god had meant all men, all things to be free, That's the way our life should be,
> So stand up and fight for what you think is right,

> A boy told me upon return to my world,
> There will be freedom for every black and white girl,
> For every boy there will be a toy ...
> So to this world full of joy , I woke because my dream had ended
> Sang out loud, Because suddenly I was proud
> Because I was what I a am, a man called the tam,
> I'm talking about freedom!
> And how long will it take?
> Freedom, and how long must I wait?
> (Joe Bataan, "Freedom", 1969)

With this number, Joe Bataan aligns with the ongoing black freedom struggle, positioning himself at the crossroads between Civil Rights and Black Power. His dream of "black and white children, walking hand in hand" can be read as a reference to the assassinated Martin Luther King ("I heard a voice from the clouds up above") who in his famous 1963 speech had said: "I have a dream that [...] one day right there in Alabama little black boys and black girls will be able to join hands with little white boys and white girls as sisters and brothers." But, just when he thought that "our children had found the promised land" (like King who had "seen the promised land"), Bataan faces reality ("I fell from the sky...my dream had ended"), and doesn't shy away from telling what it takes to make his dream come true ("Stand up and fight for what you think is right") and also asserts self-pride ("sang out loud, because suddenly I was proud") which was one of the key tropes of the Black Power movement. As Bataan's "Freedom" advocates for unity between black and white, the song was in line with the philosophy of the Black Panthers, who denounced the racial separatism of cultural nationalists as divisive.

Local Black Panthers liked the album but after its release Bataan was criticized for the sleeve-notes, which included the line: "The music revolution has gone from rags to riches as Joe Bataan makes headlines overwhelming the music business with his fourth album, ..., as Joe Bataan becomes the George Washington of latin soul music." Bataan remembers that he got a call by a Black Panther, questioning the content of the text:

> They said, 'Joe, we're trying to get rid of the white heroes "Why you didn't use George Washington Carver [a famous African American scientist]?' And then I realized that I never thought of that because I was ignorant. You start to get angry because we didn't have Black history in school. All we have was George Washington, Abraham Lincoln, you know, white history.

The anecdote demonstrates not only that Joe Bataan's music was infused by the rebellious spirit of the times and that he cared about what activists would think about it. It also proved that Black Power activists of the era were keenly aware of the impact Joe Bataan had on their core constituency, the black ghetto youth, which propelled them to try to raise his consciousness on the issues they cared about. Bataan, for his side, continued the habit of including socially conscious songs on each of the albums that were released during the highly politicized late 1960s and early 1970s which marked the peak of the Black Power era. On *Singin' Some Soul*, he not only included the Afro-Latin pride anthem "Young, Gifted, and Brown", but also "Unwed Mother", in which Bataan sings about the sorrows and struggles of a single mother who "grew up in the slums of the city", and now "lives by the station where nobody goes, cares for the baby, and makes all the cloth, a young little mother with tears in her eyes, caring for her baggage when she cries." But, as Bataan continues in the spirit of "keep on keepin' on" that defined soul: "She's gotta make it through, life's gonna be tough, and the road's gonna be so rough, little mother hold your head up high, no time for you to cry, no time to fret, there's still hope yet. … a new day is gonna come for you and your baby girl, in a better and a brighter world!" With "Unwed Mother," Bataan revealed a sensitivity to the often-silenced social realities of women of color, who faced both racism in mainstream society and entrenched sexism in African American and Latino migrant communities, which was extremely rare among male artists in the Latin and soul music scenes of the era.

As black and Puerto Rican radicals became increasingly aware of Bataan's interethnic appeal[10] and his willingness to use it for political means, "Young Lords and Black Panthers started to come to our concerts", as he remembers. In 1970, Bataan performed on a fundraiser for the Young Lords at the Apollo with Felipe Luciano's Last Poets and the Young Rascals (Fig. 9). Reflecting on his relations with the movement, Bataan said, "I was not an activist, but it seems like many activists liked my music and my ability to unite the black and Puerto Rican ghetto youth on the dancefloor by speaking about what was going on." In 1973, Angela Davis had been invited by the government of the GDR to speak at the socialist World Youth Festival in East Berlin and was asked by the organizers to bring a musician. And so after Davis had seen Bataan playing at a rally of the Young Workers Liberation Party, some of her comrades approached him:

> They were like 'Let's bring him! He's an activist sort of like.' They said, 'Joe we're going to Berlin and to Russia. You wanna come with us?' So I talked to my band. Many people said, 'Joe don't go! They gonna label you a communist.' I said, 'I ain't no communist. If there's a

---

10 Bataan's 1972 album *Saint Latin's Day Massacre* further exemplifies his flexible, bi-lingual reach-out to both communities, as it includes straight salsa such as "Para Puerto Rico Voy" in which he sings in Spanish and also soul songs in English like his cover version of Isaac Hayes' "Shaft", the title song of the famous Blaxploitation movie".

chance for me to see the world, I wanna do it'. After entering East Berlin via Checkpoint Charlie, everything suddenly turned grey. When we entered the stadium with Angela Davis, they looked at us as if they've never seen black people with Afro. After Angela Davis gave her speech, she introduced me. I had written a sing which was based on the theme of the festival 'Peace, Friendship, Solidarity.' So I performed the song, in English, Spanish, Russian, and German... 'Frieden, Freundschaft, Solidarität'. When I finished singing that song, the whole place stood up. Even the president, Honecker. They gave me standing ovations with Angela Davis.[11]

Joe Bataan was picked by Angela Davis to join her delegation for this trip behind the iron curtain because of his reputation as the "voice of the street", New York's people's singer who represented the interethnic alliances left-wing radicals like Davis advocated for. After achieving success on the up-and-coming Fania Records as a non-Latino and at the same time gaining popularity among African American youth with his unmistakable Latin soul sound in the 1960s, Bataan continued to explore uncharted grounds in the 1970s. When he broke with almighty Fania, Bataan founded Ghetto Records, an independent label dedicated to the raw salsa and soul fusion sound of El Barrio that he labelled *salsoul*. On the sleeve-notes of his 1973 album *Salsoul*, Bataan alludes to the challenges he faced as a rebel on the monopolized New York Latin music scene: "Revolution in mind and body can be a tough fight. To be independent and free to think at the same time to commit oneself and to be able to survive can be difficult." Defiantly, he affirms his "endurance in life despite all obstacles, because no man should be chained by his environment." With *salsoul*, Bataan not only underlined his status as a renegade bridgebuilder but also created a synonym for interethnic alliances that inspired groups such as the Salsa Soul Sisters, a New York-based black and Latina feminist group founded in 1974. Eventually, Bataan's word creation also gave the name to Salsoul Records, which would become a successful label in the disco and house eras. On this label, just a few weeks after the release of "Rapper's Delight" by the Sugar Hill Gang in September 1979, Joe Bataan recorded the single "Rap-A-Clap-O." Thus, Bataan's song became one of the first rap recordings ever and, after an appearance on the popular West German TV show "Musikladen", a hit in the European charts. The B-side of "Rap-A-Clap-O" features a version in Spanish, arguably

---

11 In 1973, the GDR hosted the 10th World Youth Festival (*Weltjugendspiele*) with 25.600 participants from 140 countries and more than 8 million spectators between July 28 and August 5, a magnitude that gained the event the reputation as "Woodstock of the East". After the GDR was involved in the international solidarity campaign to free Angela Davis in 1972, she accepted the invitation to participate and was welcomed as the festival's most prominent guest by the country's leadership around Erich Honecker. Bataan's multilingual song "Peace, Friendship, Solidarity" was released on the 1973 album *Salsoul*, where it is introduced with Bataan saying "I'd like to dedicate this song to the 10th Youth World Festival in East Berlin and to struggling people all over the world."

turning it into the first Latin Rap record and highlighting once again Bataan's role as a pioneer of interethnic dialogues and styles (Rivera *New York Ricans*).

3.5 Black Power in El Barrio: Nuyorican Poets and Young Lords

Whereas Joe Bataan's involvement in radical politics was singular, the role of Latin soul and boogaloo in the forging of African American-Nuyorican alliances in the Black Power era was significant. The abrupt end of the boogaloo era in 1969 did not put a halt to the interethnic collaborations it had helped to foster. It was in the same year that the New York chapter of the Young Lords Organization was launched by a small group of young radicals from Spanish Harlem, including Nuyoricans Mickey Meléndez, Pablo "Yoruba" Guzmán, David Pérez, Felipe Luciano, and the African American woman Denise Oliver (Fig. 8), who had been mentored by the Afro-Panamanian activist and writer Carlos Russell at Old Westbury College (Steinitz "Hemispheric Ambassador").

The Young Lords were founded in 1968 in Chicago by former gang leader José "Cha Cha" Jiménez, following his conversations with Black Panther Party leader Fred Hampton who called for the formation of "rainbow coalitions" between African Americans and other oppressed ethnic groups. Consequentially, Jiménez transformed his street gang by the name of Young Lords in a political action group, mobilizing Puerto Rican gang members against racism and for Puerto Rican independence. One of their first activities consisted in organizing a month of soul dances to collect funds (Flores-Rodríguez 62). Attracted by the combination of revolutionary Puerto Rican and black nationalism with socialism, the activists from New York were encouraged by Jiménez to found their own Young Lords chapter, which they did, rapidly gaining popularity not only among Spanish Harlem's Puerto Rican youth but also among African Americans, which constituted one quarter of their membership. This was due to the fact that the New York Young Lords, whose original leadership was also majority black, were built on the long history of interethnic coexistence that had shaped the realities of Spanish Harlem, the neighborhood where they started their first actvities as a political direct-action group.

Denise Oliver, who had grown up in Queens, became the only African American to form part of the Central Committee of the New York Young Lords. Her father was a a former Tuskegee airman and a leftist actor with a PhD in Literature and Drama, her mother was a school teacher. Oliver recalls that the interactions between African American and Puerto Rican youth on the dancefloors were a crucial factor in the making of the alliances that gave birth to the Young Lords:

> Soul music, Latin soul, the boogaloo, all of that played a key role in the Lords too. ... You can not separate the African American experience in New York from the Puerto Rican experience in New York. ... People who lived together, who then hang out together who then partied together. As a member of the Young Lords, they tend to try to isolate you as just political, but you know we had boyfriends, we went to parties. The whole Latin boogaloo movement... We went out dancing, almost every night. And we all danced Latin boogaloo, blacks and Puerto Ricans. We danced in the streets, we went to clubs, we were walking around with radios, you know, the music was something that brought people together.

The successive emergences of Latin boogaloo and the Young Lords as related expressions of black-brown solidarity seem to confirm Felipe Luciano's assessment that "art always precedes revolution, you're not going to have attacks on a system unless there's first an aesthetic change, and then a change of consciousness". Luciano had grown up in a Afro-Puerto Rican family who had instilled in him a sense of black pride from an early age in defiance of widespread anti-black racism in the Puerto Rican community:

> I grew up with a very different consciousness than most Puerto Ricans did, even those who were black. My grandmother came here in 1920. She used to wear a bandana around her head. She cooked in an African style. And she used to tell me that I was the prettiest black man she had ever seen. My mother and my father were proud of being black. My father loved jazz. My mother loved jazz. They both had black friends. A lot of Puerto Ricans have no intimate relationships with blacks. Quite the contrary, in my family, we were intimately, umbilically connected to black people. You end up with a blanket of of race security around you that's so intense that no one can knock it down. I never felt badly about my nose, my lips, my hair, my skin color. I think I was the first one to say I'm a black Puerto Rican. And that got a lot of Puerto Ricans mad at me. Why don't you just say Puerto Rican? I said, because Puerto Rican is a nationality. But we are also black. And we should not deny it. So, in my family we were black and proud before James Brown even thought about it.

Before becoming the first chairman of the New York Young Lords in 1969, Luciano had been involved in the Black Arts Movement, indicating the crucial role of African American influences in the emergence of Nuyorican radicalism: "When I came out of jail in 1966, I was so imbued with the black aesthetic, Black Arts Movement, and the teachings of Amiri Barka that I wanted to be part of it. At that time, I wasn't interested in Puerto Rican arts, I wanted to be part of the Black Arts." After release from prison, Luciano got in touch with Gylan Kain and other African American poets and writers associated with the Black Arts Movement who gathered at the Harlem-based East Wind.[12] Not sure if he would be accepted as a Pu-

---

12 At East Wind, Luciano started to give a political education class called "Black Power": "At that time, Stokely Carmichael had written a book along with Charles Hamilton called *Black Power*, and I

erto Rican in an all-African American group of radicals, Luciano recalls how he approached Kain:

> I said, I'd like to work with you guys. And to my surprise, I was accepted wholeheartedly. They were really very nationalist. But they accepted me without even without even blinking an eye. Now, was it because I was black? Was it because I had an Afro larger than many of them? Or that my politics was a politics of Negritude and black nationalism? I don't know. But I know one thing. I felt totally at home.

Thus, Felipe Luciano, along with Gylan Kain and David Nelson, became a founding members of The Original Last Poets, a spoken word group that was launched on May 19, 1968 (the 43rd birthday of the late Malcolm X) at Mount Morris Park (now Marcus Garvey Park) in Harlem. With their specific style of rapping, their radical poems on white racism and black revolution in the language of New York's ghettos, and, not least, their blending of African American and Puerto Rican perspectives through the inclusion of Luciano, The Last Poets are considered by many to be the legitimate forefathers of hip-hop, to which Puerto Ricans have also contributed significantly. In several poems, as the bilingual "Jíbaro, My Pretty Nigger" (*The Last Poets* 1971), Luciano addressed the specific situation of being black and Puerto Rican, adding a genuinely Nuyorican perspective to these emblematic expressions of socially conscious poetry in times of Black Power radicalism. Being the only Puerto Rican in an African American group, Luciano played a crucial role for interethnic dialogues as a transcultural communicator between both communities and a voice for uniting black and Latino struggles, which was heard in Spanish *and* Black Harlem. According to Luciano, his time with The Last Poets ended, when he was urged to help organize the Puerto Rican community by Gylan Kain: "He said, Felipe, these are your people. You've done your work here. You got to go back." In search for advice, Luciano, hurt by the dismissal of the black nationalists to whom he felt he belonged, traveled to Baton Rouge, Louisiana, to meet his close friend, former SNCC chairman and militant Black Power advocate H. Rap Brown:

> He was able to convince me that the only way to affect revolution is to put yourself there. He said: 'Art is one thing, politics another thing, but art creates the revolution. You can bring both things together. You're ready, and you got to make them ready.' So I went back to Spanish Harlem, and I went back with the black aesthetic.

---

knew Stokely very well, so I read the book and I used that, and I used Descartes, I used, Nietzsche, I used Plato, I used what I was learning with people like Carlos Russell at Queens College at the time. I combined all of these elements to produce what I call my form of black nationalism".

Driven by countercultural impulses from the Black Arts Movement, as seen in Felipe Luciano's participation in The Last Poets and brought together by the sounds of Latin soul and boogaloo, as described by Denise Oliver, the dialogues that evolved between New York's Puerto Rican and black youth in the late 1960s found their political expression in the Young Lords. As Johana Fernández emphasizes, the Young Lords became "one of the first Latino formations that saw itself as part of the African diaspora; ... and that would commit itself to the struggle against racism in the United States and insist that poor African Americans and Latinos shared common political and economic interests" ("The Young Lords" 1). A crucial point in the Young Lords' identification with the African American freedom struggle here was the the practice of whitening and the anti-black racism hidden behind the myth of racial equality that prevailed in both Puerto Rico and New York's Puerto Rican community. As Pablo "Yoruba" Guzmán emphasized, racism was often downplayed by Puerto Ricans, many of whom said: "'Well yeah, those Blacks got a hard time, you know, but we ain't going through the same thing'. This was especially true for the light-skinned Puerto Ricans, Puerto Ricans like myself, who are dark-skinned, who look like Afro-Americans, couldn't do that, 'cause to do that would be to escape into a kind of fantasy. Because before people called me a spic, they called me a nigger" (236). Accordingly, the anti-racist struggle of African Americans had an exemplary role in the organizing of the Young Lords, as Guzmán wrote:

> We know that the number-one group that's leading that struggle [for liberation] are Black people, 'cause Black people – if we remember the rule that says the most oppressed will take the vanguard role in the struggle – Black people, man, have gone through the most shit. Black people, along with Chicanos and Native Americans, are the greatest allies we can have. So we must build the Puerto Rican-Black alliance. That is the basis for the American Revolution for us. (237)

Just like the sounds of soul, the rise of the Black Power movement appealed to a politicized youth in Spanish Harlem, who began to draw connections between the simultaneous liberation struggles in the U.S. and the Third World and the claims of Puerto Rican nationalists for independence from the U.S. Committed to an agenda of revolutionary internationalism and the building of interethnic alliances with other oppressed groups, the Black Panther Party "represented the model for revolutionary struggle, resistance, and radical chic," to Puerto Ricans and other non-African American groups as Chicanos/as, Asian Americans, Native Americans, and even poor whites, as Jeffrey Ogbar describes in his essay on "Rainbow Radicalism" (194). Corresponding with the border-crossing spirit of the Latin boogaloo, the invitation of the Black Panthers to other marginalized communities to become part of interethnic "rainbow coalitions" with the common goal of overcoming white supremacy and capitalism resonated among young Nuyoricans, who had grown up facing the same forms of discrimination as their African American peers.

Confronted with a legacy of anti-black racism within the Puerto Rican community, adopting the aesthetic representations of Black Power and soul style became an important element of Young Lords politics, as Johanna Fernández points out: "By growing their Afros and proclaiming that 'black is beautiful', the Young Lords, like the Black Panthers and many others of African descent, were challenging the unexamined racist logic of both Puerto Rican and American cultural norms and their psychologically damaging dimensions among Afro-descended people of color" (*The Young Lords* 162). As was the case with the Latin boogaloo, older generations of Puerto Rican immigrants often resented the ways the Young Lords embraced blackness, as was evident, for example, in the disparaging way they spoke about *los peluses* – a term that, as a reference to long unkempt hair, was a chiffre for the fashion of the Afros. (*The Young Lords* 162)

In Spanish Harlem, the Young Lords made themselves a name because of their grassroots campaigns to improve the devastating living conditions of a neighborhood that was suffering from all forms of structural neglect by city authorities. In the so-called "garbage offensive", Young Lords forced the city to take care of the problem of uncollected garbage in the streets, followed by a campaign to improve access to health care for the residents of El Barrio. In cooperation with local Black Panthers, the Young Lords also started to organize free breakfast programs, an initiative that had already gained the BPP respect and admiration across the nation. When the First Spanish United Methodist Church in Spanish Harlem refused the Young Lords' request to use the building for their breakfast program in late 1969, the organization reacted by occupying the building for over a week, sparking a wave of support by Spanish Harlem residents, as Benny Bonilla recalls: "We used to go to the church and bring food to the activists." During the days of the occupation which started December 28, 1969, and was ended by a police raid on January 7, 1970, the site became the "People's Church", where new visions of Nuyorican identity and solidarity were articulated, as for example when Pedro Pietri gave the first public reading of his influential poem "Puerto Rican Obituary", signaling the birth of the Nuyorican poets movement (Fernández, *The Young Lords* 181). According to Johanna Fernández, "they kept passersby informed with a loudspeaker affixed to the building's exterior on which they played the speeches of Malcolm X, [Puerto Rican independence activist] Pedro Albizu Campos, and Fred Hampton [who had been assassinated three weeks earlier], interspersed with political music", that included songs such as Eddie Palmieri's "Justicia" and Curtis Mayfield's "Mighty, Mighty (Spade and Whitey)" which also contains the phrase "I got to say it loud, I'm black and I'm proud" (177). Pictures and references on the linkages between the Puerto Rican and African American freedom struggles,

Malcolm X, and the Black Panthers, were a recurrent theme in the Young Lords newspaper *Palante*. Further underlining their emphasis on black-Puerto Rican coalition building, the curricula of Young Lords political education classes, taught in so-called liberation schools by activists like Denise Oliver and Iris Morales, also included a combination of lessons on African American and Puerto Rican histories and thinkers. As the Young Lords' Minister of Information Pablo Guzmán argued, "it is important for us to study the history of Blacks in the Americas, because it is part of Puerto Rican history, in terms of Black slaves in Puerto Rico and how they came into the culture, and in terms of better understanding the development of Blacks in the United States, who are the major force in the Amerikkkan revolution" (qtd. in Morales 109).

The engagement with soul, Black Arts and Black Power became a defining element in the making of 1960s and 1970s Nuyorican counterculture. The Young Lords and Nuyorican poets such as Piri Thomas, Victor Hernández Cruz, Pedro Pietri, Papoleto Meléndez, and Felipe Luciano coincided in their "characterization of African Americans as vanguards of a global struggle" (108) and in their practice of a "transaffective solidarity" that is defined by its "persistent proclaiming of affective relation and community across national, linguistic, and ethnic borders" (109), as Anne Garland Mahler has argued in her book on *Tricontinentalism* and revolutionary alliances in the 1960s and 1970s. Nuyorican participation in the Black Arts Movement was also addressed in a special issue of *Umbra*, a magazine on literature and culture founded by Black Arts activists and writers that regularly included contributions by Nuyorican poets such as Victor Hernández Cruz. The issue was titled "Latin Soul", and featured several articles which dealt with "cross-cultural connections between blacks and Latinos" (Hernández 335) in the Black Power era, addressing "how much the music of the African diaspora played a mediating role" as "Latino/a poets examined their own relationship to blackness during the Black Arts Movement," as Rod Hernández holds (345). While the editors of *Umbra*'s special issue acknowledged that "Latin Soul" is rooted "in the Black and Puerto-Rican areas of New York where both groups often jam to the same music: Latin and Soul" (333), their use of the term hints at a broader understanding of "Latin Soul" as a concept that decribes dialogues between African Americans and Latin American immigrants and challenges the black-white dichotomies that dominate racial discourses in the United States. In this sense, Latin soul and boogaloo not only represented new hybrid musical genres that underscored New York's role as a crucial site of Afro-hemispheric transculturations but were also symbols of non-essentialist black-brown solidarities that paved the way for new constructions of *afrolatinidad* and evidenced the salience of cosmopolitan practices in the Black Power era.

4 Panama: Soul, Black Internationalism and Afro-Caribbean Liberation at the Hemispheric Crossroads

"Everybody's talking about the soul invasion, it's a new sensation, it's a new vibration, it's a groovy generation!" This is how Panamanian soul singer Ernie King described the general feeling in late 1960s Panama in "Soul Invasion", a song he recorded for the group Los Invaders from Colón. While soul music in Panama was immensely popular across ethnic lines, those who were especially attuned to the latest developments in African American popular music from the United States were the descendants of black labor migrants from the Anglophone Caribbean who had been hired by the U.S. government at the beginning of the 20th century for the construction of the Panama Canal (1904–1914) – a project that, after the victorious Spanish-American War, cemented the status of the United States as upcoming hegemon of the region and constituted a key component on its path to becoming a world power. As participants in this large migration movement, the grandparents of Ernie King had moved from Jamaica to Panama, hoping for new opportunities as employees of the U.S. government. Ernie King (a stage name he adapted as a reference to the influence of New Orleans soul singer Ernie K-Doe) was born in 1943 as Ernesto Eduardo Reid[13] in Colón, which had become the center of the West Indian community in Panama as it became the Caribbean gateway to one of world traffic's most important passages when the Canal was opened.

Like many other Afro-Caribbean immigrants[14], the parents of King continued the family's migratory circuit from Panama to New York when King was six years old. As an adolescent he started to follow the teachings of Malcolm X, converted to Islam and became a Black Muslim. After he had gotten into trouble with the U.S. law, King was sent back to Colón in the late 1950s where he became a leading member of a youth gang by the name of the Diggers (in reference to their heritage as grandchildren of the Canal workers who did the "digging"). He began to use his skills as a singer that he brought from his time in New York and started to perform with local doo-wop groups like The Crowns, The Twilights, and The Lyrics, which were springing up all over Panama and the Canal Zone at the time (King). In the

---

13 Until his passing in 2023, Ernie King bore his Muslim name Kabir.
14 The Panamanian descendants of Afro-Caribbean immgrants are referred to alternately but synonymously as Afro-Caribbean Panamanians, West Indians, or *afro-antillanos* (based on the different self-descriptions members of this community chose for themselves over the decades).

https://doi.org/10.1515/9783110665550-006

late 1960s, after leaving Los Invaders and becoming singer of Los Fabulosos Festivals, Ernie King gained reputation as one of the leading vocalists of the *combos nacionales* – a new musical movement that revolutionized popular music in Panama, translating soul music from the United States into local contexts by combining it with Anglo-Caribbean calypso music, Panamanian *típico* rhythms and the latest *son montuno, guaracha,* Latin boogaloo, and salsa styles from New York, Puerto Rico and Cuba (Fig. 10). Ernie King's career was at its peak and close to reach another level when his band The Festivals, along with The Exciters, opened the show for James Brown at his only appearance in Panama in 1972. King, who used to "dance like J.B. in the streets" and had "a huge Afro" (Fig. 11) inspired by his idol, performed right before James Brown and his band the J.B.'s entered the stage: "The Godfather was backstage looking at me, listening to me... After the show, he approached me, so I got scared he would destroy me but he said: 'You can make it in the States. You have a soulful voice. I want you to come with us and become part of the James Brown revue.'" Instead of going on tour with the J.B.'s, King opened a barber shop in Panama City which was popular among black GI's stationed in the Canal Zone because of his expertise in Afro hairdos. In 1975, Muhammad Ali, curious about Panama's black Muslim barber, paid him a visit during his stay.

Ernie King's account reveals how imperialist policies, histories of multiple migrations, the transnational impact of black popular music from the United States, and the trajectories of translocal agents interplayed in the making of a vibrant soul scene in Panama that reinforced the strong sense of connection that the Afro-Caribbean community had developed with the cultural and political expression of African Americans in the Civil Rights-Black Power era. Due to the construction of the Panama Canal, large-scale Caribbean immigration and the establishment of a U.S.-occupied "neocolony" (Corinealdi "Envisioning Multiple Citizenships") in the Canal Zone, there is no country in Latin America where interactions between African Americans and other black populations have been as direct and intense as in Panama. The following chapter shows how a long history of dialogues between Afro-Panamanian and African American travelers, activists, intellectuals, GIs, and musicians contributed to the rise of soul and Black Power in Panama during the reign of populist General Omar Torrijos who became the leader of an anti imperialist campaign to recuperate the Canal from U.S. control in the late 1960s and 1970s.

4.1 Colón: Global Traffic and Black Cosmopolitanism

Panama is often overlooked in accounts of the intra-diasporic dialogues and transnational flows that define the Black Americas, notwithstanding its unique location at one of the world's major transportation hubs and its role as a hemispheric crossroads between the Caribbean, North and Latin America. As recent contributions such as those by Sonja Stephenson Watson (2014) and Kaysha Corinealdi (2022) demonstrate, research on the experiences of Afro-Panamanians "between overlapping, linked, and often conflicting histories and realities" (Nwankwo, "Introduction" 223) provides complex insights into the meaning of ethnicity, nation, and citizenship in the Americas. What brought the condition of Panama as a site of hemispheric transculturation into being was its geographic location on the isthmus where only 40 miles separate the Caribbean from the Pacific Sea. The possibility to create a passage that could revolutionize world traffic triggered several projects: the U.S.-led construction of a railroad between the Caribbean and the Pacific in the 19th century (which was the fastest and safest way to travel from the east to the west coast of the United States in the second half of the 19th century), the first intent to build a canal by the French Ferdinand de Lesseps in the 1880s (which failed due to miscalculations, hunger and a deadly yellow fever epidemic among the workers) and, most importantly, the finalization of the Panama Canal at the beginning of the 20th century by the United States. All of these ventures were only possible through the recruitment of migrant workers from Barbados, Jamaica, Martinique, and other Caribbean islands, 150.000 to 200.000 of whom settled in Panama during the construction of the Canal alone, doubling Panama's population at the time (Corinealdi, *Panama in Black* 6) and representing the "most important modern migration of African descendants within Spanish America and the Caribbean" (D. Duke 75). As a consequence of these migration waves, a heterogeneous community from diverse parts of the Caribbean emerged in Panama. In face of the various layers of race- and citizenship-based exclusion, the immigrants in the U.S.-controlled Canal Zone and the surrounding Panamanian republic were confronted with, they created "localized platforms for transformative change that affirmed the centrality of Afro-diasporic life in national and global politics" which Kaysha Corinealdi defines as practices of "Afro-diasporic world-making" and "local internationalism" (6).

The construction of the Panama Canal was part of a deal with local elites, in which the U.S. government promised them support in their efforts to become independent form Colombia to which the isthmus originally belonged. In exchange, the United States was granted complete control over the territory where the Canal was to be a built: a zone between Colón and Panama City that extended roughly five miles on each side of the Canal and split the county in two parts. As Julie Greene points out, "the republic became a protectorate of the United States and a model for the sort of neocolonialism that would dominate U.S. efforts to control the Caribbean and Central America in the twentieth century" (73). Thus, after a brief and unsuccessful protest by Colombia, Panama became a state at the mercy of the United States, putting a large question mark behind its alleged independence and sovereignty from the beginning. Hence, the demonization of the Canal and the transnational migrants who had come to Panama to build it have been at the core of nationalist discourses that intended to construct the romantic imagination of a homogenous Panamanian nation based on colonial, Catholic, and Hispanic heritage as a a proposal against Panama's transnationality, the vilified "transitismo", as Luis Pulido Ritter has argued ("Transnacionalismo y Modernidad" 28). Within these exclusive imaginaries the black, Anglophone, and protestant immigrants, many of whom worked for the detested *gringo* occupiers, represented the ultimate Other – a threat to the national project.

Colón, the capital of Afro-Caribbean life on the isthmus, embodied everything Panamanian nationalists despised. While practically on Panamanian territory, the city was almost entirely surrounded by the U.S. Canal Zone. Ships from New York, New Orleans, San Juan, Havana and other parts of the world had to dock here before passaging through the canal or returning to their ports of origin. With the ships came peoples, ideas and sounds that influenced the culture of Colón's diverse population, the majority of which was made up of a Caribbean community from various islands, but also Chinese, Indian and Jewish immigrants.

From the very beginning of the West Indian experience in Panama, black popular music has played an extraordinary role for the evolving dialogues with African Americans. In the interwar period, jazz music had already become an important platform for exchanges between Harlem and Colón, with musicians and records travelling constantly between both sites (Putnam "Jazzing Sheiks"). As the trajectory of jazz musician Luis Russell from Bocas del Toro via Colón to New Orleans where he became the leader of Louis Armstrong's orchestra shows, there was also a lively exchange with New Orleans. Both cities, which were connected by weekly steamship lines were designed by French architects and often compared to each other for their vibrant nightlife scenes (Pérez Price). Pulido Ritter holds that the diasporic transnationality of Colón recreated in music the historical foundation of a black cosmopolitanism, the consciousness of belonging to a transnational community: "If Paris was in the 19th century [...] the capital of Europe, Colón was [...] the musical capital in the Central American region for its role as intermediary, connecting languages, rhythms and diasporic spaces of the Atlantic" ("Lord Cobra" 9). Eric Walrond, the British Guyana-born author of *Tropic Death*, spent his youth in Colón before he continued his journey to New York and joined the Harlem Renaissance, where he became acquainted with, among others, the activist Marcus Garvey, who had also worked on the Canal. In a bibliographic note, included in his short story "Godless City", Walrond said: "I am spiritually a native of Panama. I owe the sincerest king of allegiance to it" (qtd. in Pulido Ritter, "Eric Walrond" 18).

As Colón became an integral part of a circum-Caribbean "migratory sphere that stretched from northern Venezuela to southern Harlem", as Lara Putnam argues, "not only did individual lives and family units cross national boundaries, but so, too, did social networks, formal institutions, and cultural consumption" ("Nothing Matters" 107). Border-crossing awareness of political developments related to matters of racial discrimination and black protest in the different locations of this trans-Caribbean sphere were part and parcel of these processes. Linkages between New York and Colón, two major destinations of West Indian migration, were especially close. In consequence, the familiarity, and often identification, with African American affairs shaped Afro-Caribbean culture and politics in the decades after the finalization of the Canal significantly. Reinforcing the ties with black movements in the U.S. and the Caribbean, Marcus Garvey and his New York-based Universal Negro Improvement Association (UNIA) gained a significant followership in Panama: local chapters were founded in the Canal Zone and Colón, people read UNIA's newspaper, *Negro World*, and in 1920 a mass strike of the West Indian canal workers organized by Garveyites demonstrated his influence in Panama. In 1927, 50.000 West Indians welcomed Marcus Garvey at the port of Colón when he was deported from New York ("Nothing Matters" 107). Putnam puts these developments in transnational perspective:

> [...] migration and migrants' activities created a West Indian–centered black internationalist world in the first decades of the twentieth century; [...] this world came under attack as a result of the rise of narrow, racially defined nationalisms and imperial closures in the interwar years; [...] the attacks reinforced 'race consciousness' among migrants, spurring increasingly explicit black internationalist critiques of imperial and neocolonial power. (109)

The popularity of Marcus Garvey's Pan-Africanism and other manifestations of black nationalism among West Indians in Panama persisted after his death in 1940 and was intrinsically linked to the omnipresence of anti-black racism in the U.S. and the Canal Zone and the rise of anti-West Indian sentiment in Panama, instigated by leaders such as President Arnulfo Arias of the nationalist Partido Panameñista.

Although World War II was not fought on Panamanian soil, it did change life in Colón fundamentally. Under the impression of Pearl Harbour, the U.S. Army and Navy reinforced their troops in the Canal Zone significantly to prevent a potential Japanese or German attack. In the Cold War era, the Canal Zone would become the largest U.S. military base in Latin America, used as an important logistical center during the Korea and Vietnam Wars. The massive increase of U.S. troops caused an economic and cultural boom in Panama. As Cobo Dixon, a union organizer who grew up in Colón remembers: "Entonces sus barcos llegaban aquí, una pequeña ciudad de 16 calles y nueve avenidas, inundada de soldados y todo el mundo hacía negocio, el limpia botas, el que vendía comida, el del almacén, las bandas de música, las prostitutas, todos, era una inyección económica."[15] There were designated clubs and casinos such as the Hotel Washington, New Yorker, Club 61, Strangers Club, Atlántico, and the Paris, which the GIs were allowed to visit during their excursions into the nightlife of Colón – but under no circumstances were they to stay in bars that had signs which said "off limits", as these were only allowed for Panamanian citizens. If they were caught there, they would get severe beatings by the feared military police (Castro).

Due to the increased demand for entertainment by thousands of GIs stationed at the U.S. military posts in the surrounding Canal Zone and sailors on shore leave, the music they brought and claimed became an important platform for the dialogues that evolved in the bars, brothels, casinos, dancehalls, and clubs of Colón. Tito Johnson, whose grandparents had come to Panama from Barbados and Jamaica, and who spent his teenage years in Colón before moving on to New York, shares his memories on the musical encounters with the GIs and sailors from other shores:

> In my teens, this is when rock'n'roll hit the scene. The rocking 50s. The Korean War was just over. And there was peace. And the soldiers that were stationed in the bases close to Colón, would come to Colon on the weekends and leave. And they would party. We had a wonderful time. We were dancing rock'n'roll, with the Americans. The Chinese owned basically all the bars in Colón. So this Chinese in particular, in that block where we used to hang out, asked the American GIs to bring their records and to put it in the jukebox. So these soldiers would bring the latest hits of rhythm and blues, of rock'n'roll from the States and Charlie, the Chinese guy, would put it in the jukebox there. So when they would come off the base in the weekend, they would go to the bar, putting their music and dancing their dances. And we watched, we learnt how they danced and we followed it. Of course, a lot of girls were in the bars because many of them wanted to get married and leave with an American GI. And we just picked up the American style also. I lived in a strip where they had about five bars and they were always filled with people in the weekends and in particularly, in the holidays. So they had a particular bar and they had jazz musicians coming by contract for six months.. So we were exposed to jazz, R&B, rumba from Cuba, calypso and even the Brazilian samba. A ship from the Brazilian navy was docked at the Cristobal Port right there during the Carnival. And they decided to participate in this Carnival in Colón. And they dressed up in their costumes, something we have never seen before in Colón. And they really stole all the show. This Brazilian guy from the navy opened Colón streets and from that time, samba got stuck in Colon. The music, the rhythm. Samba in Colón. Mixed with the conga from the African descendants, mixed with the rumba from the Cubans and the American jazz.

---

15 "Their ships came here, a small town of 16 streets and nine avenues, flooded with soldiers and everybody was doing business, the shoeshine boy, the shoeshine boy, the grocer, the shopkeeper, the grocer, the brass bands, the prostitutes, everybody, it was an economic boom." *Translation of the author in this and all further quotations.*

4.2 Racism, Nationalism, and West Indian-African American Alliances in the Era of Decolonization

While the accounts of cosmopolitanism in Colón show the important role music played in the migrants' daily lives, there is no question that they faced a hostile environment on both sides of the demarcation line between the Canal Zone and the Panamanian republic. From the moment of its establishment, the U.S.-controlled Zone became somewhat of a Deep South state transplanted to the isthmus. The U.S. Canal Zone authority introduced a system based on Jim Crow-style segregation which dominated all spheres of public life: hospitals, schools, hotels, recreational areas, shopping facilities, bathrooms, courtrooms, offices and public transport were completely segregated in areas for "coloreds" and "whites" (Bryce-Laporte 102). Like in the U.S., school segregation and the race-based restriction of access to educational facilities of quality became a major feature of perpetuating inequality in the Canal Zone (Westerman). Irwin Frank, a white Zonian, as the inhabitants of the Zone were called, remembers:

> I never in my life sat next to a black student. Schools were totally segregated; it was probably as bad as apartheid in South Africa [...], they rode not just in the back of the bus, they rode in different buses. Segregation was complete and it's what got the canal built. [...] I did not know as I grew up that the word nigger was a derogatory term. Just never knew it, it was just a figure of speech like calling this a table. (qtd. in Dombrowski 2011)

Afro-Caribbeans as a source of cheap, unskilled labor were exploited heavily, working under the direction of white U.S. Americans, mostly from the South, as Biesanz points out: "On the theory that Southerners knew how to handle Negroes the administration hired its supervisory force largely from the South; they imposed a system of racial relations similar to that back home" (Biesanz 23). A separate wage system was established based on the division of labor into "goldroll" and "silverroll" wages, ostensibly paid on the basis of skill. In practice, the gold and silver rolls became a form of racialized pay, with white U.S. workers receiving much higher wages on the gold roll and non-white, predominantly West Indian, canal workers working on the silver roll regardless of their specific qualifications. The imposed racial segregation permeated all aspects of life in the Canal Zone and had long-lasting effects on race relations between West Indian workers and white Zonians: "Southern patterns of racial etiquette have been adopted by most Americans on the Zone, [...]. On the level of personal contact, most whites feel called upon to keep the Negro 'in his place'" (Biesanz 26).

While the disparity of wages and the humiliating experiences of daily discrimination caused deep resentments against the U.S. government and white Zonians among Afro-Caribbeans in the Canal Zone it also reinforced solidarity and coalition-building with African Americans who were subjugated to identical forms of racial oppression, in the U.S. *and* in the Canal Zone. Technically, the U.S. citizenship of African American employees in the Canal Zone granted them specific privileges, but in practice, these were denied. Giving in to complaints of white employees, Canal authorities even ordered the removal of the few people of color on the gold roll to be transferred to the silver roll. In the face of rampant discrimination at all levels of the Canal authorities and the racist attitudes of white Zonians, demands by African American workers to be treated equally were usually turned down, as Patrice C. Brown showed in her publication on the African American experience in the Zone:

> Citizenship mattered, but so did color, despite the official canal policy statements to the contrary. If an employee was white and an American citizen, he benefited from the system. However, if an employee was an African American, he encountered problems in securing the 'rights' that went with American citizenship in the Canal Zone. [...] they had traveled to a foreign land only to face the same problems found at home.

Whereas these experiences were deeply frustrating for the affected African American employees, they contributed significantly to the development of a mutual sense of connectedness with the plight of West Indian migrants, paving the way for the forging of transnational alliances between activists of both communities during the anticolonial and antiracist struggles that defined the decades after World War II.

While life under Jim Crow segregation in the Canal Zone was a constant hardship, West Indian hopes for freedom of discrimination in the Panamanian republic were shattered in the early 1940s, when conservative President Arnulfo Arias launched a nationalist campaign under the slogan "Panamá para los Panameños" ["Panama for the Panamanians"], casting West Indian, Chinese, East Indian and Jewish migrants as "razas prohibídas" ["forbidden races"]. In 1941, the Panamanian government imposed a new constitution which revoked citizenship of the "undesired aliens" whose loyalty to the Panamanian nation was put in question. Inspired by Latin American *hispanismo*, pseudoscientific racism and European fascism, Arias' xenophobic "Panameñista" policies were based on a Eurocentric and homogenizing concept of Panamá's national identity that promoted a mestizo, Catholic, and Hispanic self-image – an alleged *crisol de razas* which included the local Afro-Hispanic population, the so-called *afro-coloniales*, but explicitly excluded Anglophone *afro-antillanos*. According to Renée Craft, Arias' agenda constituted a form of "racist nationalism that projected its rage against the United States onto West Indian bodies" (42). Arias drew heavily on widespread "anti-Yankee" sentiment among Panama's mestizo middle class and combined it with anti-black racism against Afro-Antilleans who, as English-speakers and employees of the U.S.

Canal authority with wages that often doubled the income of average Panamanians who worked outside the zone, were accused of collusion with the imperialist United States. Afro-Panamanian educator and activist Selvia Miller recalls that

> they used to call some of us the *tontos útiles* [useful idiots]. Because historically, most of our parents, grandparents, worked for the Panama Canal Commission in those days. So they were discriminated by the North Americans because they were not white. On the other side, they were also discriminated by Panamanians because they were seen as aliens.

Panameñismo despised Anglophone West Indians as anti-nationalists as Sonja Stephenson Watson explained: "While Afro-Hispanics were viewed as 'compatible' with the cultural foundation of the nation, Afro-Caribbeans were viewed as a threat to the homogenous image that Panamanian nationalists desired to propagate during the early 20th century" (Stephenson Watson 233–234). These discourses also resonated among native Afro-Panamanians who rejected West Indian Canal Zone workers and their alleged loyalty toward racist U.S. bosses as submissive "tío tom" behavior, straining relations between both black communities for decades to come (Donoghue 101–102). Anti-West Indian sentiment among Afro-Hispanics was reinforced by strong disparities in job opportunities and income, as due to their lack of English skills they were less competitive in the best paid jobs available in the facilties, companies, and amusement halls of the Canal Zone. Tito Johnson stresses how the divisions between Panama's two black communities played out:

> They had a word called *chombo.* They use this to distinguish themselves from the West Indians. I mean, guys who were blacker than us, they were direct descendants of Africans. We were Africans too, but we spoke English, there was a resentment. Because when you got a job in the Panama Canal Zone, you got payed because you could communicate with the Americans better and you had a living quarter that was furnished for you. And you made a lot more salary than the local people.

Though Arias' constitution was short-lived – West Indians regained their citizenship rights in 1946 – the traumatic experience of parallel race-based exclusion and marginalization in the U.S.-administered Canal Zone and the Panamanian republic had long-lasting effects: Language-based discrimination became a major issue in the experience of West Indians who were increasingly forced to leave their homes in the Canal Zone, settling in Colón and the emerging black neighborhoods of Panama City: Rio Abajo, Parque Lefevre, Calidonia, Marañón. Their English-speaking children who entered the Panamanian school-system had to overcome all forms of discrimination, as Selvia Miller confirms:

> The children of the West Indian descendants, who studied at the Panamanian schools, were forbidden to speak English in schools. English was just supposed to be a subject. Not part of their culture, not their mother language. Because they will be suspended, punished. So when you walk in the schools, you will find signs that would say *prohibido hablar ingles* [forbidden to speak English]. So people started to change the pronunciation of their names, which were in English. And they changed it to Spanish. And they started speaking to their children in Spanish, in order for them to be not discriminated and not to be treated as they were treated.

This experience of living "between a rock and a hard place", Jim Crow segregation in the Canal Zone and nationalist xenophobia in Panama, not only strengthened West Indian Panamanian community building but also reinforced existing drives to seek for allies beyond the Isthmus: in the broader African diaspora and, more specifically, among African Americans whose experiences of racialization resembled their own. As these developments coincided with the rise of antiracist and anticolonial movements in the U.S. and the Third World after World War II, they gained special momentum in cosmopolitan Panama where most international trends had instant repercussions.

The post-war period witnessed a growing sense of assertiveness and militancy among second- and third- generation West Indians, who were born in Panama or the Canal Zone. They often rejected the perceived servility, submissiveness and accomodationism of their parents and grandparents, whose initial admiration for the U.S. as modernizing force and provider of job opportunities had been met with contempt and treatment as second-class citizens by the U.S authorities and white Zonians (Donoghue 107). Younger generations became "deeply frustrated at the prospect of American textbooks praising democracy, tolerance, equality, compared to their own situation" (Biesanz 27) and started to develop diverse strategies of resistance. The influence of the African American freedom struggle, which entered a pivotal stage in the mid-1950s, proved crucial in the development of black activism in Panama. Anti-racist alliances with civil rights activists from the U.S., the increased presence of African American GIs after World War II, constant news coverage of developments in the U.S. by the military radio stations of the Canal Zone, and U.S. black popular culture were important sources of information and inspiration for local activists. Melva Lowe de Goodin (Fig. 12), an achieved author on matters of Afro-Caribbean identity and English language in Panama, emphasizes the importance of news from the U.S. as diffused through the Panama Tribune and radio stations, when she grew up in the segregated Canal Zone in the 1950s and 1960s: "Images and news from the Civil Rights Movement enhanced our self-esteem and of course we identified. Although we were kind of privileged economically in comparison with those who lived in the cities, we were always conscious that there was a struggle" (*personal interview*).

Against the backdrop of a new sense of determination and internationalist awareness that defined civil rights activism in the U.S. and Panama after World War II, prominent leaders of the West Indian community such as George Westerman and Sidney Young established contacts with African American activists, intellectuals and politicians mobilizing support for their efforts to end the discriminatory practices by the Canal authorities. In consequence, U.S. civic organizations like the NAACP and labor unions such as the United Public Workers of America (UPWA) started to tackle Jim Crow-style gold and silver roll segregation in the Canal Zone in the mid-to-late 1940s. In 1946, West Indian and Panamanian Canal Zone workers founded Local 713 as a chapter of UPWA, thus creating a multiethnic organization of various diasporic communities determined to overcoming segregation and securing better living conditions in the Canal Zone. Local 713 activists managed to mobilize international support for their campaign: In 1947, West Indian and Panamanian labor union organizers and U.S. civil rights activists joined forces for the organization of a Panamanian tour by African American singer and activist Paul Robeson, who was a leading figure of the transnational black movement, widely admired for his outspokenness on race-related issues throughout the African diaspora (Zien). As part of the local anti-segregation campaign, Robeson performed in Colón and Panama City, but refused to sing in the Canal Zone: "I would not have [sung] on the Canal Zone to the white people there, no matter what they offered. I never have [sic] and never will sing as long as I live in places where my people are segregated in the audience" (Zien 115). As Katherine Zien detailed, Robeson along with W.E.B. Du Bois and UPWA secretaries launched the "Citizen's Committee to End Silver-Gold Jim Crow in Panama" in 1948, deepening the ties between African American and West Indian activists from Panama. Due to allegations of Communist ties, Local 713 was ultimately disbanded but its transnational and multiethnic anti-racist activities provide an example of the processes of "diasporization" which Frank Guridy has described as "diaspora in action, [...] the ways Afro-diasporic linkages were made in practice" (*Forging Diaspora* 5).

In the following years, scholar and activist George Westerman promoted a series of concerts by African American artists in ton Panama, which, according to Zien, emphasized black cosmopolitanism and constituted "a distinct type of activism" that "deployed the transnational mobility and visibility of African American artists to foster new conjunctures of race relations in Panama and the Canal Zone after World War II" (119). Through intense lobbying, George Westerman established close ties with African American leaders from the U.S. such as Harlem congressman Adam Clayton Powell, NAACP leader and Supreme Justice Thurgood Marshall, and Ralph Abernathy, enlisting their support for ending racial discrimination in the Canal Zone (Conniff 155). The case of Lester Greaves, a West Indian convicted to a 50-year sentence for rape of a white woman in 1946, became another rallying issue for black activists from Panama and the U.S. Greaves had allegedly been framed for breaking the taboo of sexual relations between black men and white women and became a symbol of "apartheid injustice" in the Canal Zone to local West Indian activists and black U.S. supporters such as Robeson, Powell and the NAACP, who had joined the campaign for Greave's release (Donoghue 116–117). These post-war collaborations strengthened relations between the U.S. Civil Rights movement and Panamanian West Indians significantly, heralding the extraordinary impact of the African American freedom struggle on Panama's black movement in the following decades.

4.3 The 1950s and Beyond: Afro-Panamanian Community Building in New York

A large portion of Anglophone migrants from the Caribbean had not arrived in Panama with the idea of settling there indefinitely but hoping to gain the necessary economic means and citizenship rights for eventually relocating to the United States. Judith Stewart, whose father Waldaba Stewart became the first Panamanian-descended New York stated senator for Brooklyn in 1968, recalls: "When I was a kid, it was always clear that someday we would go to the States. That was always the plan." Whereas West Indian remigration from Panama to the U.S., mostly to New York, had been a widespread phenomenon since the construction of the Canal, these movements of people increased significantly after the conclusion of the Remón-Eisenhower treaty in 1955. The treaty included some concessions to Panamanian claims against the U.S. government and Canal Zone administration, but at the cost of the West Indian community whose economic situation was affected detrimentally by the implicated measures. The treaty had specifically negative implications for West Indians: non-U.S. Canal Zone employees were obliged to pay income taxes to Panama; Canal Zone employees who resided in Panamanian neighborhoods as Calidonia, Río Abajo and Parque Lefevre lost their rights to shop at the non-profit commissaries of the Zone, eliminating an important source of income for West Indians, who often sold high-quality U.S. products from the Zone commissaries in Panama. Reinforced by an overall lack of professional and educational opportunities for blacks and accompanied by an increased policy of depopulation by Zone Governor John Seybold – who forced many West Indian residents to move out of the Zone to Panama, where they were received with anything but open arms – these unfavorable developments led many West Indian Panamanian families to migrate to the United States. As George Priestley holds, thousands of Afro-Caribbean Panamanians migrated as a "direct result of their expulsion from the Canal", "feeling abandoned by the United States and relatively shut out of the economic opportunities opening in Panama" (Priestley 53).

In the 1950s and 1960s, Brooklyn became the primary destination of a generation of highly ambitious Anglophone Afro-Panamanians who moved to the North in search of better education and economic advancement, only to find themselves embroiled in the turbulences of the African American freedom struggle that was gaining intensity on the very same campuses and urban centers they had headed to. The Crown Heights and Bedford-Stuyvesant neighborhoods in Brooklyn became a focal point of West Indian Panamanian migration to New York, the area around Franklin Avenue eventually gaining a reputation as "Little Panama". In her rich study on the emergence of a transnational Afro-Panamanian community, Kaysha Corinealdi argues that "the presence of other Black migrants from throughout the Caribbean increased the appeal of Brooklyn for Afro-Caribbean Panamanians" ("When Panama came to Brooklyn"). In Brooklyn, Panamanians converged with African Americans, immigrants from the Anglophone Caribbean, Haiti and Puerto Rico, with whom they shared the knowledge of US imperial governance (ibid.). Due to their trajectories of circular migration, their multilingual, cross-cultural, and cosmopolitan backgrounds, Afro-Caribbean Panamanians become important interlocutors between other immigrant groups from Latin America and the Caribbean and African Americans, with whom they shared, among other things, the experience of racial segregation and the English language. As Corinealdi emphasizes, Afro-Caribbean Panamian immigrants in Brooklyn were uniquely positioned at the intersection of overlapping diasporas:

> As migrants, they brought histories of previous homes and connected them to the racial and ethnic politics of New York. They were, therefore, familiar with diaspora (as Afro-Caribbeans), migrants who understood national politics (as Panamanians), and self-defined Black women and men ready to engage in hemispheric conversations about race. ... To be Panamanian in Brooklyn blurred the distinctions among Latinx, African American, Latin American, and Caribbean identities. The multidiasporic Blackness that Afro-Caribbean Panamanians encompassed remained outside any defined racial or ethnic category in early 1950s New York. ... fully understanding Afro-Caribbean Panamanians required addressing the layered history they embodied. These layers included hemispheric citizenship debates, multiple migrations, and a direct experience of US neocolonialism. ("When Panama came to Brooklyn")

English-speaking Panamanians of Caribbean descent interacted with African Americans much more easily than other immigrant groups from Latin America and the Caribbean. George Priestley, Afro-Panamanian sociologist and community leader who had migrated from Panama to New York in 1961, argues that West Indian Panamanians had been "'pre-sensitized to African American culture'" (Opie 11) through their encounters with African American GIs in the Canal Zone. Priestley recalls how he was introduced to African American and Puerto Rican friends upon his arrival to the U.S., who used to take him to clubs that "were largely African American clubs." (11). Driven by day-to-day interactions with a highly mobilized African American community and exposure to events related to ongoing black liberation struggles, many members of the West Indian Panamanian migrant community in the U.S. became involved in the Civil Rights and Black Power movements. Stepping in the footsteps of Afro-Panamanian psychologist Kenneth B. Clark from Colón – who had arrived in the U.S. as early as 1919 and became known for conducting research on the negative effects of racial segregation on the psyches of blacks that the NAACP used in the *Brown vs Board of Education* case of 1954 – some members of the vocal Afro-Panamanian migrant community participated in the U.S. black movement and became important mediators between African Americans and the West Indian community in Panama.

The biography of Carlos Russell illustrates the often-overlooked role of Afro-Panamanian migrants as bridge-builders between African American, Caribbean, and Latin American experiences. Born in 1934 to parents who had migrated from Barbados and Jamaica to Panama during the construction of the Panama Canal, Russell moved to the United States in 1955. Recollecting his first experience as an Afro-Panamanian migrant in the United States, he states: "When I arrived in the U.S. the first thing I saw in the newspaper was a picture of Emmett Till, all messed up...that was when I knew I had to get involved in the black movement. [...] In the U.S., blacks were much more focused on opposing racial society, which is what turned me on to the black movement there" (*personal interview*). As Russell's account illustrates, the U.S. black movement attracted many Panamanian West Indians who felt frustrated by the slow pace of political progress and lack of opportunities for Afro-descendants in Panama and admired the confrontational direct-action approach of the U.S. black movement. After settling in Brooklyn in the early 1960s, Carlos Russell got involved with black internationalist intellectual circles who were sowing the seeds for the emergence of the Black Power and Black Arts movements later in the decade. He became a member of the Brooklyn branch of the prestigious Harlem Writers Guild and started to work as an editor of the *Liberator* magazine for which he interviewed Malcolm X in 1964 (Russell "Exclusive Interview"). In the mid-to-late 1960s, Russell served as an advisor to Martin Luther King, became acqainted with African American leader such as Jesse Jackson and Angela Davis in the organization of Black Power activities, and in 1968 founded Black Solidarity Day, which is still observed in New York black activist circles (Steinitz "Hemispheric Ambassador"). As a professor at Old Westbury College, he also became a mentor to the Young Lords, hinting at the importance of his experiences with the diverging meanings of race in the United States and Latin America, as Denise Oliver recalls: "He opened the doors to a much broader understanding of blackness that was not limited to the United States, but included blackness in Mexico, blackness in Central America, blackness in Latin America as well as the Caribbean." According to Felipe Luciano, the experience of Russell and other Panamanians helped the Young Lords in articulating a critique of anti-black racism in the Puerto Rican community: "The Panamanians in this city were the first migrants from a Latin American country to say that they were black, which was revolutionary in those days. ... There's no doubt that Carlos Russell was a bridge-builder between African American and Latino communities because of his experience as black migrant from a Spanish-speaking country like Panama" (qtd. in Steinitz, "Hemispheric Ambassador" 87).

In the 1970s, Carlos Russell and other prominent members of the Afro-Panamanian community in the U.S. such as Cirilo McSween, Waldaba Stewart, and George Priestley become important allies of Panamanian nationalist leader Omar Torrijos efforts to recuperate the Panama Canal that ultimately led to the Torrijos-Carter Treaties in 1977. They used their close relationship with African American leaders such as Jesse Jackson and the Congressional Black Caucus as platform for intense and sustained lobbying for the recuperation of the Canal, proving their often-questioned affiliation with Panama and further deepening existing ties between black communities in both countries (Priestley).

Panamanian migrants in the United States were not only involved in transnational and anti-racist politics, but also contributed their versatility in diverse musical traditions from different hemispheric contexts in the making of new, innovative sounds, as the trajectories of musicians such as Louis Armstrong's bandleader Luis Russell and Joe Panama show. Hinting at a "Panamanian connection", Benjamin Lapidus has argued that, although often overlooked and misidentified as African Americans due to their English names, Afro-Panamanians and their "musical multiculturalism" (151) played a key role in New York's international Latin music scene. Musicians from Colón such as saxophone player Mauricio Smith (who recorded with Mongo Santamaria, Tito Puente, Joe Cuba, Dizzy Gillespie, and many others), and singer Camilo Azuquita (who became known for his collaborations with Kako and his Orchestra), but also Ruben Blades (who became one of Fania's main vocalists in the 1970s and 1980s), underline the protagonism of Panamanians in New York's boogaloo and salsa scenes. The constant traffic between New York and Panama also contributed to the emergence of a local soul scene in Panama and the popularization of Panamanian bands such as Love, Warmth, and Affection in 1970s Brooklyn. Concluding, New York's Afro-Panamanian community was instrumental in creating a highly frequented channel of communication between both sites through which symbols, slogans, and sounds travelled, providing a source of inspiration and information for those who had stayed in Panama.

4.4 The Turbulent 1960s: Anti-Imperialism and Black Power in Panama

Panama in the 1960s, in tune with international developments marked by decolonization, the advances of the African American freedom struggle, and the beginnings of a global youth revolt, witnessed the parallel rise of two conflicting and overlapping movements. One was driven by the anti-imperialist vision of a Panama without U.S. occupation and a Canal under Panamanian control. The other, which operated more from the margins and did not manifest itself in a mass political organization but rather in a change of attitude and new cultural expressions, was about the struggle against the various forms of racial discrimination Afro-Panamanians of Caribbean descent continued to face.

The so-called Flag Riots in January 1964 signaled the beginning of a new era in U.S.-Panamanian relations. After U.S. students had refused to follow-up on a previous agreement to fly a Panamanian flag next to the stars and stripes at Balboa High School in the Canal Zone, riots broke out in Panama City and Colón, with protesters attacking U.S.-owned businesses and U.S. citizens and U.S. army snipers killing several Panamanians. Always under suspicion of holding allegiance to the United States by Panamanian nationalists, many Afro-Caribbeans, frustrated at the persistence of Jim Crow segregation in the Canal Zone, joined the struggle. The young General Omar Torrijos positioned himself as the leader of a renewed anti-imperialist campaign to gain control over the Canal. Selvia Miller from Colón recalls that her father became involved with Torrijos' *Partido Revolucionario Democrático*, "because he considered that since he was born in Panama, even though his mother and his father were from Barbados and Jamaica, he was born in Panama and he felt that he had all the rights to be treated as a Panamanian, because he was born here".

Events took a dramatic turn in the fateful year of 1968, when a military coup deposed President Arnulfo Arias, with Omar Torrijos eventually taking complete power in 1969 and initiating his so-called *proceso revolucionario*. In search of allies for his populist and nationalist agenda, which challenged the country's conservative and wealthy *mestizo* elites and the U.S. occupation of the Canal Zone, Torrijos embraced formerly excluded and marginalized sectors of society, most prominently Afro-Caribbean and Afro-Hispanic Panamanians. He promoted blacks such as Romulo Betancourt and Juan Materno Vásquez to high posts in his government, others ascended to leadership positions in the armed forces, members of the Afro-Panamanian migrant community in the United States such as Cirilo McSween and Carlos Russell became crucial allies in his lobbying efforts for the recuperation of the Canal. Condemning racial discrimination in the Canal Zone, Torrijos' strategical alliance with anti-racist struggles became a powerful propagandistic

132 — 4 Panama: Soul, Black Internationalism and Afro-Caribbean Liberation

tool for discrediting U.S. occupation and heralded an era of new opportunities and inclusion for Panama's West Indian community (Priestley 54–55).

Many Afro-Caribbean Panamanians supported the nationalist project of Torrijos while at the same time identifying with the struggle of African Americans against precisely the same forms of racial segregation they were subjugated to as workers in the Canal Zone. This led to the paradoxical situation where Afro-Caribbean youth who participated in the struggles to end U.S. rule in Panama sympathized with African American GIs who wore the uniform of the "enemy", challenging the generalized anti-Americanism and hatred of anything "gringo" among many Panamanians. During the Vietnam War, military bases in Panama had become hotbeds of Black Power activity, part of a larger development in which African American GIs increasingly questioned their over-proportional involvement in a war against another people of color.[16] Afro-Panamanian activist Dosita Wilson de Bryan – who had spent the early 1960s involved in militant nationalist activism at the Instituto Nacional ("I know how to prepare molotov cocktails") and the second half as participant of black movements in New York City – explains the attitude of Afro-Panamanians toward African Americans stationed on the military bases: "We were not against the GIs who often looked like us. We were against the U.S. occupation of the Canal Zone and racism in Panama". Black community organizer, lawyer, and writer Alberto Barrow recalls how the clenched fist salute became a signal of solidarity and mutual identification between Afro-Panamanians and African American GIs:

> Se encontraron caminos comunes, escenarios comunes. Habían soldados negros aquí obviamente, esos soldados transitaban en Panamá en la ciudad, había un tema de identidad del puño alzado, de reconocer al otro, de saludar al otro. Yo recuerdo a los soldados negros saludándose entre ellos pero también saludándonos a nosotros con el puño y nosotros devolviéndoles el saludo.[17]

Friendly relations between black GIs and West Indian thwarted the overall hostility U.S. army members were met with on Panamanian soil and reinforced accusations by Panamanian nationalists that West Indians loyalty to the nation was not to be trusted. Shared experiences of racialization and common struggles for equality in the Canal Zone provided an important base of mutual understanding for Afri-

---

16 Muhammad Ali had given voice to this sentiment with his refusal to become drafted, famously stating in 1967: "I ain't got no trouble with them Viet-Cong."

17 "Common paths were found, common scenarios. There were black soldiers here obviously, those soldiers were transiting in Panama in the city, there was an issue of identity related to the raised fist, of recognizing the other, of saluting the other. I remember the black soldiers saluting each other but also saluting us with their fist and us returning the salute".

4.4 The Turbulent 1960s: Anti-Imperialism and Black Power in Panama — **133**

can American GIs and West Indian encounters in Panama. As Melva Lowe de Goodin recalls, the music the soldiers brought had mobilizing effects on Afro-Panamanian youth:

> We grew up listening to expressions of black music from the U.S. My father deeply appreciated African American music and had a huge collection of records. On Sundays we would listen to religious gospel music and the rest of the week to popular music, jazz, rhythm and blues, soul. But at that time, radio was even more popular than records. Everybody listened to the radio, so we really became enchanted by many of those singers and what was going on in the States. (*personal interview*)

U.S. military radio stations proved to be important incubators of soul music in Panama. An even more important source of information and entertainment for the Afro-Caribbean was provided by a local radio station with full English program by the name of H.O.G. which was launched to counteract the dominance of the U.S. Armed Forces radio station. With West Indian DJs like Joe Gavini, Vince Monchini, and Joss Russell, H.O.G. became the most popular station among Panama's Afro-Caribbean community, providing extensive airtime to black American popular music and daily broadcastings by community personalities such as Hugo Wood, who was a staunch Garveyite and used to dedicate specific attention to black struggles in the U.S. and other parts of the African diaspora (Patterson). As Bruce Codrington, a community organizer and activist in the Canal Zone, who would become known as manager of the The Exciters in the late 1960s, recalls: "Hugo Wood taught us about Malcolm X, Martin Luther King, the Panthers. He opened my eyes."

The emergence of black militancy among the West Indian youth sent shockwaves through the Canal Zone and Afro-Caribbean neighborhoods in Colón and Panamá City. Widespread frustration with white supremacy as experienced in the Canal Zone and the passivity of their parents and grandparents, had significant impacts on younger, more radical generations of Afro-Panamanias. Hinting at the impact of "soul style" in late 1960s Panama, Michael Conniff writes: "Young persons of West Indian descent picked up the language and style of American blacks, including techniques of confrontation virtually unknown in Panama. The U.S. imports probably came with black servicemen stationed in army and navy bases. Canal youth wore Afro hairdos and Swahili robes and adopted other symbols of the black power movement" (165). Despite of heavy restrictions on political activities in the Canal Zone, local organizer Alberto Smith Fernández founded *Asociación Afro-Panameña* in the late 1960s, modeled after U.S. Civil Rights and Black Power organizations. According to Michael Donoghue, the local adherents of U.S.-style Black Power, who were regarded as "rebels", "boat-rockers", and "trouble-makers" by older West Indians and Zone officials, "gave another Black

Power salutes and high-fives, and refused to defer automatically to whites in the manner of their fathers" (122–123). The new Black Power-inspired militancy among West Indian youth was condemned by moderate community leaders such as George Westerman: "We reject any misguided militants who may emerge from black power sources abroad encouraging local youths to identify with them and anti-white sentiments, or to engage in disruptive efforts which could lead to violence and chaos in this country" (Conniff 165). However, the young black activists, deeply critical of "Uncle Tom-behavior" carried on, showing that the old leadership had lost some of its authority.

In the late 1960s and early 1970s, Canal Zone authorities were confronted with increased direct-action protests against segregated facilities as the Canal Administration building and high schools. Frequent protest marches and acts of insubordination in the Canal Zone coincided with increased racial tensions on the military bases, where African American GIs struggled against persistent discrimination. In October 1972, *Concerned Brothers*, an association of African American GIs joined forces with white allies and young Afro-Panamanian activists in a protest rally against practices of racial segregation at the Elks Club, where only white GIs were allowed to gather. In an article published in the Panamanian newspaper *Matutino*, Cecil Innis, leader of *Concerned Brothers,* is quoted voicing his critique against the discriminatory practices and the crimiminalization of black protest by the U.S. authorities in the Canal Zone: "Cada vez que dos o tres negros se unen, dicen que siempre hay disturbios" ["Whenever two or three blacks get together, they say there are always riots"] (*Matutino*, October 23, 1972). The Zone Administration's Internal Security Office, haunted by the impression of the Canal as a "racial tinderbox" (Donoghue 124), even started evicting young black activists to Panama after they turned 18, as Melva Lowe de Goodin remembers: "Outright political activism was not accepted. Canal Zone authorities very strongly penalized everybody involved in 'rabblerousing'". Black struggles against Jim Crow in the Canal Zone also faced stiff resistance by white Zonians who wanted to preserve their white supremacy-based privileges.

Soul music played a crucial role in the increased manifestations of Afro-Panamanian assertiveness. Selvia Miller holds that the West Indian youth in Colón "assumed black identity through African American music. They used to call themselves soul sisters and soul brothers. So the soul sisters and brothers used to dress in a different way." In the same vein, activist-scholar Gerardo Maloney underscores the significance of soul music in the emergence of Black Power-inspired youth movements in Panama and the Canal Zone:

> En la ciudad de Colón, y también en las comunidades de los trabajadores antillanos en la antigua Zona del Canal, la influencia de la música negra de los Estados Unidos, al igual que del

Caribe sí fueron fuentes importante en el desarrollo de una identidad racial,y la organización de movimientos sociales en contra del racismo y la discriminación racial, lo que nos incorporó a un movimiento de alcances internacionales, que caracterizó la generación de ese momento. [...] Esa música penetró mucho. "Say it loud (I'm black and proud)" de James Brown fue una canción ícono, se convirtió en un himno, porque fue un canto a la identidad y en Panamá esa identidad llegó directamente, porque nosotros siempre tenemos familia allá y la gente nos mandaba las fotos, nos mandaba cosas. [...] En Panamá, yo creo que fue muy importante esa música porque alimentó enormemente la consciencia de la gente joven ... Entonces yo diría que la gente afroantillana que vivió en la lucha, en consciencia étnica alimentada por el movimiento de Garvey fueron mayormente los protagonistas de los sectores de la influencia de la música del soul.[18] (*personal interview*)

4.5 Panama Soul: From Nights of Fun to Combos Nacionales

The increased availability of imported vinyl records from the United States and cheap record players was a crucial factor in the emergence of a vibrant soul scene in Panama. These records, distributed on 45rpm singles, became essential in the emergence of so-called *nights of fun* in Colón and the Rio Abajo, Parque Lefevre, Calidonia neighborhoods of Panama City. Initially, *nights of fun* were dance parties organized by Afro-Caribbean youth organizations such as Ernie King's Diggers or The Debonairs as fundraisers for their activities (Reina). According to Alberto Barrow, these were "bailes populares, la forma pobre de organizar una fiesta en la comunidad" ["popular dances, the poor way to organize a party in the community"]. The ingredients of a typical *night of fun* were palm leaves and blue or red-light bulbs for decoration and intimacy, a record player, a DJ, which during that time went by "Johnny Arbuja" (Sealy), and the latest singles of soul music imported from the U.S. as Gerado Maloney remembers:

Normalmente *night of fun* se hacía en la parte de abajo porque las construcciones de las casas en lugares como Río Abajo eran sobre un alto, entonces había una parte abajo y allí se ponían

---

18 "In the city of Colón, and also in the communities of West Indian workers in the former Canal Zone, the Influence of black music from the United States, as well as from the Caribbean, were important sources in the development of a racial identity, and the organization of social movements against racism and racial discrimination, which incorporated us into a movement of international scope, which characterized the generation of that time. [...] That music penetrated a lot. James Brown's "Say it loud (I'm black and proud)" was an iconic song, it became an anthem, because it was a hymn to identity and in Panama that identity came directly, because we always have family there and people sent us photos, they sent us things. [...] In Panama, I think that music was very important because it fed enormously the consciousness of young people. So I would say that the Afro-Antillean people who lived in the struggle, in ethnic consciousness fueled by Garvey's movement were mostly the protagonists of the soul music influences." (Maloney, t.m.)

luces rojas, se ponía palma y ahí la gente ponía su tocadiscos, cobraba 25 centavos para recoger fondos, se vendía comida, y esa era una Night of Fun. Eran eventos sociales de la comunidad.[19]

Carlos Brown, bass player and leader of The Exciters who was born and raised in Rio Abajo remembers: "We had a big old home, and downstairs we did *night of fun*, it was about dancing, and blue lights, and dark lights, you understand, groovy." As Brown emphasizes, next to soul, calypso from the Anglophone Caribbean was also very popular among Panamanians of West Indian descent and played at these events. *Nights of fun* mirrored the emergence of soundsystem culture in 1950s Jamaica, which, according to Anand Prahlad "brought people together in large yards [...] where 'the music of Jamaica and Black America could be played without restraint', where they could dance, party, and have a good time" (6). With the global expansion of the record industry, soundsystem culture would become an integral part of black cultural resistance throughout the Americas, not only in Jamaica (Stolzoff.) but also in Brazil, where black youth was introduced to the sounds and styles of soul on so-called *bailes black* during the Black Rio movement of the 1970s, as addressed in Chapter 5.

Afro-Panamanian community activist Ines Sealy recalls that *night of fun* "was introduced by West Indians, but if the Latins wanted to have a good time they could come." Here, she gives a hint on how these dances became the sites for the bridging of formerly established racial and ethnic boundaries: *nights of fun* also attracted growing crowds of Panama's Spanish-speaking population who became introduced to the formerly unknown musical worlds of their Afro-Caribbean neighbors. These cultural flows were anything but unidirectional. When audiences became more mixed, and *nights of fun* were somewhat nationalized as manifested in the establishment of the term *naitofón* in Panamanian Spanish, DJs started to adapt to these changes by including Afro-Latin genres such as salsa and boogaloo from New York, Cuba, and Puerto Rico to their sets, turning dancefloors into contact zones of diverse Afro-diasporic sounds from the United States, Latin America, and the Caribbean (Barrow). The cross-cultural interactions related to the popularization of *naitofón* in the mid-1960s heralded the emergence of the *combos nacionales.*

---

19 "Normally, *night of fun* was held in the lower part because the construction of the houses in places like Rio Abajo were built on pillars, so there was a lower part and there they would put red lights, they would put palm trees and there people would put their turntables, they would charge 25 cents to collect funds, they would sell food, and that was a *night of fun*. They were community social events." (Maloney)

Panama's Afro-Caribbean youth did not conform itself with listening and dancing to new sounds from abroad. The appearance of the *combos nacionales* had its roots in the 1950s when a young generation of Afro-Caribbean musicians, many of whom had enjoyed musical formation or were members of gospel choirs of West Indian protestant churches, picked up on a new trend form the United States: doo-wop. Mirroring developments in Spanish Harlem at the same time, the impact of Frankie Lymon and The Teenagers proved to be crucial. In 1957, the band had come to Colón to play at a carnival parade. They performed at Colegio Abel Bravo to promote their main show, as Carlos Castro, who was a student in Colón at that time, vividly remembers: "Era un pelado de 15 años, todo el mundo lo adoraba." ["He was a kid of 15 years, everybody loved him."] Mirroring developments in Spanish Harlem's at the same time, Lymon's appearance sparked a boom of R&B and vocal groups in Colón, Panama City, and the Canal Zone. Among these bands were The Playboys, Los Ron Coloniales, Los Skyliners, The Astronauts, The Golden Boys, The Twilights, The Lyrics, The Crowns, and many others, giving teenagers like Ernie King, who sang in many of these groups, the opportunity to earn some money at gigs for GIs in the Canal Zone or in venues such as Teatro Rio or Club 24 in the nightlife of Colón. True to the motto "if you can make it in Colón you can make it anywhere", expressed by radio DJ Irving Harris hinting at the exigent audiences of the city, one of these vocal groups reached international fame: The Gay Crooners performed in the USA, Central and South America, shared the stage with The Platters, Sammy Davis Jr., Frank Sinatra, Nat King Cole, Dinah Washington, Tina Turner and B.B. King, and toured several years with Little Richard, playing covers of U.S. doo-wop, R&B, and soul songs like "Soul Man", and own productions (Maloney *Los Gay Crooners*).

While The Gay Crooners were the only band to became internationally famous, the vocal groups developed a growing local followership as the demands of their U.S. audiences at the military stations and the incoming records allowed them to follow developments in black popular music (which in the early-to-late 1960s meant the rise of soul music), in real time. Ricardo Staple, who started his musical career as a guitarist for The Skyliners in 1958 and became known as a drummer for Los Soul Fantastic in the late 1960s, also recalls the importance of S.C.N., the radio station of the U.S. army, in his musical upbringing:

> Recuerdo que los muchachos nos pegábamos a la radio para escuchar esas fabulosas armonías de grupos como The Temptations, solistas como Sam Cooke, Jackie Wilson y Smokey Robinson; era algo brutal, algo que rayaba en lo devocional. Uno los escuchaba con tal deteni-

> miento y concentración que tú sentías cómo te penetraban en la carne, la sangre, el alma misma.[20] (qtd. in Irving 11)

According to Ricardo Staple, the emergence of the so-called *combos nacionales* in the mid-to-late 1960s took place when the vocal groups, many of which peformed a-capella, followed the shift from doo-wop to soul in US black popular music, using more instruments such as horns, drums, electric bass and guitar (11). Reflecting the political, social and cultural transformations that were taking place in Panama and the United States, epitomized by the parallel rise of Omar Torrijos and the release of James Brown's "Say it Loud – I'm Black and I'm Proud", 1968 was the year in which the phenomenon widely referred to as the *combos nacionales* took off. Staple emphasizes that the *combos*, while soon becoming a multi-ethnic and inclusive affair, had their origins in Panama's West Indian community: "La herencia antillana era todavía muy poderosa en las décadas de los 50 y 60. Eramos de veras 'negros finos', orgullosos, educados en toda disciplina, desde las ciencias hasta la música"[21] (qtd. in Irving 9). While "negros finos" was a derogatory term that also expressed the envy and resentment that many native Panamanians felt toward West Indians given their multilingualism, better education, and higher incomes, the *combos* were also a symbol of the self-confidence and community pride with which a young generation confronted these resentments. As the first *combos* releases from 1968 to 1970 demonstrated, U.S. soul music and style became the primary language through which young Afro-Panamanians expressed their new attitude.

Starting in the city of Colón, the rise of the *combos nacionales* in the mid-to-late 1960s was related to increased financial and technical resources. The Colón-based Jewish businessmen Moises and Jacob Heres were among the first to invest in the new sound. As compiler Roberto Ernesto Gyemant holds, "entrepreneurs such as the Heres brothers [...] functioned as incubators for a number of important combos, providing instruments and paying for recording sessions at Discos Istmeños studio" (*Panama!*). Running two record stores in Panama City and Colón, the Heres brothers were well aware of the popularity of soul music among Panamanian youth. With early releases such as "Necia de mi corazón" (1966) by Little Fran-

---

20 "I remember that we kids were glued to the radio to listen to those fabulous harmonies of groups like The Temptations, soloists like Sam Cooke, Jackie Wilson and Smokey Robinson; it was something brutal, something that bordered on devotional. You listened to them with such attention and concentration that you felt how they penetrated your flesh, your blood, your soul itself" (Staple).

21 "The West Indian heritage was still very powerful in the 1950s and 1960s. We were truly 'negros finos', proud, educated in every discipline, from science to music" (Staple).

cisco Greaves, the first Panamanian soul release in Spanish, the Heres brothers' label Sally Ruth became a driving force in the emergence of a new, distinctly Panamanian soul style that went beyond covering hits from the U.S. billboards and became the trademark of the combos. Powered by the skills of Chinese Panamanian sound engineer Eduardo "Balito" Chan at Discos Istmeños recording studio, labels such as Sally Ruth, Loyola, Taboga, and later Tamayo, had a steady output of singles, shaping the hybrid *combos* sound for the years to come.

Along with the steady influx of the latest U.S. vinyl records and the soul music played on radio stations such as S.C.N. and H.O.G., constant interactions with African American GIs stationed on the Canal Zone became a major influence in the making of the *combos* sound. The young bands, who made a living playing gigs at the casinos and clubs of the Canal Zone, not only had to adapt to the demands of their audiences (who wanted to hear soul music), but in some instances also integrated African American GIs in their bands, as Stanley Boxhill[22], who became known as a trombone player for the Soul Fantastics and The Exciters, remembers: "I played in an integrated band so to speak. We called ourselves The Ascots. The keyboard player was from the Airforce, the singer also was a soldier, the drummer too, the guitar player was from over here." The account of Carlos Brown, founder, leader, and bass player of The Exciters, confirms that contact and collaboration with the GIs was a key influence for his and other *combos* in the late 1960s:

> We started playing soul music in the Canal Zone. We went over to play in a club by the name of El Rancho, in Panama City, a place where only the GIs used to go, on the borderline. We used to play for them. And there was a Mexican-American from the US military band, he used to come and play with us, the saxophone. Anytime we played, he was with us. They worked eight hours but what they do with the freetime is their decision. Nighttime is their time. Panama was not restricted to them so they could always come and play. We used to speak only English in the band, no Spanish. That made communication with GIs much easier. And we used to play in every which post, in every which club the US army had in Panama. The Clayton, the NCO, the Sargeants Club, Non-Comissioner, Fort Davis, you name it. From Panama to Colón, all the posts. We were the No. 1 band to play for them and then the soldiers started to put together their own bands. We also played with them, right on the posts.

Illustrating the significant impact of African American culture and *soul* – as a style, and a discourse – references to "soul" and "blackness" became a current feature of *combos* releases from the late 1960s and early 1970s. Songs such as "Black Soul" by The Beachers, "You Got Soul Girl (You Are Super Bad)" by Harvey Bender and The Groove Makers, "Soul Girl" by The Happy Sound, "Soul Power" and "Black

---

22 In the present, Stanley Boxhill runs The Diggers Descendants, a calypso band which honours the legacy of Afro-Caribbean migrant workers who built the Panama Canal, the diggers.

Tribute" by The Goombays, and "Soul Train" by the Soul Fantastic evidence the salience of allusions to *soul* as a code for U.S.-inspired representations of blackness. In "Soul Chombo", Frederick Clarke not only cites Sam and Dave's "Soul Man" but also inverts the meaning of "chombo", a derogatory term for Afro-Caribbean Panamanians, by turning it into a self-conscious assertion of black pride and identity, giving voice to a new attitude of defiance. With "Mi Bella Panama", a band called Soul Revolution showed that allegiance to "soul" and the nation was not mutually exclusive. While "soul" is referenced as a certain positive quality in these releases, the song "Black Power" by The Persuaders is one of the few explicit mentions of the movement, highlighted with a clenched black fist on the cover of their album. In the song, the vocalist Anselmo Innis announces:

> Whenever the time comes, we gonna yell the song,
> Black Power!
> If you wanna have peace, we'll have peace,
> if you wanna have hate, we will hate.
> But to those who don't like it,
> we don't care what you think about it!
> Black Power!
> (The Persuaders, "Black Power", 1970)

By self-consciously offering peaceful coexistence in case of being tolerated and accepted but at the same time warning that hate will be returned with hate and challenging those "who don't like it" that "we don't care what you think about it", The Persuaders gave voice to the new attitude of defiance that emerged among Panamanians of Afro-Caribbean descent in the Black Power era.

While the first *combos* were in their majority composed of musicians of Afro-Caribbean descent and their sound reflected the special exposure of this community to soul music from the United States, the consecutive inclusion of genres representing other aspects of the multicultural Panamanian society was an important factor in their popularity across ethnic and linguistic lines. By also including Afro-Hispanic and *mestizo* Panamanian musicians, the *combos* and the music they created became important sites of interethnic collaboration. The *combos*' multiethnic composition and the diversity of influences they combined played a decsive role, when General Omar Torrijos started to embrace these bands as symbols of national unity after seizing power in 1969. Just as Torrijos recruited leading Afro-Caribbean intellectuals for his cabinet as part of his populist, anti-oligarchic agenda, he also saw benefits in supporting the rise of the *combos*, as several musicians of the period confirm. Torrijos built concert halls, arenas, and stadiums where combos were allowed to play and frequently invited bands to play at his events, giving unprecedented visibility to formerly excluded Afro-Caribbean musicians and performers. Ernie King holds that "General Omar Torrijos always had an inclination toward West Indians. When he heard the sound of us black Panamanian guys he endorsed us." Carlos Brown of The Exciters shared the same experience:

> During the Torrijos government the *combos* would become a big thing. When Torrijos came, the blacks got more participation, he opened spaces, which was, of course, good for us. Sometimes he would take advantage of us, we were scheduled to play in a club, but Torrijos had his own TV station and he would say: 'Tomorrow you got to be on my show.' You can't tell him no, you gotta take up all of your equipment, and when you're finished, take it to the studio. As Torrijos liked us, we got exposure all over the country by getting on TV.

Torrijo's support for the *combos* was also based on the fact that these groups spread modern and popular music that was not imported but produced in Panama – hence the emphasis on *nacionales* – and thus fit well with his anti-imperialist and nationalist rhetoric. An announcement for a celebration of the 4th anniversary of the 1968 "revolution" featuring the Festivals and the Beachers, evidences how the Torrijos regime enlisted the combos for political means ("Celebre el IV Aniversario de la Revolución, bailando hoy en el Jardín Rancho Grande con Los Beachers y Los Festivals"). Whereas Torrijos's minister of Justice Juan Materno Vásquez, a zealous nationalist, despised the U.S. influences in the combos and eventually forced The Exciters to use the name *Los Dinámicos Exciters* and demanded that The Beachers changed theirs to *Los Playeros* (C. Brown), what was apparently tolerated, at least in the beginning of the process, was the fact that the *combos* also became a platform for articulating attachment to a black movement from abroad, a reference that challenged the homogenizing discourses of Panamanian nationalism and encouraged identification and solidarity beyond the nation.

While the *combos* were undoubtedly inspired by "soul style" from the United States, evidenced by their aesthetics, most importantly the Afro hairdos and distinct ways of clothing, dancing, and talking, they drew from diverse sources. A look at the ways the labels promoted the sounds featured on these records reveals the flexibility in terms of language and genres which characterized the *combos:* A and B sides featured different styles described as "soul", "latin soul", "soul boogaloo", "balada soul", "bossanova soul", "calipso", "balada son", "son calipso", "salsa típica", "guaracha", "guajison", "mambo swing", "hard rock", "rock lento", "merengue", "samba", "tamborito", "son bolero", or simply "potpourri.". The rise of the *combos* was very much related to this heterogeneity, as Gyemant suggests:

> Equipped with new, electrified instruments, the younger generation listened closely as the music coming over U.S. Army Radio and arriving in the record stores changed: new sources of inspiration included Richie Ray and Eddie Palmieri, the Chi-Lites, the Temptations, and the Four Tops, Santana, Curtis Mayfield and James Brown. [...] Almost overnight, the Panamanian

> seemed to have found a music that represented their diverse tastes and experiences: favourite groups such as the Silvertones, the Festivals, the Exciters, the Beachers, the Mozambiques, the Soul Fantastic, and the Goombays appeared on local television and were booked for engagements all over the country. [...] The Combos Nacionales' mix of latin rock, guarachas, doowop, calypsos, tropical funk and true latin soul defies categorization even today. (*Panama!*)

These groups, encouraged by demanding and contrasting audiences on the U.S. military bases and in the clubs and concert halls of Colón and Panama City, were able to switch between soul, calypso, cumbia, típico, salsa, boogaloo or fuse all of these styles. This versatility reflected Panama's cosmopolitanism. While gigs for GIs in the Canal Zone and the bordering nightife areas in the terminal cities were important, *combos* also started to perform at so-called *saraos*, concerts organized by students in the gyms of their schools, as Gerardo Maloney describes: "Eran las fiestas estudiantiles musicales que se hacían en los principales centros de educación popular los días viernes en la tarde en donde los que tocaban eran los *combos nacionales.*"[23] At the *saraos,* the audiences were mostly Spanish-speaking Panamanian natives, encouraging the *combos* to adapt their styles and vocals accordingly. As a result, many *combos* started to feature one Spanish-native speaker for the Latin numbers and an Anglophone singer for the soul and calypso tunes, as was the case for The Invaders from Colón where Ernie King alternated with Carlos Grenald (resulting in a division of tasks that in this case also led to a sometimes violent rivalry for the role of lead singer, as both confirmed in interviews). Carlos Grenald, a singer of mixed Afro-hispanic and Afro-Caribbean descent from Bocas del Toro, who achieved national success with Los Silvertones after his time with The Invaders, recalls:

> Siempre alternabamos los vocalistas. En estas bandas yo era responsable de las canciones en español, salsa, cumbia y boleros. Cuando tocabamos soul o calypso, le tocaba a otro que sabía major el inglés. Ernie King con Los Invaders, Carlos Allen y Roy Joe Clark con Los Silvertones. Cuanda tocabamos para los gringos ellos reclamaban soul, cuando tocabamos para los latinos pedían salsa y era mi turno. Pero siempre hubo rotación en un mismo baile.[24]

---

23 "*Saraos* were the student parties that took place in the main centers of popular education on Friday afternoons and those who played there were the combos nacionales." (Maloney, *personal interview*)

24 "We always alternated vocalists. In these bands I was responsible for the Spanish songs, salsa, cumbia and boleros. When we played soul or calypso, it was someone else who knew better English. Ernie King with Los Invaders, Carlos Allen and Roy Joe Clark with Los Silvertones. When we played for the gringos they asked for soul, when we played for the Latinos they asked for salsa and it was my turn. But there was always rotation in the same dance." (Grenald)

Through this flexibility, groups such as Los Silvertones, led by saxophonist Carlos Bermúdez, had very successful releases in different genres as with a soul balad like "Oh...! Gee", sung by Carlos Allen, and a cumbia-típico-salsa crossover track like "Tamborito Swing", performed by Carlos Grenald. Calypso, a genre that originated in Trinidad and Tobago and had become an important platform of social and political comment throughout the Anglophone Caribbean, was another important source in the *combos* productions. Bands such as Los Beachers from Bocas del Toro, the only *combo* which is still running today, adopted soul aesthetics and influences but became especially successful with a new brand of calypso, as featured in their hit "Africa Caliente". After initiating his career with the Orquesta Black Star, a reference to Marcus Garvey's failed Black Star Line, Lloyd Gallimore founded Los Beachers which became famous for his distinct Hammond organ sounds, inspired by Booker T. & The MGs from the US soul label Stax (Gallimore). Through collaborations, Los Beachers also gave increased visibility to pioneers of Panamanian calypso such as Lord Cobra, Lord Panama, and Lord Byron who became the first to release bilingual calypso tracks in Spanish and English, epitomizing the linkages that connected Panama with the West Indies. True to the tradition of conscious lyrics in calypso, Lord Cobra with the Pana-Afro Sounds criticizes the lack of black unity in his Sally Ruth recording "Black Man", referencing the icons of Pan-Africanism Marcus Garvey and Haile Selassie and revealing that the Black Power movement was only one among several sources of information and inspiration in 1960s and 1970s Panama:

> From I was a child it is puzzling me, why black man can't live in unity...
> Chinese for Chinese, Indian for Indian, black man against black man...
> In the days of Marcus Garvey, he freed the negros from slavery,
> and from the time the negros get free, they say to hell with Marcus Garvey...
> have had outstanding negro leaders, who tried to keep us together...
> Men like Menelek and Haile Selassie,
> these are the names that must go down in history...
> Chinese for Chinese, Indian for Indian, black man against black man...
> (Lord Cobra, "Black Man", 1978)

Afro-Cuban styles and the rise of boogaloo and salsa in New York had a similarly significant impact on the *combos*, as they increasingly expanded their appeal to Panama's Spanish-speaking population and Afro-hispanic Panamanian musicians started to form groups like Los Mozambiques, which were dedicated exclusively to salsa. Panama, especially during carnival season, was part of the regular tour circuit of Nuyorican musicians such as La Lupe, Hector Lavoe and Willie Colón. Benny Bonilla of the Pete Rodriguez Orchestra recalls: "I will never forget when we played the Teatro Rios in Panama City and thousands of Panamanians sang our hit 'I like It Like That'" (Bonilla). In Panama, the musicians from New York would perform with internationally acclaimed local salsa musicians like Francisco "Bush" Buckley, whose Afro-Caribbean background defied the common categorizations which held that Anglophone Panamanians were more attuned to soul and calypso: "Me consideraban raro porque, aunque crecí en un ambiente de antillanos anglófonos, lo mío siempre ha sido la percusión y la música latina, sobre todo la salsa."[25]. One of Bush's alumni was Rubén Blades, who, after moving to New York would become Panama's representative in the Fania All-Stars. Panamanian singer Camilo Azuquita from Colón, in his collaborations with Kako and His Orchestra ("Panama's Boogaloo"), Típica 73, Sonora Ponceña, Rafael Cortijo and Roberto Roena would made himself a name as one of the New York Latin music scene most acclaimed voices in both, boogaloo and salsa. The special connection between New York, Puerto Rico and Panama is also evidenced in a number of songs such as Charlie Palmieri's "Panama's Bugalu", Willie Colón and Hector Lavoe's "La Murga", The Latinaires' "Panama", Francisco "Bush" Buckley's "Puerto Rico y Panama", and the song "El Nazareno" in which Puerto Rican *sonero* Ismael Rivera cherishes the black Jesus statue in a church of the Panamanian coastal town Portobelo, granting Rivera status as a Panamanian folk hero.

4.6 The Exciters: Soul Music and Black Empowerment

None of Panama's *combos*, embodied the interrelatedness between music and the struggle for Afro-Panamanian emancipation in Panama more than The Exciters. Carlos Brown, their founder and leader, was born in 1944 in Rio Abajo to a father of Jamaican descent and an African American mother from Boston. Brown's relationship with the United States had always been close. As many of his contemporaries, the beginnings of his musical career were influenced by the doo-wop vocal groups that started to perform in the U.S. military bases. Following developments in the United States, his band was initially entirely dedicated to soul music in the 1960s, and, like many other *combos* started to include other influences later:

> All of these groups got popular here imitating the latest sounds from the U.S. We started The Astronauts Fig. 13. with some guys from the Canal Zone, Gamboa. Not all of us were West Indians, our lead guitar player was Antonio Rodriguéz. We played mostly for the army posts. Monday, Tuesday, Wednesday.... we played all of the soul music, you name it, we played all of these sounds from the US, mostly cover versions, because this is what they wanted to

---

25 "I was considered strange because although I grew up in an environment of English-speaking West Indians, my thing has always been percussion and Latin music, especially salsa."

hear. James Brown was always our major influence. In Panama he was number 1! In the beginning, we and The Festivals were the only *combos* to play strictly soul music. When we became popular nation-wide, we also started to include Panamanian típico, Latin, calypso.

In 1968, Carlos Brown got to work as a manager of Palacio Musical, one of the record stores of the Heres brothers in Panama City. He recalls, "it was mostly soul music the people wanted to hear, and soul music was all over the airwaves". In his position as sales manager of a record store, he was the first to receive the latest releases from the U.S., which would become sources of inspiration for the recordings of his band which renamed from The Astronauts to The Exciters. Their first recording was "The Bag", a variation of James Brown's "Papa's Got A Brand New Bag", released on Loyola: "We used to play it for the GIs on the military posts and they loved it. Anytime they asked for it, they were crazy about 'The Bag'. [...] So after our initial success, we used to play in every which post, in every which club the US army had in Panama." (ibid.). Following up on their debut success, The Exciters recorded cover version of U.S. soul hits like "Stop, Look, Listen" by the Stylistics, "Different Strokes" by Syl Johnson (featuring a cover of Joe Cuba's boogaloo song "Sock It To Me" on the backside) and "The Brown", a tribute to James Brown. Including cumbia, salsa, and calypso-influenced own compositions and Spanish soul ballads like "Ojos Verdes" in the early 1970s, The Exciters established themselves as a leading force on the Panamanian music scene (Fig. 14).

In 1970, Ralph Weeks, a soul musician who was born and raised in the Canal Zone and had migrated with his family to New York ten years earlier, was on a short stay in Panama when a friend took him to a concert of The Exciters. Although it was the first time he came back to his home country after 10 years, people recognized him as the interpret of the song "Something Deep Inside" he had recorded with his band The Telecasters. A band member of The Exciters approached him if he wanted to come back to Panama for a show and a recording, which resulted in the release of "Algo Muy Profundo", a Spanish version of "Something Deep Inside", as Weeks recalls: "When I went to Panama, I decided to translate it. Because I knew that there are a lot of people there that don't speak English. One day I was at the record store and this lady came in and she wanted the song but she couldn't pronounce the name. So I told the guy she wants 'Something Deep Inside.'" The Spanish version "Algo Muy Profundo" would became one of The Exciters' biggest hits. Weeks appearances at The Exciters' shows during his short stays in Panama would give them an international touch. On an advertisement for a concert with The Exciters, The Festivals, and The Soul Fantastics in the newspaper *Crítica* from February 10, 1972, he is pictured with "Miss Soul" Sonja Stultz and announced as "atracción especial directo de New York: Ralph Weeks" (Fig. 16). When Carlos

Brown left Panama for New York in the 1970s, he would collaborate with Ralph Weeks and form the band Love, Warmth, and Affection, demonstrating once again the importance of multidirectional flows between the two locales in the creation of new genres and the translation of musical content from one context to the other.

What distinguished The Exciters from other *combos* was their sense of mission and their actual involvement in matters of black empowerment, which was connected to the influence of Bruce Codrington and his brother, Egbert Wetherborne, leader of the black leftist student group *Guaycucho*, both of whom infused the band with political consciousness. Codrington, who had grown up in the Canal Zone and worked for the Panama Canal Company, was a very influential activist and leader of the West Indian community who organized workers in the Canal Zone to fight against racial discrimination, openly identifying with the African American freedom struggle: "Black Power was everything to me" (Codrington). As Carlos Brown remembers, "he was a businessman, but he had this very strong connection with the black movement in the US. You know, these guys like him, the university graduates, they were really involved. [...] Bruce was an icon, a main person, with The Exciters." Under the leadership of Codrington, The Exciters supported activities of Alberto Smith Fernández' *Asociación Afro-Panameña* and participated in the foundation of *Instituto Soul*, a cultural association for the advancement of black Panamanians in Colón.

In the early 1970s, the influence of Bruce Codrington and other black activists on The Exciters proved critical when the Torrijos regime identified the open association of Afro-Caribbean youth with the Black Power movement as a threat to national unity. The ambivalence of Torrijos' race politics manifested itself in hostility against expressions of black pride in times of new opportunities for Afro-Panamanians, epitomized by a campaign against blacks with an Afro hairdo which started in 1970. A short note in the English-language newspaper *The Panama Canal Spillway* from April 10 of the same year, read: "Canal Zone residents are reminded of an executive decree, signed recently by President Demetrio Lakas, prohibiting the entrance into Panama of men wearing extra-long hair and who are slovenly in their dress. The Panama National Guard is enforcing the decree and all are cautioned that no one is exempt from the rule" (1). Considering the absence of any significant hippie community in the Canal Zone, the prohibition of people with "extra-long hair" to enter Panama was a clear message to the Afro-Caribbean Canal youth among which the Afro had become a popular symbol of black pride and identification with the African American freedom struggle – very much like in other African-descendant communities throughout the Americas. What followed was a campaign which implicated a daily assault on blacks with Afro in the streets of Panama City and Colón, who were forcedly shaved by members of the military and the National Guard.

Under the direction of their manager Bruce Codrington, The Exciters responded to the campaign against the Afro. In 1971, they started to organize what would become one of the most visible manifestations of Black Power-sentiment during the Torrijos era: the "Miss Soul Queen" beauty pageants, or "La Reina Soul" as they were called in Spanish. These events, inspired by the U.S. slogan "Black is beautiful" featured black Panamanian women with Afro hairstyles, challenging prevalent white beauty standards and the police repression against the Afro. As Miss contests were very popular during carnival time in Panama, but lacked Afro-Caribbean representation, these celebrations of black beauty were intended to fill this gap, evidencing the strong influence Black Power had on combos like The Exciters, as Carlos Brown stresses:

> What motivated us was the Black and Proud movement over there. We had to identify with what was going on over there, over here we also had prejudice against our community. 'Say it Loud, (I'm black and I'm proud)' was a very popular song here. We used to idolize James Brown by then. And we had some guys around us who were heavily politically involved. Activists like Bruce Codrington and Carlos Russell. They were following the U.S. black movement and everything that was going on over there. We sympathized with the US Black movement. Our thing was the music. But we supported the movement and we said on carnival times when you have the big parades all you see is only the white girls coming down. So we said: 'What about the black?' What we did was we created the Soul Queen contest, in Panama and Colón, a pageant with several black girls from Panama and Colón and it became huge, with many followers. [...] We were playing soul and soul is black. So we called it Miss Soul instead of Miss Black.

The "Miss Soul" events turned into an important part of the yearly carnival parades in Panama City and Colón where they were accompanied by concerts of The Exciters and other *combos*. Miss Soul Queens like Sonja Stultz (1972) and Sheila Penso (1973) became community celebrities who symbolized black pride. In Panama, where the Afro hairdo had been persecuted by presidential decree, the coronation of "Reinas Soul" tested the limits of accepted levels of blackness, provoking harsh reactions by Panamanian nationalists who criticized the divisive effects of importing U.S. manifestations of black pride into the Panamanian nation (Castro, "Notas al margen" 175). Activists like Alberto Barrow, however, applauded The Exciters: "Cuando ellos armaron la Reina Soul era un acto contestatario, era un acto de rebeldía, era un acto de confrontación al racismo en la Zona del Canal y en Panamá."[26] Miss Soul Queen contests were held each year during carnival season until

---

26 "When they put together the Reina Soul it was an act of protest, it was an act of rebellion, it was

1977, when a committee, integrated by Alberto Barrow, Ines Sealy and other community members, decided to change the title of the event from "Miss Soul" to "Panameñisima Reina Negra" in order to attract broader sections of the Afro-Panamanian community to the contest, specifically Afro-Hispanic Panamanians. The change of title reflected the wish of the organizers to contribute to the efforts to forge unity between both of Panama's black communities, hinting at the ways soul and the adoption of Black Power symbols among Afro-Caribbean Panamanians sparked debates on integration and Panamanian national identity, discussed further in Chapter 6.

In 1972, The Exciters and Bruce Codrington, once again, underlined their status as key players of soul music in Panama when they overcame a plethora of financial and organizational hurdles and managed to bring James Brown to the country. As Bruce Codrington recalls, it was Carlos Brown – who band members used to call "the pressure man" – who approached him with the initial idea: "He came to me and said: We have to bring James Brown to Panama. And I said: Are you crazy? But then we just did it. We got in touch with our contacts in the U.S. to negotiate with the James Brown organization. So they called and asked, can you get the equipment and the money? I said, we'll arrange for everything. Then they said: Let's do it!"

There was no government support for the event, so Codrington became involved in intense community fundraising to pay the 30.000 Dollar for the contract with James Brown. When everything was set for two James Brown shows on September 30 and October 1, 1972, "Torrijos government messed it up," as Carlos Brown remembers: "We had Roberto Durán Arena, we had that set for two days, and the government decided that they wanted to do some kind of political activity on these very days." After they had to call the James Brown management at very short notice (the concert was still being promoted in *Crítica* on September 29), they had to pay a large contract penalty to the James Brown organization. However, The Exciters wouldn't give up on their dream of instigating "una revolución de la mente" by bringing James Brown to Panama, as they had announced on the sleeve notes of their 1972 album *Potpourri*. They were able pay the penalty and collect the money once again with the help of donors from the black community who understood the significance of presenting the icon of soul music in Panama.

On October 29, 1972, the efforts of The Exciters and their manager Bruce Cordrington came to fruition, when James Brown and his ensemble finally arrived in Panama. The Exciters had organized bus shuttles from the Heres-owned Palacio

---

an act of confrontation against racism in the Canal Zone and in Panama." (Barrow, *personal interview*)

Musical record store to the Tocumén airport where the fans welcomed their idol who came with his own jet. After the arrival, a motorcade with James Brown and the J.B.'s paraded along the main streets of the city with huge crowds saluting him from the boardwalks. The appearance of "El Rey de la Música Soul" as he was announced in the newspapers, was a major social event in Panama, as Carlos Brown remembers: "James Brown was treated like a president. He got royal treatment in Panama." Brown's stay featured two sold-out concerts at Gimnasio Nuevo Panama which were openened by The Exciters and The Festivals (featuring Ernie King, see introduction to this chapter), the two Panamanian combos that were most prolific in the interpretation of soul music (Fig. 17). At both shows, James Brown, Lyn Collins and the other members of his band played in front of crowds of 10 to 20.000 Panamanians from all ethnic backgrounds, leaving long-lasting impressions on all those present (almost all the Panamanians interviewed for this study, claimed to have attended the concert).

Omar Torrijos, who had been responsible for the last-minute cancellation and the significant loss The Exciters suffered due to the contract penalty, also wanted to share in the attention and enthusiasm that James Brown had generated with his visit to Panama, as Carlos Brown recalls: "James Brown wanted to leave the day after the concert, but before he left, we had to meet General Omar Torrijos, so we took him to the headquarters. James Brown and Torrijos had a big meeting there and they talked and talked. As he was late for the plane, Torrijos called and stopped the plane on the airport, send him up with escort and everything." While the whole undertaking was a financial disaster for The Exciters, Carlos Brown didn't regret it: "We opened the show for James Brown and were the ones who brought him. So for our reputation it was extremely important." The event was also highly significant for Afro-Panamanian activism and community building: James Brown's concert in Panama became a demonstration of black empowerment, as it was an event organized by leading black Panamanian entertainers, funded by wealthy black Panamanian donors, featuring the undisputed transnational icon of black pride and black popular music.[27]

---

[27] The James Brown concerts were not the only appearance of African American soul musicians in Panama. Between 1972 and 1974, The Dramatics (also brought by The Exciters), The Oncoming Times, and The Jackson Five also performed in Panama.

4.7 The 1970s: Torrijos, Afro-Panamanian Activism and the Fear of Black Power

Whereas the success of Panamanian soul was closely related to the ways the *combos nacionales* were embraced and opened spaces as part of General Omar Torrijos' nationalist strategy, his policies were ambiguous for Afro-Panamanians who, informed and inspired by Black Power, were determined to overcome the vestiges of white supremacy in Panama and the Canal Zone. As part of his efforts to enlist West Indian support for his platform of social justice, inclusion, and recuperation of the Canal, Torrijos denounced racial discrimination in the Canal Zone and voiced support for the struggles to end Jim Crow, promising equality for blacks in a country without U.S. occupation. While embarrassing to the United States, it gained him considerable support among Afro-Caribbean Panamanians who had developed deep mistrust of the U.S. authorities, many of them aligning themselves with the Panamanian nationalist struggle against U.S. rule over the Canal, exposing widespread suspicions of West Indians' alleged loyalty to the U.S. as a myth.

In the 1970s, Torrijos' regime supported the creation of several civic organizations as ARENEP (*Acción Reivindicadora del Negro Panameño*), directed by Gerardo Maloney, and APODAN (*Asociación de Profesionales, Obreros y Dirigentes de Ascendencia Negra*) which were formed to combat racial discrimination. Afro-Caribbean activists participated in Torrijos' efforts to mobilize black support for his efforts to recover the Canal and in the negotiations that led to the Torrijos-Carter Treaties. These efforts were supported by popular music singer Leroy Gittens from Colón, who, after returning from the U.S. to Panama, next to Cirilo McSween, Carlos Russell, and other Afro-Panamanian migrants in the United States helped to establish contacts with African American leaders like Jesse Jackson, who visited Panama in 1977 after the plebiscite on the Canal treaties had been ratified (Priestley 54–58).

Despite the clear positioning of many Afro-Caribbean Panamanian activists on the side of the Panamanian struggle to end the U.S. occupation, discrimination and suspicion regarding their allegiance to the nation continued under Torrijos' regime. West Indian activism was encouraged, but only as long as it was consistent with Torrijos' nationalist agenda and refrained from denouncing Panamanian manifestations of racism, as Michael Conniff observed: "Black movements might prove useful in discrediting Zone society, but they could reflect badly on Panama, too" (167). The persistence of anti-West Indian sentiment under Torrijos was particularly evident in the way the regime responded to expressions of black pride in late 1960s and 1970s Panama. *Mestizo* elites and Panamanian nationalists rejected influences from the Black Power movement among *afro-antillanos* as manifestations of U.S. imperialism and a threat to national unity. While the *combos* were featured in national televsion and given ample opportunities for concerts and recordings under Torrijos, the symbolic identifcations with U.S. soul styles they helped to popularize in Panama, provoked harsh reactions, as manifested in the repressive campaign of the security forces against the Afro that started in 1970.

Alberto Barrow, author, lawyer, and a leading figure of the contemporary Afro-Panamanian movement, was born in 1952 as a descendant of immigrants from Jamaica and Barbados in Panama City's black working-class neighborhood of Calidonia. He remembers the time, when sporting an Afro could have serious consequences: "A nosotros se nos perseguía para cortarnos el cabello, nos cortaban, nos correteaban."[28] In 1970, Barrow even missed his graduation ceremony as a law student at the Instituto Fermin Naudeau for refusing to cut his Afro:

> Yo me negué a cortarme el cabello, entonces no se me permitió ir a la ceremonia. Creo que yo fui el único que se rehusó a cortarse el cabello. Es que habían pocos negros en ese colegio, entonces entre los pocos negros, yo tenía afro, habían otros pero con el cabello un poco más bajo.[29]

Barrow was part of a generation of radical Afro-Caribbean Panamanian students who were influenced by the African American freedom struggle: "En los años 1967, 1968, 1969 estamos leyendo a Malcolm X, Eldridge Cleaver, Angela Davis, estábamos siguiendo muy de cerca todo el movimiento en Estados Unidos, todo el movimiento contra la guerra en Vietnam."[30] Under the leadership of black radical student leader Egbert Wetherborne, Barrow became a member of *Guaycucho* in the early 1970s, a revolutionary left-wing organization with mostly, but not exclusively West Indian membership, deeply critical of the traditional left's failure to address racism, as he points out: "Nosotros sabíamos que eso de la lucha de clases tenía una especificidad que se llamaba la negritud. Otros sectores de la izquierda nunca entendieron eso."[31] Hinting at centuries of Latin American anti-black racism disguised behind homogenizing *mestizaje* and *hispanidad* discourses, Guaycucho also denounced Torrijos' intents to portray racism as a problem imported to Panama by the U.S. occupying force: "Entonces aquello que estaba ocurriendo en el norte lo estábamos viendo, pero el racismo estaba aquí en Panamá tambien,

---

28 "We were chased to get our hair cut, we were cut, we were run around." (Barrow)

29 "I refused to cut my hair, so I wasn't allowed to go to the ceremony. I think I was the only one who refused to cut my hair. There were few blacks in that school, so among the few blacks, I had an afro, there were others but with slightly shorter hair." (ibid.)

30 "In the years 1967, 1968, 1969 we are reading Malcolm X, Eldridge Cleaver, Angela Davis, we were following very closely the whole movement in the United States, the whole movement against the war in Vietnam." (ibid.)

31 "We knew that the class struggle had a specificity called blackness. Other sectors of the left never understood that." (ibid.)

no es que lo inventaron y lo trajeron del norte. Desde luego había una situación en el área del Canal, pero eso estaba aquí y estaba desde hace mucho tiempo, desde la construcción del Canal de Panamá si no antes."[32]

Many Afro-Panamanians who had gone to the U.S. to study and work in the 1960s returned to their home country in the years following Torrijos' takeover to participate in the opportunities that had opened up for black professionals under the new regime. Melva Lowe de Goodin, who had spent the late 1960s on a scholarship at University of Wisconsin and, like many of her Panamanian peers, had been strongly influenced by the African American freedom struggle during her years on U.S. campus, belonged to this group. She was shocked to find that her then-husband, a man from Ghana with whom she had spent two years teaching at the University of Zambia, was met with hostility at the Panama airport because of his Afro and the dashiki he was wearing – an experience many returnees from the United States shared. Later, she married Orville Goodin, an Afro-Panamanian economist who, like many other Afro-Panamnians of his generation who became government officials under Omar Torrijos, served as Vice-Minister of the Treasury, and participated in the negotiations of the Torrijos-Carter Treaties. Reflecting on the mixed legacy of Torrijos, Lowe states:

> As much as he opened the country for high-level blacks, he also empowered lower level military groups to get into black communities, and when they saw black youngsters growing Afros they forced them to shave them off. The military saw these expressions as a threat. [...] Under Torrijos, there was a generalized feeling against blacks who were identifying too strongly with black movements. So at the same time Torrijos empowered certain groups of blacks, there were also forces within the military that disempowered blacks. (*personal interview*)

In the mid-1970s, Melva Lowe (then de Ocran) was directly involved in a dispute with the minister of Justice and later Supreme Court Justice Juan Materno Vásquez who was a driving force behind the persistence of anti-West Indian sentiment under Torrijos. Materno Vásquez, who belonged to Panama's Spanish-speaking black community and was one of the most influential players in Torrijos' government, took a hostile stance against *afro-antillanos* which was rooted in an aggressive Panamanian nationalism that demonized the Afro-Caribbean community as anti-national elements. The way the combos adapted black influences from the U.S. and normalized the use of English in popular culture had always been a thorn in his side, which allegedly led him to insist that more Panamanian folklore

---

32 "So we were seeing what was happening in the north but racism was here in Panama too, it is not that they invented it and brought it from the north. Of course there was a situation in the Canal area, but that was here and it was here for a long time, even before the construction of the Panama Canal." (ibid.)

music was played on the radio and that the bands use Spanish names. Importantly, he questioned West Indians' contributions and loyalty to the nation by hinting at their admiration of soul and calypso instead of local folklore.

In 1974, Materno Vásquez had published *El País por Conquistar*, in which he accused West Indian Panamanians of lacking patriotism and posing a threat to the nation due to their use of English language, their reluctance to assimilate to the country's Hispanic traditions and collaboration with the U.S. American occupiers. His diatribes against West Indians, who he described disparagingly as "de piel oscura, costumbres raras, e idioma inglés," ["dark-skinned, with strange costums, and English-speaking"] and "sin vinculación espiritual con la nación panameña" ["without spiritual bond with the Panamanian nation"] were also reflected in his views on the increasing expressions of black pride in this community. According to Materno Vásquez, "Black power and negritude had no place in Panama." (Conniff 167).

Giving voice to the new assertiveness that Afro-Panamanians had developed in the late 1960s and early 1970s, Melva Lowe, along with *Asociación Afro-Panameña* leader Alberto Smith Fernández responded to Materno Vásquez accusations with two articles, published in *Revista Nacional de Cultura* in 1976, that sparked a debate which epitomized the racial frictions in the Torrijos era. In her article "El idioma inglés y la integracion social de los panameños de origen afro-antillano al carácter nacional panameño" ["The English language and the social integration of Panamanians of Afro-Antillean origin into the Panamanian national character"], Lowe acknowledged that there are more elements that distinguish West Indians from native Panamanians than the use of the English language and protestant religion, namely that they respond more to soul music and to calypso than to Panamanian folklore and Latin music (24). Citing government officials whith discriminatory statements that accuse "jamaiquinos" (used as a generic term for all Panamanians of Caribbean descent) of being anti-Pananamian and allies of the "gringos" against the aspirations of the Panamanian people to exercise sovereignty over the Canal Zone ("los Jamaiquinos son anti-nacionales, anti-panameños. Ellos son los aliados de los gringos contra las aspiraciones del pueblo panameño en ejercer su soberanía sobre la Zona del Canal"[33], 24). Lowe claimed that white Panamanian shared with the *gringos* more than they would ever admit, namely an attitude of racial superiority toward the West Indians. She stated that the attitude that exists in Panama towards the West Indians was not only based on the fact that they don't speak Spanish as their mother tongue, but that its integration policy

---

33 "Jamaicans are anti-national, anti-Panamanian. They are the allies of the gringos against the aspirations of the Panamanian people to exercise their sovereignty over the Canal Zone." (Lowe 24)

154 —— 4 Panama: Soul, Black Internationalism and Afro-Caribbean Liberation

also reflected a racist discrimination against blacks. According to Lowe, West Indians presented a double problem to the state: their race and their foreign culture (38). As for the relationship between *afro-antillanos* and so called *afro-coloniales* (native Afro-Panamanians), which also played into the conflict with Materno Vásquez who was black, Lowe criticized the ways both black communities had been pitted against each other although they both faced racial discrimination, manifested in different forms (28). Lowe held that Materno Vásquez used Afro-Caribbeans as a scapegoat for Panamanians' hatred against the U.S. occupation of the Canal (35). Hinting at the benefits of the English language which facilitated the forging of ties with the African diaspora, specifically with African Americans, Lowe voiced the expectation that the black revolution in the United States would have its effects in Panama, something she already saw in the Afro, but also in the repressive responses of the state which evidenced the racist attitudes she denounced:

> El peinado afro ha sido una de las manifestaciones concretas que ha tenido la revolución afro-americana en Panamá. Hombres y mujeres que anteriormente tenían pena de lucir peinados en el estilo natural de su cabello, ahora están luciendo el afro con orgullo. Sin embargo, la respuesta del estado panameño hacia este fenómeno nos demuestra claramente esa política discriminatoria de la cual estamos hablando. Guardias nacionales se volvieron barberos y cortaron el cabello de los hombres con afros o moñitos que andaban por la calle. Hubo instancias en que se introdujeron a hogares para llevar a cabo esta campana, que fue dirigida principalmente contra los negros. En otra parte la campana fue fortalecida, pues en la oficina de pasaportes un anuncio advirtió que no se daría pasaportes a hombres con afros; no a hombres con cabello largo, solamente a los con afros. ("El idioma inglés" 40)[34]

In "El Afro-Panameño Antillano frente al concepto de la Panameñidad" [The Afro-Panamanian Antillean facing the concept of *Panameñidad*], the second essay in the issue, Alberto Smith Fernández explained why it was impossible for conscious black Panamanians of Caribbean descent to identify with the static bourgeois version of Panamanian nationality, which, according to him, excluded West Indian contributions methodically and systematically in favor of an irrational glorification of the colonial Hispanic legacy (46–47). He held that the reluctance of *afro-an-*

---

34 "The Afro hairstyle has been one of the concrete manifestations of the Afro-American revolution in Panama. Men and women who were previously ashamed to wear their natural hairstyles are now proudly sporting Afro hairstyles. However, the response of the Panamanian state to this phenomenon clearly demonstrates the discriminatory policy we are talking about. National Guardsmen became barbers and cut the hair of men with afros or moñitos walking down the street. There were instances when they entered homes to carry out this campaign, which was directed mainly against blacks. Elsewhere the campaign was strengthened, for in the passport office a notice warned that passports would not be given to men with afros; not to men with long hair, only to those with afros" (Lowe, "El idioma inglés" 40).

tillanos to identify themselves with the archaic and folkloric concept of the 'national' should be interpreted as mechanisms of protest and responses to situations of internal colonialism (56) and the discriminatory practices of Panamanian nationalism which were based on the accusation of posing a threat to the purity of the Hispanic Panamanian nationality (50). This is why, according to Smith Fernández, most West Indians could not relate to important figures of Panamanian nationalism and rather identified with personalities from the international arena, most notably with leaders of the African American freedom struggle:

> El apotegma "Black is beautiful" ... lanzado por el taumaturgo W.E.B. Du Bois, enfatizado por el carismático Marcus Garvey, predicado por el elocuente Martin Luther King Jr. y cantado por el estridente James Brown ha permeabilizado la conciencia del antillano...El antillano parte hacia la panameñidad desde su base empírica; es decir desde su condición de negro... El afropanameño antillano, en virtud de esa muy particular característica suya de hablar y comprender inglés... ha podido captar el evangegelio social y revolucionario predicado por los negros americanos como el abolicionista Frederick Douglass (1817–1895); el pedagogo Booker T. Washington (1858–1915); el religioso Martin Luther King Jr. (1929–1968), el audaz Marcus Garvey (1887–1940); y los revolucionarios sociales Malcolm X (1925–1965), Stokely Carmichael y H. Rap Brown ... El afropanameño antillano comprendió que la plataforma ideológica de estos renombrados hombres era perfectamente idéntica a la suya. La afinidad idiosincraica con dichos pensadores era más cónsona a su realidad nacional que las emanadas de las lucubraciones de Justo Arosemena, Eusebio A. Morales o Belisario Porras. ...A nadie le debe sorprender el hecho de que el antillano haya escogido como héroes a figuras de factura internacional.[35] (57–58)

With their defiant rejection of the demand for assimilation, affirmation of a distinct language and culture, and articulation of a frame of reference beyond the na-

---

35 "The apothegm "Black is beautiful" ... launched by the thaumaturge W.E.B. Du Bois, emphasized by the charismatic Marcus Garvey, preached by the eloquent Martin Luther King Jr. and sung by the strident James Brown has permeated the consciousness of the Antillean...The Antillean starts towards Panamanianness from his empirical base; that is to say from his condition of black....The Afro-Panamanian Antillean, by virtue of that very particular characteristic of speaking and understanding English...has been able to grasp the social and revolutionary evangelism preached by black Americans such as the abolitionist Frederick Douglass (1817–1895); the educator Booker T. Washington (1858–1915); the educator Booker T. Washington (1858–1915); the educator of the Afro-Panamanian Antillean (1858–1915); and the educator of the Afro-Panamanian Antillean (1858–1915). Washington (1858–1915); the religious Martin Luther King Jr. (1929–1968), the bold Marcus Garvey (1887–1940); and social revolutionaries Malcolm X (1925–1965), Stokely Carmichael and H. Rap Brown ... The Afro-Panamanian West Indian understood that the ideological platform of these renowned men was perfectly identical to his own. The idiosyncratic affinity with these thinkers was more in tune with his national reality than those emanating from the lucubrations of Justo Arosemena, Eusebio A. Morales or Belisario Porras.... No one should be surprised that the Antillean has chosen as heroes figures of international invoice" (Smith Fernández 57 f.).

tion, namely the African American freedom struggle and the African diaspora, Lowe and Smith had launched an attack on the foundations of exclusionary and discriminatory Panamanian nationalism that caused great unrest and outrage. The two following numbers of *Revista Nacional de Cultura* featured indignated responses to the essays of Lowe and Smith by the uncle of Panamanian salsa singer Ruben Blades, cultural critic, poet, and diplomat Roque Javier Laurenza, and Juan Materno Vásquez himself (addressed in Chapter 6).

The interventions of Lowe and Smith reflected on the ways Panama's Afro-Caribbean community drew from international sources, specifically from U.S. black popular culture and polics, in their struggles for empowerment. Informed by their experiences with both, U.S.-style racial dichotomy as imposed through Jim Crow segregation and Latin American invisibilization and marginalization of blackness through *mestizaje* and homogenizing discourses of *hispanidad*, Afro-Panamanian artists, authors, and activists in Panama and the United States continued to play an important role as hemispheric translocutors between movements and cultures in the Caribbean, North and Latin America in the 1970s and beyond.

Inspired by the Black Power and Black Arts movements, authors such as Carlos Guillermo Wilson, Carlos Russell, and Gerardo Maloney produced poetry and literature that gave voice to the multiple layers of racialization and resistance in the Americas (Stephenson Watson). As mentor to the Young Lords, advisor to Martin Luther King and other figures of the African American freedom struggle, Carlos Russell was an important bridge-builder between Panama and the U.S. In 1979, ARENEP organized a public commemoration of Martin Luther King and Malcolm X, featuring the appearance in Panama of King's widow Coretta King and Atillah Shabazz, the daughter of Malcolm X (Maloney "Malcolm X)".[36] In 1980, Maloney, along with US-based Panamanian scholar Roy Bryce-Laporte, organized the second

---

36 In an *Estrella de Panamá* article on the meaning of Malcolm X for Afro-Panamanians, Maloney wrote in 2017: "No importa si hemos tenido que expresarnos en inglés, francés portugués o español, o si nuestra "patria" ha sido América Latina, las Islas del Caribe o Norteamérica; nuestras experiencias han sido esencialmente las mismas: una existencia dura, difícil y socialmente costosa.[...] Nosotros creemos que Malcolm X, vive y vivirá en la conciencia de todos nosotros y mas allá de la piel , mientras existan aún injusticias que acabar, derechos que conquistar y libertad que alcanzar. Y el día que el negro y otros pueblo alcancen esas condiciones de plenitud y armonía, Malcolm X vivirá con más fuerza en nuestra memoria." ("Malcolm X") ["Whether we have had to express ourselves in English, French, Portuguese or Spanish, or whether our "homeland" has been Latin America, the Caribbean Islands or North America, our experiences have been essentially the same: a hard, difficult and socially costly existence. ...] We believe that Malcolm X lives and will live in the consciousness of all of us and beyond the skin, as long as there are still injustices to end, rights to win and freedom to achieve. And the day that Black and other people reach those conditions of wholeness and harmony, Malcolm X will live even more strongly in our memory."]

Congreso de la Cultura Negra de las Américas held in Panama, hosting a range of influential Afro-descendant intellectuals and activists from different hemispheric contexts and Africa (Ratcliff). Also in 1980, Melva Lowe was involved in the foundation of the *Museo Afro-Antillano* and *Sociedad de Amigos del Museo Afro-Antillano de Panama* (SAMAAP) which has become one of the most important centers of Afro-Panamanian community activism, fostering dialogues with the Caribbean islands the large migrations of the early 20th century originated in and also reaching out to Afro-Hispanic Panamanians (Duke). This legacy is carried on by transnational activists such as Yvette Modestin who grew up in Panama and is now living in Boston, from where she coordinates the diaspora activities of the transnational network *Red de Mujeres Afrolatinoamericanas, Afrocaribeñas y de la Diáspora* and where she also runs *Encuentro Diaspora Afro*, an organization dedicated to the forging of alliances between black communities from the Caribbean, North, and Latin America.

5 Black Rio: Raising Consciousness on the Dancefloor

During the early-to-mid 1970s, soul music from the U.S. took dancefloors in Rio de Janeiro's Zona Norte by storm. Each weekend, thousands of mostly Afro-Brazilian aficionados frequented the so-called *bailes black* in order to dance to the latest vinyl records of James Brown, Aretha Franklin, Wilson Pickett, The Temptations and other soul stars. When national media took notice that what would become known as the Black Rio movement was not only about dancing to imported soul records but had also become a breeding ground for the popularization of political slogans and aesthetic representations of Black Power among Afro-Brazilian youth, repudiation by Brazil's right-wing military rulers, intellectual elites, and left-wing anti-imperialists was unanimous. Rio's municipal secretary of tourism Pedro de Toledo Pizza declared Black Rio a commercial movement with a racist philosophy (Oliveira 6). Even Gilberto Freyre, the seasoned mastermind of Brazil's nationalist *democracia racial* ideology and supporter of the military regime, felt compelled to speak out against the evils of soul music.

What had caused the demonization of soul in Brazil? Black consciousness discourses from the U.S. were met with hostility by Brazil's nationalist intellectuals and elites as they challenged the hegemonic ideology of *democracia racial*, which denied the existence of anti-black racism and the related marginalization of black Brazilians. As the Black Rio movement shows, the transnational appeal of soul music made sure that Black Power did make its way to Latin American contexts, despite the widespread rejection of U.S. influences. The symbolic appropriation of U.S. forms of blackness, as featured in Black Rio, constituted a rupture with established racial hierarchies and traditional stereotypes and an important step towards the formation of antiracist black movements throughout Latin America in the 1970s.

5.1 *Democracia Racial* and the Politics of Comparative Race Relations

Although U.S. African American influences would only reach major Afro-Brazilian audiences in the late 1960s and early 1970s, there had been a long history of exchange on matters of race relations between Brazil and the U.S., which dates back to the early 20th century. Contrasting lynch mobs, segregation, and racial oppression in the U.S. with allegedly harmonious coexistence between black, brown, and white in Brazil, constituted a core element of the nationalist *democracia racial*

https://doi.org/10.1515/9783110665550-007

5.1 *Democracia Racial* and the Politics of Comparative Race Relations — **159**

ideology, which was first articulated by Gilberto Freyre in the 1930s. The narrative of Brazil as "paraiso racial" held that the culture of *mestiçagem* had rendered the category of race irrelevant, making the country an example for tolerance and the erasure of prejudice for the world, and especially the U.S. to follow. Until the 1960s, this was a vision which was even shared by some U.S. African American intellectuals who travelled to Brazil in order to learn more about race relations there (Seigel; Stam and Shohat).

Embracing Afro-Brazilian forms, such as samba, carnival, candomblé, and capoeira as symbols of national culture and unity, was an integral part of this ideology – its prominent role served as proof for the progressive and inherently antiracist character of Brazilian society. Nationalizing Afro-Brazilian culture also ensured a large degree of social control over the country's black communities (Marx 170–171). By concealing the existence of structural anti-black racism and picturing Brazilian society as exemplary in its achievement of harmonious race relations, *democracia racial* discourse and the related "prejudice of having no prejudice" (Fontaine 125) proved to be a major obstacle for the formation of a broad antiracist movement in Brazil. In contrast to the United States, it was extremely difficult to mobilize blacks against racial discrimination where, according to the dominant ideology, skin color didn't matter, and class was the sole reason for the deep social inequalities that shaped the country. Early forms of Afro-Brazilian organization as the *Frente Negra Brasileira* in the 1930s and Abdias Nascimento's *Teatro Experimental do Negro* in the 1940s and 1950s failed to reach mass bases among Afro-Brazilians, in part due to their elitist approaches (Hanchard 106–108).

It was in the turbulent 1960s, when important impulses for the formation of what would become Brazil's contemporary *movimento negro* were given. A series of publications by Brazilian sociologists, such as Florestan Fernandes and Fernando Henrique Cardoso of the so-called Escola Paulista, in which they deconstructed the foundations of *democracia racial* ideology by refuting the alleged benevolence of Portuguese slavery and proving the persistence of racial inequality in Brazilian society, coincided with the rise of a powerful black movement in the U.S. and anti colonial struggles in the Third World. Inspired by new concepts of racism and blackness articulated in these contexts, small circles of Afro-Brazilian activists came to see *democracia racial* as a national myth which disguised deep-rooted forms of anti-black racism in Brazilian society that manifested themselves in the social marginalization of the country's Afro-Brazilian population, widespread negative stereotypes of blackness and the existence of a white-only political and economic elite in a country in which people of African descent constitute a large portion of the population. While African national liberation movements from Lusophone countries, such as Angola and Mozambique, constituted important influences, the U.S. Civil Rights and Black Power movements proved to be the most relevant source of inspiration for Afro-Brazilian activists (Sheriff 187–188). Televised images of black mobilizations in the U.S., the international visibility of African American icons as Martin Luther King, Malcolm X, Stokely Carmichael and the Black Panthers, the return of *movimento negro* leader Abdias Nascimento[37] and other Afro-Brazilian activists and musicians from the U.S. to Brazil, and, last but not least, the global impact of soul music contributed to the massive diffusion of U.S.-inspired blackness discourses.

Despite these developments, Brazil remained a most unlikely place for the emergence of a black mass movement in the 1960s and 1970s which challenged the status quo of race relations. Since 1964, the country was ruled by a right-wing military regime which fiercely advocated *democracia racial* as a national ideology and repressed any expression of dissent as subversive activity. It comes as no surprise that possible influences of militant Black Power discourses from the U.S. on Afro-Brazilians were seen as a serious threat by the ruling elites who feared nothing more than social unrest and applied censorship on any mentioning of racial discrimination in Brazil. The inclusion of race-related data in the census was prohibited and police authorities were ordered to prevent any contacts of local black activists with the U.S. Black Power movement (Stam and Shohat 278). While the general climate of repression impeded open political activity, Black Power did make its way to Brazil in the early 1970s. It remained unnoticed for quite some time, mainly because in the beginning, the feared messages of black consciousness and black pride were not spread on political rallies but on the dancefloors of Rio de Janeiro's predominantly black neighborhoods.

5.2 From Harlem to Rio: Toni Tornado

In 1971, the arrival of the Black Power revolution on Brazilian soil was televised: When Afro-Brazilian soul singer Tony Tornado entered the stage at the 6th annual *Festival Internacional da Canção* in Rio de Janeiro, wearing an Afro, raising his fist for a Black Power salute and singing the song "Black Is Beautiful", he caused a national scandal. For his subversive intervention, Tornado was arrested on stage by the military police right after his show. By performing Black Panther-inspired militancy and what had become popular and widespread representations of black pride in the U.S. during the mid-to-late 1960s, he had crossed the narrow limits

---

37 During his stay in the U.S. in 1968/69, Abdias Nascimento was received by protagonists of the Black Power movement such as Amiri Baraka and Black Panther leader Bobby Seale who had a significant influence on his political thought (Almada *Nascimento* 97).

of artistic freedom granted by the military regime. Only a year before, Tornado had returned from New York City, where he had spent five years as an illegal immigrant. As a Harlem resident, he was constantly exposed to soul music and the dynamics of the black freedom struggle. During his stay, he became familiar with the local Black Panther chapter and even got to know Black Power leader Stokely Carmichael personally (Pelegrini and Alves).

Upon his return to Brazil in 1969, Tornado started a career as a soul musician in which he capitalized on his Harlem experience: Alongside Tim Maia, who had also spent time in New York, he became an important figure of the emerging Brazilian soul scene. In appearing with an Afro haircut, wearing a special kind of colorful clothing and putting his blackness on the agenda, he was one of the first musicians to introduce the Brazilian audience to the style of African American soul culture (ibid.).

In 1970, Toni Tornado released the message song "Sou Negro" which translates "I'm Black" and was based on the instrumental of the James Brown-produced single "From the Love Side" by Hank Ballard (Fig. 18). For Brazilian popular music standards, the lyrics were outrageously defiant: "Sou negro sim. Mas ninguém vai rir de mim!" ["Yes, I am black. But nobody will laugh about me!"] In its raw and funky sound and politically charged content, this song constitutes a paradigmatic example for the translation of soul music and Black Power discourse in Brazilian contexts. With his provocative appearances, critical comments on *democracia racial*, and more message songs like "Se Jesus Fosse Um Homem de Cor (Deus Negro)" ["If Jesus was a man of color (Black God)"] (1976), Tornado continued to disrupt the notions of Brazilian blackness. He was always suspected by Brazilian police to be financed by black radicals from the U.S. in order to found a Rio branch of the Black Panther Party, which lead to constant harassment by the police including numerous interrogations and arrests – a situation which finally made him leave the country again for political exile in Czechoslovakia (Pelegrini and Alves).

Toni Tornado's creative appropriation of soul music is representative of the impact of African American genres on Brazilian popular music. From the 1960s on, some of Brazil's major stars like Roberto Carlos, Jorge Ben, Gilberto Gil, Wilson Simonal, Elis Regina, Caetano Veloso, and Sergio Mendes were all influenced by jazz, blues, soul, and funk from the United States. Tornado and fellow U.S. returnee Tim Maia contributed heavily to the genesis of Brazilian soul as a genre of its own, which was also represented by the likes of Gerson King Combo, Carlos Dafé, and Banda Black Rio, among others (Palombini). While the migratory movements of translocal actors such as Toni Tornado and Tim Maia were crucial to the emergence of hemispheric soulscapes, in the case of Brazil, the increased mobility of sounds through the expansion of the record industry proved even more relevant.

5.3 Bailes Soul: Rio Becomes *Black*

Between 1969 and 1973, the Brazilian market witnessed a massive growth in the import figures of U.S. records and the distribution of electronical mass media which was related to economic upturn, increased purchasing power, and a modernization campaign under military junta leader Emilio Medici. For this reason, Rio de Janeiro's youth was very familiar with the latest rock and pop releases from the USA and Great Britain. One of the first DJs to start playing soul music alongside these styles on his radio program was Newton Duarte, better known as Big Boy. In the late 1960s, he and his colleague Ademir Lemos began hosting a weekly dance event called "Baile da Pesada" at the Canecão club in Rio's well-heeled southern zone, which quickly became very popular (Dunn 160). This also had to do with the fact that word got around among Afro-Brazilian youths that the two white DJs Big Boy and Ademir Lemos also had soul music in their repertoire. According to Sidney Araújo Lima from the working class neighborhood of Osvaldo Cruz, the Baile da Pesada quickly became a meeting point for black youth from the Zona Norte like him:

> Every week we went to Canecão to listen to the latest soul records by Big Boy and Ademir Lemos. They organized dance competitions at the Baile da Pesada and if you came out on top, you could win an imported soul record from the USA as a prize. As I was a very good dancer, I earned my first records that way. We soon had the desire to organize dance events where you didn't have to wait until the rock sets were over to finally listen to soul again, because we only wanted to hear this music. (*personal interview*)

And so, in 1969, Sidney Araújo Lima became *discotecário* (DJ) Dr. Sidney. He and his friends organized a street party in Osvaldo Cruz, where he played his first soul records. As it was a huge success, he teamed up with his friends and formed one of Rio's first sound systems with *Alma Negra* [Black Soul]. In the following years, enthusiastic DJs like Dr. Sidney and Mr. Funky Santos became the protagonists of a movement which bore resemblances to Jamaican soundsystem culture, as the working-class neighborhoods of Rio's Zona Norte witnessed the emergence of so-called *bailes black* (or *baile soul*), giving birth to what would become known as the Black Rio movement. As the soul dances drew larger crowds of mostly Afro-Brazlian youth each weekend, the soundsystems started to organize their events in large samba schools, clubs or gyms.

Following the example of pioneers like Dr. Sidney and Mr. Funky Santos, who had succeeded in popularizing soul music among Rio's Afro-Brazilian youth, many local DJs formed *equipes de som* with telling names like *Afro Soul, Revolução da mente* and *Black Power,* which played soul and funk records exclusively from the U.S. By the mid-1970s, there were hundreds of *bailes black* operating throughout

Rio, which were frequented by something between 500.000 and 1.5 million people – each weekend (Palombini 99). Very much like in Jamaican soundsystem culture, there was huge competition among the *discotecários*, about who would present the latest and hippest records on the dancefloors. There were numerous ways of transferring soul records from the U.S. to Rio's dancefloors. While major U.S. labels distributed their releases on the Brazilian market, there were also DJs who paid crew members of airlines for buying records during their stays in the U.S. As soul singer Ed Motta recounts, there were even DJs who made 35-hours back-and-forth trips to the U.S. in order to purchase the latest releases before any other competing DJ would have them (Thayer 90).

5.4 Soul, Empowerment and *movimento negro*

One of the venues that started to host *bailes black* in the early 1970s was the Renascença Clube – a social club in Rio's Zona Norte where samba concerts and *miss mulata* competitions had taken place since its foundation in the 1950s. Afro-Brazilian engineering student Asfilófio de Oliveira Filho, better known as Dom Filó, played a crucial role in the emergence of Black Rio when he called into life *Soul Grand Prix*, one of the city's most successful *equipe de som* [soundsystem]. In 1972, he launched his regular event "Noite do Shaft" – a reference to the first black superhero of U.S. Blaxploitation cinema – at Renascença Clube, which in contrast to samba events at the same location, was almost exclusively frequented by black audiences. What differentiated Dom Filó's "Noite do Shaft" from other existing soul parties was its distinct emphasis on raising consciousness and spreading the scandalous message of "Black is Beautiful". As a way of empowering Afro-Brazilian youth, sophisticated slideshows with several beamers juxtaposed pictures of the present dancers with "photos taken from African American magazines like *Ebony* and *Essence*, showing black women, men, and families with Afro styles images along with subtitles stimulating self-esteem, the importance of studying and forging black unity", as Carlos Alberto Medeiros remembers ("Black Rio" 239). Dom Filó, acting as somewhat of an activist MC and teacher, regularly used his microphone and dropped some of his didactic messages from behind the turntables, which encouraged the audiences to get involved in the antiracist struggle and practice critical thought (Oliveira).

Like many other politicized Afro-Brazilian youngsters who endured under the conditions of a repressive military regime and were frustrated with the absence of a powerful national black movement, Filó, a student and activist at Rio's Candido Mendes University, was deeply impressed by the rise of U.S. African American freedom struggle in the 1960s (ibid.). To him, appropriating soul music and the related aesthetic representations of black pride became a way of showing identification and solidarity with the Civil Rights and Black Power movements and raising awareness for denied racial discrimination in Brazil. According to Filó, he was not as interested in the search for African roots as other Afro-Brazilian activists and also many white progressive intellectuals of the era, as he could relate much more to the modern and urban sounds and looks from the black ghettos of the USA. He understood *Soul Grand Prix* as a revolutionary enterprise in which soul music was used as a way to elude the regime's censorship (ibid.). Dom Filó's immensely successful approach of blending black consciousness with dancing pleasure became a trendsetter for the Black Rio movement.

For those who wanted to express dissent with the Brazilian model of racial hierarchies, soul music offered an alternative to traditional samba, carnival, and other black cultural forms which had been 'nationalized' as emblems of Brazilian unity and popular culture, as George Andrews notes (172). The *bailes black* attracted especially Afro-Brazilian youth for they offered new ways of embracing black identity that contrasted sharply with the widespread stigmatization of blackness that was hidden behind the color-blind discourse of *democracia racial.* In a social context, in which whiteness was set as the ideal to which Brazilians of all colors aspired, a song like James Brown's Black Power anthem "Say It Loud – I'm Black and I'm Proud" (1968), which would become the most played record of Brazil's soul movement, had revolutionary and self-liberating potential as *movimento negro* veteran Carlos Alberto Medeiro remembers. According to Medeiros, James Brown's iconic status as Soul Brother No.1 was undisputed in Rio's soul scene, where his latest songs, outlooks, and dance moves became the measure of all things (*personal interview*). The language gap did not prevent Afro-Brazilians from receiving the messages of black pride which were transported by soul music, as Bryan McCann points out: "Certain totemic phrases from the Soul records as black power, black is beautiful – became buzzwords in the Soul dances. What they lost in specific meaning they gained in power, precisely because of their foreign allure" (48). Visual material as the afore-mentioned slideshows and screenings of movies which conveyed Black Power imaginaries such as *Wattstax* and *Shaft* also played a significant role in bridging linguistic barriers and spreading symbolic representations of black assertiveness on the *bailes.*

The collective consumption of soul music and visual material of African American culture resulted in the appropriation of the Black Power aesthetic by Rio's Afro-Brazilian youth. During the early-to-mid 1970s, the Afro hairstyle, which was called *cabelo black power,* became the most visible and widespread sign of showing solidarity with the U.S. black freedom movement and implicitly expressing dissent with the status quo of race relations in Brazil (Alberti and Pereira 72). Identifying with U.S. representations of blackness also manifested itself in Rio's

5.4 Soul, Empowerment and *movimento negro* — **165**

soul fans addressing each other as "brothers", "sisters" and "blacks" [braz.-port: *bleques*], differentiating themselves from Brazilian denominations as *pardos* o *pretos* (Alberto 4). In 1977, Gérson King Combo, another important figure in the Brazilian funk and soul scene who had gained a reputation as "James Brown brasileiro", released the song "Mandamentos Black", in which he articulates his version of translating U.S.-inspired blackness in a Brazilian context and calls on Afro-Brazilians to take pride in their identity as *bleques:* "Brother! Assuma sua mente, brother! ... O certo é seguir os mandamentos black, que são, baby: dançar como dança um black/...falar como fala um black ... ter orgulho de ser black."[38] While the song was basically about how good it felt to assume black identity, the Policia Federal suspected Gérson King Combo of becoming the leader of a radical black movement and preparing a favela rebellion, which led to various arrests and the dissolution of a crowd of thousands who had gathered at Clube Magnatas in Rio for a concert of King Combo with his band União Black in 1977 (*personal interview*). Like other Brazilian soul musicians, Gerson King Combo experienced how narrow the confines of accepted cultural activity were for Afro-Brazilians, once they left the realm of samba.

Although aesthetic and commercial aspects, and entertainment defined Black Rio's success as a youth movement, it also had deeply political connotations. The setting of the *bailes black* provided Afro-Brazilian activists with opportunities to covertly raise awareness for matters of black identity and the racist implications of *democracia racial*, avoiding the censorship of the ruling military regime. Luís Antonio da Silva, one of the founders of the Afro-Brazilian funk group Abolição, recalls how the consumption of soul became crucial for constructing a critical black consciousness and mobilizing black Brazilians against persistent forms of structural racism: "O grupo Abolição surgiu com o propósito de apresentar Soul music. Com o despertar das ídeias, partimos pra outras atividades, com o objetivo de reunir e conscientizar o povo black"[39] (Risério 31).

Black activists tried to use the soul dances for their own purposes. It was their goal to bring people beyond the level of symbolically appropriating aesthetic representations of Black Power into getting involved in the political struggle against racial discrimination. Carlos Alberto Medeiro became an important bridge between Black Rio and black movement when he started to use the soul dances as

---

38 "Brother! Assume your mind, brother! ... The right thing is to follow the black commandments, which are, baby: dance like a black dances/...talk like a black talks...be proud to be black." (Gerson King Combo "Mandamentos Black").

39 "The group *Abolição* started with the purpose of presenting Soul music. With the awakening of the ideas, we set off for other activities, with the aim of bringing together and raising awareness among black people" (Risério 31).

sites for mobilization: and political education: "[G]roups were formed in areas that were more distant from the sound systems to discuss race relations in Brazil and beyond, including cases of discrimination, films, books, and articles about that topic." ("Black Rio" 239). Following the example of *bailes black*, black activists like Medeiros, who founded the *Instituto de Pesquisa da Cultura Negra* in 1975, started to organize soul parties, which not only featured movies from the African American struggle in but also the opportunity to purchase movement literature as *The Wretched of the Earth* by Frantz Fanon, *The Autobiography of Malcolm X, Black Power* by Stokely Carmichael, or *Soul On Ice* by Eldridge Cleaver (Sterling 5–6).

The appropriateness of Black Power discourses and soul music from the U.S. as catalysts for Afro-Brazilian mobilization was subject of intense debates on the campus of Rio's Candido Mendes University, as Michael Hanchard describes in *Orpheus and Power*, his landmark study on Brazil's *movimento negro*. There were two opposed schools of black political thought among activists in 1970s Rio: While the so-called *africanistas* insisted on African history, culture, and liberation movements as the sole relevant sources of inspiration for Afro-Brazilian activism and rejected any influence from the United, the so-called *americanistas* advocated for a political vision which emphasized the connectedness of black struggles in the Americas and the vanguard character of the African American freedom movement and its cultural manifestations. Whereas *africanistas* congregated at the *Sociedade de Intercâmbio Brasil-África* (SIMBA), the *Centro de Estudos Afro-Asiáticos* (CEAA) and the IPCN led by Medeiros became centers for *americanistas* (Hanchard 88–89). Accordingly, it came as no surprise that IPCN, in an effort to reach out to Rio's soul-enthused black youth, celebrated its first anniversary in 1976 with a public screening of the documentary *Wattstax*. The documentary provided transnational audiences with powerful images of this symbiotic moment in the relationship between soul music and black nationalism and was one of the most-played movies on Rio's *bailes black*. The paradigmatic scene, in which Reverend Jesse Jackson raises his fist for a Black Power salute and calls on the spectators at the Los Angeles Coloseum to intonate his "black litany" ("I may be on welfare, but I am Black, Beautiful and Proud... I am somebody" (*see introductory paragraph, chapter 2*), was reenacted at IPCN's anniversary celebration, as audiences in Rio de Janeiro raised their fists and responded to Jackson in unison: "I am somebody." According to activists' accounts, this call-and-response scheme between the African American Reverend on the screen and Afro-Brazilian soul fans – many of whom didn't speak English – became somewhat of a ritual whenever the film was shown on a *baile black* (Ribeiro 168–169).

IPCN cadre and other *americanistas* within the movement saw the popularity of U.S. soul music and the related representations of black pride as a chance to break with prescribed modes of Brazilian blackness as represented in carnival and samba music, which had lost their function as expression of black dissent when they became converted into symbols of national unity and *democracia racial* by the government's cultural policies. To black activists, who had unsuccessfully tried to reach out to the masses for decades, the collective consumption of soul music represented a point of departure for a process of "conscientização" of Afro-Brazilians, as Medeiros points out (*personal interview*). Activists' hopes for the mobilizing and consciousness-raising potential of soul were expressed in the following lines, which were published in the left-wing underground magazine *Versus:*

> Primeiro a descoberta da beleza negra. O entusiasmo de também poder ser black. A vontade de lutar como o negro-norteamericano, em busca da libertação do espírito negro, através do Soul. ... Num segundo momento, uma consciência incipente começa a surgir. O trabalho, as condições de vida, a igualdade racial começam a receber destaque.[40] (qtd. in Vianna 29).

Arguing that the "soul movement was more about transgressing social conventions than about political organizing", Christopher Dunn holds that Black Rio brought "into focus some of the defining characteristics of the Brazilian counterculture" (173) during the military dictatorship. Black Rio transcended the city limits and had a long-lasting impact on Afro-Brazilian popular music and mobilizations. Building on the ties with the African American popular culture and politics established through Black Rio, Salvador de Bahia as the center of Afro-Brazilian culture, witnessed the emergence of the-so-called *blocos afros,* percussion ensembles dedicated to the advocacy of black consciousness that have shaped Bahia's carnival culture and influenced icons of *Música Popular Brasileira* such as Margareth Menezes, Gilberto Gil, Caetano Veloso, Daniela Mercury, and Carlinhos Brown significantly (Pinho). The first and next to Olodum most influential *bloco afro* was Ilê Aiyê, an all-black cultural group which provoked outrage at their first appearance at the Bahia carnival in 1974 when they performed the song "Que Bloco è Esse?" that included the catchphrase "Temos cabelo duro, somos Black Power" ["We got kinky hair, we are Black Power"] (Risério). Black Rio and the related influence of the Black Power movement have also been crucial in the formation of a broad antiracist Afro-Brazilian movement which materialized in 1978, when activists who had become politicized through soul founded the *Movimento Negro Unificado* (MNU) in São Paulo, creating the first national black organization since the *Frente*

---

40 "First the discovery of black beauty. The enthusiasm to also be black. The will to fight like the black North-American, in search of the liberation of the black spirit, through Soul. ... In a second moment, an incipient consciousness begins to emerge. Work, living conditions and racial equality begin to be highlighted".

Negra Brasileira of the 1930s (Alberti and Pereira 85). The intergenerational legacy of Black Rio also manifests itself in the late 20th and early 21st century emergence of hip-hop and *baile funk* as Afro-Brazilian countercultures.

6 Soul vs. *cultura nacional:* Race, Nation, and *anti-Afro-Americanism* in Latin American Identity Discourses

In the Black Power era, soul music was one of the most popular black music forms across the Western hemisphere. This was not only the case among African American youth in the United States where its impact was unparalleled but also among second-generation immigrants from Puerto Rico in New York, among the Afro-Caribbean community of Panama, the youth of Rio de Janeiro's majority black Zona Norte neighborhoods, and many other locales of the African diaspora in the Americas. While the emergence and hemispheric proliferation of soul coincided with the rise of black nationalism and the transition from Civil Rights to Black Power in the African American freedom struggle, the genre, its protagonists, and its adherents complicated and transcended the tenets of black nationalist ideologies and were not per se tied to the agenda of any particular strain of the ideologically diverse and heterogeneous Black Power movement. Rather, soul music functioned "as a primary site of negotiation and articulation over the form and appearance of black liberation struggles", which, according to Michael Hanson, "can be read as a meta-narrative of the shifting terrain of political self-consciousness and resistance over time" (342). Despite the strong "inter-animation of politics and sound" that shaped the era and the specific capacity of black music "to communicate a particular political sensibility" (ibid.), soul often eluded black nationalists' efforts to enlist it as a propagandistic tool in their advocacy of a male-centered "fixed, iron-clad Black aesthetic" (Ashe 615) that was based exclusively on the African American experience in the United States.

Much like the Black Power movement that soul reflected and served as inspiration for, the genre was much broader, more inclusive, more flexible, more feminine, more hybrid, and more transnational than its nationalist, essentialist, and reductive interpretations were able to grasp. Soul was also an expression of African American agency in modernity in a way that many cultural nationalist advocates of a return to "authentic" African traditions and roots rejected. Interestingly, soul was rejected in Latin American contexts in part with very similar arguments against the contamination of autochthonous national cultures. Here, however, a specific component was added, because the identification with African American culture and politics that accompanied the consumption of soul was seen by Latin American elites and intellectuals as a threat to national unity, resulting in diverse expressions of *anti-Afro-Americanism:* a specific hostility to African American cultural and political influences that resulted from a combination of anti-(US)-

https://doi.org/10.1515/9783110665550-008

Americanism and a fear of black insubordination, disguised as righteous anti-imperialism. As the translation of soul into Latin American idioms defied essentialist and folkloristic concepts of popular music and blurred the established demarcations between blackness and *latinidad*, the translation of this foreign form and the associated cosmopolitan practices of appropriating symbols and discourses from abroad and developing a sense of belonging to a transnational community became instruments of emancipation in the intersecting struggles of African American and other diasporic communities. These cross-cultural flows sparked debates on the meanings of authenticity, race, and nation in all three contexts examined here.

6.1 Latin Boogaloo: Between "African Americanness" and *latinidad*

When the youth of Spanish Harlem gave birth to Latin soul/boogaloo in the mid-1960s, elder generations of Puerto Rican immigrants, established figures of New York's Latin music scene, traditionalists, purists, and nationalists from the island hated it. The hostile reactions had different backgrounds. While the resentment against the new sound among established musicians of the 1960s New York Latin music scene had primarily economical and artistic reasons – the boogaloo youth had put them temporarily out of business with a sound that lacked their level of sophistication – the unease with the genre also had racial connotations, as it "violated the bounds that kept distinct what was Black and what was Latino" as Raquel Rivera holds ("Hip Hop, Puerto Ricans" 244). Traditionalists and advocates of Eurocentric *mestizaje* discourse found that African American influences in style, language, and music, as represented in Nuyorican culture and, particularly in Latin boogaloo, constituted a contamination of the explicitly non-black Puerto Rican Latino heritage they propagated. This attitude was reflected in an extremely hostile stance towards Nuyorican expressions of identification with African American culture, which dominated the public discourse in Puerto Rico, as Yeidy Rivero demonstrates in her discussion of the Afro hairstyle on the island. According to Rivero, the popularization of the Afro as a symbol of Black empowerment among Afro-Puerto Ricans constituted a "direct affront to the island's racist ideologies and practices [...], an in-your-face resistance to hegemonic racial discourse" (*Tuning Out Blackness* 83) which "symbolically connected Puerto Ricans on the island with the African American-Puerto Rican-Afro Puerto Rican radical mobilizations that had taken place in the United States since the early 1960s" (84). The local guardians of *mestizaje* discourse denounced the translation of U.S. blackness into

Puerto Rican contexts through Latin boogaloo and soul style because they perceived it as an imminent threat to their racial hegemony.

The dismissive and disparaging narrative regarding the boogaloo has proven long-lasting as evidenced in contemporary accounts of the evolution of Latin music that omit the Latin boogaloo era completely, downplay its role or treat it as a despicable deviation in an otherwise glorious continuum of intergenerational perfection that led from *son montuno* over mambo to salsa. The analysis of cultural critics like Cesar Miguel Rondón is illustrative of how boogaloo is often depicted as a concession to the uninformed inferior musical tastes of the U.S. audiences. In his *Book of Salsa* (2008), Rondón posits *son*, a genre based on Afro-Cuban patterns, as a timeless synonym for the different *clave*-based stages of Latin music across time which, through boogaloo, "lost the sense of hidden malice that characterized the Caribbean clave", and "became flat and thus acceptable to mainstream U.S. listeners" (28). Countering the calls of scholars like Juan Flores and Max Salazar, who have hinted at the importance of boogaloo in the making of salsa, Rondón holds that "we must not overemphasize the role of boogaloo [...] in locating the origins of the real salsalike expression. Rather, we should take the boogaloo only as a point of reference, since as a discrete singular beat it lacked substance and consequence" (28). In a reference to the 1969 decision of Fania to stop producing boogaloo, which had also become popular among African Americans, Rondón points out that "fortunately at this point the company did not try to merge these two markets" (29). Treating the 1960s black-Nuyorican sonic dialogues as a dictatorial regime that was imposed upon musicians, Rondón continues: "Already freed from hybrids such as the boogaloo [...], the son began to be played fluidly, without the unnatural tendencies or new fashionable styles that had been forced on it" (30). In his anti-boogaloo rant with clear anti-U.S.-American undertones, Rondón even manages to dismiss the success of the Joe Cuba Sextet as pioneers of the genre which he dismisses as "strident and 'gringolike' experiments" (30). Through Rondón's lens, the group lost "any clear musical direction" after the departure of singer Cheo Feliciano and their decision "to perform only U.S. music" which "turned out to be a fatal mistake for them" because, as he claims, "once the barrio sound became legitimized, audiences began to dismiss any style that did not come out of the Caribbean context" (31). Ironically, the opposite was the truth as Joe Cuba's international and interethnic fame was intrinsically linked to his vanguard role in the making of boogaloo. In a seemingly Darwinist take on musical expression in which certain musical styles are treated like diseases to be overcome, Rondón celebrates the moment the "boogaloo fever began to die down" because "once salsa's virtues imposed themselves, only the most defined styles survived" (32). In a display of ignorance regarding the transcultural fusions and multidirectional hybridizations between diverse styles and traditions that define not only salsa but also many other Afro-diasporic genres, Rondón argues that boogaloo's short-lived success was based on its ability "to capitalize on the sounds already sown by other styles. ... it was precisely that opportunism that led the boogaloo to its demise." Rondón concludes with his verdict that "the tendency to use jazz elements had little to do with the authentic popular expressions that ultimately led to salsa" (32). Rondón's interpretation of boogaloo as a "gringo-like", commercialist, superficial, unnatural, and opportunist accident which he contrasts with the virtuous, real, and authentic salsa is symptomatic for the ways debates on popular music in the Caribbean and Latin America have been driven by the condemnation of cross-cultural exchange with African Americans and the celebration of authenticity and purity. As Vernon Boggs has argued, "in their haste to assure Salsa of a 'pure' Latino identity" these interpretations "overlook the historical roots of this musical modality in American popular music, especially R&B" (16).

In the context of language-based discrimination of Latin American immigrants in the United States, the return to exclusively Spanish-language lyrics and the celebration of Caribbean heritage through Afro-Cuban *clave*-based rhythmic patterns in salsa were in fact important expression of a new pan-Latino pride and the construction of transnational identities that placed the New York Puerto Rican migrant community at the center of exchange processes in the circum-Caribbean space. However, these manifestations were not articulated in demarcation from U.S. African American culture, as essentialist interpretations suggest, but in dialogue with it – and as a result of the impact soul and Black Power had on New York's Latin music scene, as Andrés Espinoza Agurto argues in *Salsa Consciente* (41–46). In the 1970s, salsa became a crucial site for these interethnic collaborations: alongside soul performers such as James Brown, Bill Withers and The Spinners, the Fania All-Stars participated in the "Zaire 74" festival prior to the legendary "Rumble in the Jungle" between Muhammad Ali and George Foreman in Kinshasa which had a special meaning in the forging of transnational black solidarities. Salsa not only drew from African American influences in its musical arrangements and use of edgy, or "funky", horn sections. It also provided a platform for the performance of Afro-diasporic identity in hairstyles and clothing that was clearly inspired by Black Power aesthetics and soul style. When Fania's Afro-descendant performers like Roberto Roena, Cheo Feliciano, Pete "Conde" Rodriguez and Celia Cruz started to wear Afro hairstyles they contributed significantly to the popularization of this symbol of identification with the African American freedom struggle in Caribbean, Central and South American contexts. A look at the covers of 1970s and early 1980s salsa records from Puerto Rico, Cuba, Panama, Venezuela, and Colombia confirms that Afro hairstyles were not the exception but the rule among performers of the genre in this particular period of time. Salsa songs such as "Justicia" in which Eddie Palmieri demands justice for "boricuas y niches"

("Puerto Ricans and blacks"), "Negro Soy" by Kako & His Orchestra, "Moreno" by Johnny Pacheco and Pete Conde Rodríguez, "Las caras lindas" by Ismael Rivera, and "La Rebelión" by Joe Arroyo gave voice to the affirmation of Afro-Latin identity, clearly inspired by the U.S. black movement.

Whereas critics such as Rondón and many others despised the appropriation of African American elements and the use of the English language in boogaloo, they did not take issue with the celebration of African roots and Afro-Latin identity as recurrent themes in salsa. This suggests that the dismissal of boogaloo was rooted in an anti-U.S. American sentiment that directed its rage about the global predominance of U.S. popular culture against the translation of African American expressions into Latin American contexts: in short, a form of anti-Afro-Americanism. This hostility against the idiom of soul followed a wider pattern that was often related to the ways nationalist identity discourse of *mestizaje* were questioned through the building of border-crossing linkages of hemispheric black solidarity.

By bridging musical traditions, celebrating common cultural practices, and blending African American slang and Spanish lyrics, Latin boogaloo accompanied, intonated, and encouraged the building of political alliances between Puerto Ricans and African Americans, as the accounts of Young Lords activists such as Denise Oliver, Felipe Luciano, and Pablo Guzmán confirm. While Joe Bataan's recordings were an exception amid the overall scarcity of explicit political messages in the releases from the Latin boogaloo era, its emancipatory potential lay in the ways boogaloo encouraged the adaptation of African American forms in contexts that were shaped by a deep-rooted stigmatization of blackness (this holds true for the U.S. mainland and Puerto Rico). This in itself constituted a defiant act with deeply political connotations. The appropriation of African American soul styles by Puerto Rican migrants as featured in Latin boogaloo is interpreted as a form of "strategic anti-essentialism" (79) by George Lipsitz, who suggests that Nuyoricans found that "performing an identity that was not entirely their own brought them closer to their [African] roots. [...] [T]his anti-essentialist strategy revealed the heterogeneity and complexity of their group's identity sufficiently to position them to take part in subsequent national and international fusion musics [...] that enabled them to imagine and enact alliances with other groups" (79). In this light, the anti-essentialist embracing of U.S. black culture by a young generation of Nuyoricans as manifested in Latin boogaloo represented a means of showing solidarity and identification with the African American freedom struggle, but also a way of affirming Puerto Rico's neglected African heritage and challenging the Puerto Rican elites' racism and denial. In her insightful account of Nuyoricans' role in the making of hip-hop, Raquel Rivera argues that sonic dialogues between African Americans and Puerto Ricans were built on a sense of "class-based blackness" – the shared experiences of social exclusion in the ghetto that contributed to

174 —— 6 Soul vs. *cultura nacional*

the bridging of demarcations between both communities and the acknowledgement among Puerto Rican youth that they were a part of the African diaspora:

> The blackness formerly restricted by the bounds of an ethno-racialized African Americanness began expanding to accommodate certain latino groups as a population of ethno-racial Others whose experience of class and ethno-racial marginalization is in many ways virtually indistinguishable from the ghettocentric African American experience" (*New York Ricans* 99).

Thus, the emergence of transcultural and hybrid forms in the New York context, from Latin jazz over Latin soul to hip-hop, were the product of African American-Nuyorican solidarities and collaborations that were rather based on common social and historical positionings than on essentialized notions of a shared racial identity. By embracing and affirming often neglected Afro-diasporic identities and challenging both U.S. racism and homogenizing Latin American *mestizaje* discourses, the rise of Latin soul/boogaloo and the Young Lords in the 1960s contributed significantly to the emergence of Nuyorican counterculture. The resulting constructions of *afrolatinidad* transcended the boundaries of communities, cultures, ethnicities, neighborhoods, and nations, appealing to audiences throughout the Americas. Latin soul/boogaloo and the Young Lords translated African American sounds, expressions, and symbols, making them accessible to new constituents in Latin American contexts such as Puerto Rico, Venezuela, Colombia, Perú, the Dominican Republic, and Panamá.

6.2 Afro-Caribbean Transnationalism and the Boundaries of *panameñidad*

In the 1970s, soul functioned as a code in the debates on Panama's national identity, that evolved against the backdrop of Omar Torrijos' ambivalent policies that encouraged Afro-Caribbean participation while at the same time cracking down on expressions of black assertiveness and identification with the African American freedom struggle. In the debate on national identity sparked by Juan Materno Vásquez' anti-West Indian pamphlet *País por Conquistar* (1974), Afro-Caribbean Panamanians' preference of soul over Panamanian folklore is treated as an example for their refusal to assimilate. In Melva Lowe's response to Materno Vasquez' attacks, soul and the popularity of the Afro among West Indian youth is also mentioned[41],

---

41 "Además del idioma, hay otros factores en el comportamiento social de este grupo que no es cónsono con la declarada naturaleza de la cultura panameña. Por una parte, la mayoría, por ejemplo, practican la religión protestante y no la Católica que es la declarada religión del estado. Por

6.2 Afro-Caribbean Transnationalism and the Boundaries of *panameñidad* — **175**

but not as as proof of their lack of commitment with the Panamanian struggle against US domination but rather as a source of inspiration in Afro-Panamanian efforts to overcome racial discrimination in Panama. In the same vein, Alberto Smith links the impact of "Black is Beautiful" – "cantado por el estridente James Brown" – on Afro-Caribbean consciousness to a sense of connectedness with the African American freedom struggle that was sparked by the exclusionary nature of Panamanian nationalism.[42] In both sides of the argument, soul is discussed as a signifier in questions of racial and national identity. Panamanian nationalists like Materno Vásquez interpreted soul as a a tool of U.S. imperialism that had divisive effects as it kept Afro-Panamanians from assuming Panama's Hispanic national identity and culture. To black activists like Lowe and Smith, soul represented their identification with African American politics and culture and their sense of belonging to a transnational community of Afrodescendants in the Americas. As soul was a genre that originated in the country against whose domination the aspirations of Panamanian nationalists were directed and that represented an affirmation of black identity that was at odds with homogenizing concepts of national culture, the controversies around its meanings are to be understood in the context of debates on Panamanian national identity in which the boundaries of *panameñidad* have been a recurrent theme throughout the 20th century. Thus, the hostility with which Panamanian nationalists reacted to the appropriation of U.S. products generally and the translation of African American soul styles into Panamanian contexts specifically was grounded in the ways these processes touched upon two defining aspects of Panamanian nationhood: the struggle against the U.S. occupation and U.S. cultural influences and the presence of an Anglophone Afro-Caribbean community that defied the self-image of Panama as Catholic, Hispanic, mestizo nation.

Despite the strides that Afro-Caribbean Panamanians made in terms of social mobility and visibility in popular culture under Torrijos, the 1970s debates over their allegiance to Panamanian nationalism revealed how deeply rooted anti-Western Indian sentiment was among Panama's intellectual elites and how closely it was linked to expressions of anti-Afro-Americanism. Challenged by a new generation of outspoken black activists and outraged at the salience of foreign symbols and practices as represented by the *combos* and their popularization of soul, calypso, and Afro styles, Panamanian nationalists reacted with indignation. In the tra-

---

otra parte, responden más a la música Soul y al Calypso, que al Pindín o la música latina" (Lowe 24).

42 "El apotegma "Black is beautiful" ... lanzado por el taumaturgo W.E.B. Du Bois, enfatizado por elcarismático Marcus Garvey, predicado por el elocuente Martin Luther King Jr. y cantado por el estridente James Brown ha permeabilizado la conciencia del antillano" (Smith 57).

dition of former president Arnulfo Arias who had launched a xenophopic campaign in the early 1940s – during which all blacks whose mother tongue is not Spanish ("la raza negra, cuyo idioma de origen no sea el Castellano", Lowe 26), namely West Indians, were declared as "undesired aliens" and "forbidden races" ["razas prohibidas"] – Panamanian nationalists once again projected their "rage against the United States onto West Indian bodies" (Craft 42). In *El País por Conquistar*, Juan Materno Vásquez claimed that the Canal Zone posed a major threat to the nation because of its inhabitants, the white and black "zonians" who, according to him, lacked any sentiment of patriotism and committed acts of cultural aggression against the purity of the Spanish language through their use of English (Lowe 26).[43] While most white "zonians" were U.S. nationals, his diatribes were directed specifically against West Indians with Panamanian citizenship, whom he described disparagingly as "de piel oscura, costumbres raras, e idioma inglés," ["dark-skinned, with strange costums, and English-speaking"] and "sin vinculación espiritual con la nación panameña" ["without spiritual bond with the Panamanian nation"] (qtd. in Lowe 35).

When Melva Lowe and Alberto Smith denounced his racist attacks in the October 1976 issue of *Revista Nacional de Cultura*, poet and diplomat Roque Javier Laurenza, and Materno Vásquez himself responded, indignated about how "the aggressive essayists" (Laurenza 102) pretended to introduce a new element defined as the Afro-Caribbean contributions in the conformation of the national being with a "hammer blow" (Materno Vásquez, "La nacionalidad panameña" 83).[44] Both invoke the discourse of Panama as a "crisol de razas" – a Panamanian version of *mestizaje*, introduced by José Isaac Fábregas in his 1936 novel *Crisol*, which held that Panama was a nation where Europeans, Native Americans, and the descendants of enslaved Africans brought by the Spanish colonizers intermingled peacefully and harmoniously – an imaginary that not only explicitly excluded the descendants of Afro-Caribbean labor migrants and provided the ideological framework for persisting anti-West Indian sentiment in 20th century Panama but also glorified the Spanish colonial past (Pulido Ritter, "Lord Cobra" 3).

---

43 "Materno Vasquez nos señala las consecuencias sociales .... '1. La formación de nuevos grupos poblacionales a) los 'zonians' blancos y b) los 'zonians' negros sin emoción de patria. Grupos estos de un contexto espiritual anti-nacional; 2. La intromisión de la más odiosa discriminación racial en contra de los panameños; 3. Las agresiones culturales principalmente contra la pureza del idioma español.'" (Lowe 26).

44 "...sorpresivamente irrumpen en el escenario de la discusión una tendencia que pretende introducir, casi a golpe de martillo, en las bases cuturales panameñas un nuevo elemento definido como las aportaciones del Afro-antillano en la conformación del ser nacional" (Materno Vásquez, 83).

6.2 Afro-Caribbean Transnationalism and the Boundaries of *panameñidad* —— **177**

Defining the demarcation lines of *panameñidad* as a variant of western culture, Materno Vásquez holds that its "most important distinguishing features are a national language (Spanish), a Catholic sentiment shared by the vast majority of the population and cultural foundations throughout history that are part of the folklore, lifestyles, attitudes towards imperialist aggressions, traditions and national customs, all of which have shaped the idiosyncrasy of the Panamanian being" ("La nacionalidad panameña" 83).[45] In his article, Laurenza attacks Lowe and Smith for their "prejudices and despotic opinions" , which according to him manifest "a violent hostility to the Hispanic ...tradition that prevails in Panama" (102).[46] According to Laurenza, the Panamanian nation was the product of the harmonious interweaving of "indios, negros y españoles" in which "as is natural, the most powerful and best culturally provided element will prevail and its ideologies —values, forms, and style – will be the hegemonic one" (108).[47] Importantly, both authors portray blacks who have been in Panama since the colonial era, the so-called *afro-coloniales*, as an integral part of this narrative, while *afro-antillanos*, who arrived on Panamanian soil centuries later as labor migrants, are only a "very recent product of the Patriotic History" (Materno Vásquez, "La nacionalidad panameña" 92).[48] Laurenza holds the same view, stating that *afro-coloniales* "are Panamanians in their own right" while "the others" only aspire to be so in the political aspect, while "preserving other customs that they call their 'culture'" (103).[49]

---

45 "Definitivamente ya somos una nación y por ello con toda propiedad podemos teorizar sobre la panameñidad como una variante de la cultura occidental. Variante cultural cuyos rasgos distintivos más importantes lo constituyen una lengua nacional (el español), un sentimiento católico compartido por la inmensa mayoría de la población y basamentos culturales a lo largo de la historia integrantes del folklore, los estilos de vida, las actitudes frente a las agresiones imperialistas, las tradiciones y costumbres nacionales, elementos todos estos que han conformado la idiosincrasia del ser panameño" (Materno Vásquez, "La nacionalidad panameña" 83).

46 "[...] manifiesta una violenta hostilidad por lo hispánico o, mejor dicho, por la tradición de índole iberica y mediterranea que prevalece en Panama[...] rechaza todo intento de inegración cultural" (Laurenza 102).

47 "Clio, la musa de la Historia, tiene en sus manos tres ovillos –indios, negros y españoles – con los que va a tejer la complicada y sútil red de un nuevo pueblo: el panameño. Con todo, algunas hilachas, e importantes, quedarán, aqui y allá, separadas, aunque de manera armónica y siempre incluidas en el todo histórico. Como es natural, ele elemento más poderoso y mejor provisto culturalmente, es el que prevalecerá y sus ideologías –valores, formas, y estilo- será la hegemónica" (Laurenza 108).

48 "...destacar la diferencia existente entre el negro colonial, como formador de la nacionalidad panameña, y el afro-antillano panameño, como producto muy reciente de la Historia Patria" (Materno Vásquez "La nacionalidad panameña" 92).

49 "Los dos grupos poseen un pasado y un presente sobremanera distintos. Unos son panameños a carta cabral y los otros, por propia decisión, según se desprende de los ensayos que aqui se comen-

178 —— 6 Soul vs. *cultura nacional*

The relevance of West Indian contributions to Panamanian culture is neglected, with Laurenza stating that *afro-antillanos* have not introduced any of their customs into the Panamanian customs, "from cooking to dancing (107).[50] Describing Afro-Caribbean English as "un inglés hecho de retazos" ["an English made of snippets"] Laurenza questions *afro-antillanos*' correct command of the English language, stating that they "did not even bring to Panama a language and in fact constituted an element contrary to the learning of correct English" (108).[51]

Doubling down on his thesis that *afro-antillanos* were "anti-national", because "they don't feel Panamanian nationality"[52], Materno Vásquez holds that a range of illustrous Panamanian thinkers agree, that the feeling of nationality is weak among "jamaiquinos, chombos, afro-panameños o 'zonians negros" and that they have made little contributions to national culture ("La nacionalidad panameña" 87).[53] Hinting at "high rates of crime and proletarianisation, and their reluctant avoidance of coexistence and acceptance of our value systems", Materno Vásquez cites Panamanian historian Alfredo Castillero Calvo who wrote that "they appear embedded as a foreign body nucleated in a constellation of urban 'islands' slightly walled against foreign influence" and that their "problems of adaptation have been further aggravated by the increasing gravitation of recent generations towards the United States, whose cultural model has replaced the Victorian British pattern without difficulty" (87).[54] Materno Vásquez dismisses Lowe's and

---

tan, sólo aspiran a serlo en el aspecto político, somo si se dijera una especia de extranjeros que votan y que tienen derecho a puestos de elección, conservando en las demás costumbres que ellos llaman su 'cultura'" (Laurenza 103).

50 "Hasta donde alcanza mi información, los afroantillanos no han introducido ninguna de sus costumbres en las panameñas, desde la culinaria al baile" (Laurenza 107).

51 "...el afroantillano sometido al dominio inglés ...no dominó la lengua colonial y no pudo, en consecuencia, convertirla en instrumento de su más profunda intimidad. Los afroantillanos no trayeron a Panamá ni siquiera una lengua y de hecho constituyeron un elemento contrario al aprendizaje del inglés correcto. En verdad, trabajo me cuesta comprrender lo que Lowe de Ocran y Smith Fernández entienden por 'aporte cultural'" (Laurenza 108).

52 "...adoptan actitudes antinacionales porque no sienten la nacionalidad panameña" (Materno Vásquez, "La nacionalidad panameña" 87).

53 "Las indagaciones sobre el ser panameño ha merecido la dedicación intelectual de mentes muy cumbreras del pensamiento panameño. Y es sorprendente que entre toda esa pléyade de ilustres escritores haya coincidencia en la tesis de que este grupo minoritario que indistintamente se denomina jamaiquinos, chombos, afro-panameños o 'zonians negros', es muy débil el sentimiento de nacionalidad y que poco es la aportación que han hecho a la cultura nacional." (Materno Vásquez 87).

54 Materno Vásquez quoting Alfredo Castillero Calvo: "...aparecen incrustados como un cuerpo extraño nucleado en una constelación de 'islas' urbanas ligeramente amuralladas contra las influencias extrañas. Este aislamiento físico, agravado por la barrera del idioma y la divergencia de pa-

Smith's claims for recognition of West Indian culture – "the English language with the particularities they have introduced and the 'Americanized' dances and their idealized cultural values according to the English, North American or African model" – as an attack on national history and and a show of contempt for the values of what he defines as "hombre-tipo-panameño" as a product of the integration of the indigenous, *afro-colonial* and Spanish-Creole ancestors (ibid.).[55] According to Materno, it is West Indians' strong identification with foreign cultures, from the U.S. specifically, which proves that their allegiance to the nation is to be questioned. Laurenza synthesizes this line of thought claiming:

> Panamá debe evitar su anglosajonanización, el pochismo y la miaminización, envolviéndose en su lengua española y adentrándose cada vez más en su alma iberoamericana. Lo contrario, es abrir una grieta en la nacionalidad, grieta por la que el inglés afroantillano serviría al inglés de Washington de "quinta columna", arrastrando consigo una marteria política contraria al propósito nacional que es la tarea esencial de los panameños hoy. (115) [56]

Concluding, Laurenza voices the expectation that *afro-antillanos* are "a minority in the process of inexorable disappearance by force of biological fatality", which is why the critique of Lowe and Smith concerning anti-West Indian sentiment lacks any kind of relevance, "an unimportant problem, historically speaking" (116).[57] He holds that "certain folkloric phenomena and certain anachronistic

---

trones culturales ha contribuido de manera decisiva a diferir su integración a la vida nacional, como lo manifiestan, por un lado, sus elevados índices de delincuencia y de proletarización, y por otro su reticente evasión a la convivencia y aceptación de nuestros sistemas de valores. Estas dificultades de adaptación se han venido agravando a tenor de la ascendente gravitación de las últimas promociones generacionales hacia los Estados Unidos, cuyo modelo cultural ha sustituido sindificultad el patrón británico victoriano." (Materno Vásquez 87)

55 "...reclaman, que se les reconozca como elementos culturales que los identifican la lengua inglesa con los modismos particulares que le han introducido al igual que sus bailes 'americanizados' y sus valores culturales idealizados conforme al modelo inglés, norteamericano o africano. Y con sus planteamientos despotrican contra la historia nacional, al igual que denotan un desprecio por las valoraciones caras del hombre-tipo-panameño, producto de la integración de los ancestros indígenas, negro-africano-colonial y el español criollo" (Materno Vásquez 87).

56 "Panama must avoid its Anglo-Saxonization, *pochismo* [the adoption of U.S. American influences] and miaminization, wrapping itself in its Spanish language and going deeper and deeper into its Ibero-American soul. Otherwise, it is to open a crack in the nationality, a crack through which the Afro-Antillean English would serve the English of Washington as a "fifth column", dragging with it a political marteria contrary to the national purpose that is the essential task of Panamanians today." (Laurenza 115).

57 "La llamada integración de los afroantillanos que no hablan espanol es, en realidad, un falso problema. Se trata, en primer lugar, de una minoría en vías de desaparición inexorable por fuerza de la fatalidad biológica.... Un problema sin importancia, hablando históricamente" (Laurenza 116).

180 —— 6 Soul vs. *cultura nacional*

ideas will have their days numbered" because, anything that does not advance "the dignity of man does not deserve to be saved from oblivion. The progress of man is the only thing that counts ... and the rest is silence, miserable dust blown away by the wind of history" (114).[58] Rather than lamenting this process, Lowe and Smith should face reality and accept their inevitable assimilation into the Hispanic culture of the Panamanian homeland and improve their Spanish skills to voice their dreams and hopes, "without fear that such use and refinement could mean the oblivion of other landscapes and musics of the soul" (117).[59]

Laurenza's call on *afro-antillanos* not to care about the possible oblivion of "musics of the soul" in their process of inevitable assimilation indicates how "soul" is understood by the author as a symbol of a counter-hegemonic black identity and an obstacle in the forging of national unity. The aggressive responses to Lowe's and Smith's assertion of Afro-Caribbean self-determination and identification with African American culture and politics indicate that these were seen as unpatriotic acts and manifestations of the degrading effects of U.S. cultural imperialism on Panamanian national identity. Informed by soul and Black Power, Lowe and Smith had challenged dominant narratives according to which Panama was a bastion of tolerance and freedom for all races, in ways that could apparently not be tolerated.

In their essays, Laurenza and Materno Vásquez portray the Afro-Caribbean community and its cultural expressions as foreign bodies in the Panamanian nation, following a long tradition of Panamanian intellectuals negating Panama's hybrid and cosmopolitan character, which manifested itself especially in the transnational urban contact zones inhabited by black immigrants. As Luis Pulido Ritter describes in his analysis of the "nación romántica," a national discourse that understands Panama as a homogeneous entity of Spanish tradition, culture, and language, the transnationalism represented by the Canal and the Caribbean immigrants was conceived as an alien that was detached from the original, healthy and Hispanic body of the nation ("Modernidad" 13). In this context, Caribbean immigration and the heterogeneous influences it brought to Panama represent a hostile force of modernization that threatens traditions understood as genuinely Panamanian in language and culture: "El negro de origen antillano, aunque éste es

---

58 "Claro está que ciertos fenómenos folklóricos y ciertas ideas anacrónicas tendrán sus días contados... mas ¡que importa! Lo que no añada a la dignidad del hombre, no merece salvarse del olvido. El progreso del hombre es lo único que cuenta ... y lo demás es silencio, polvo miserable que se lleva el viento de la historia" (Laurenza 114).

59 "Afinen, pues, y acrezcan su dominio del mismo para plasmar sus sueños y decir sus esperanzas, sin temor de que tal uso y refinement signifique el olvido de otros paisajes y músicas del alma" (Laurenza 117).

6.2 Afro-Caribbean Transnationalism and the Boundaries of *panameñidad* — **181**

quien la ha marcado más con su presencia, especialmente, en las ciudades de Panamá y Colón, no ha sido parte de esa idea de nación romántica que se levanta en oposición a dicha transnacionalidad" (23).[60]

Challenging these narrow and nationalist notions of *panameñidad,* the *combos nacionales* gave new visibility to a formerly silenced and demonized aspect of the national reality: the strong presence of Afro-Caribbean influences in a multiethnic, diasporic, transnational and cosmopolitan Panamanian society. By using the metaphor of a popular local soup in which a great variety of ingredients have their place, Afro-Panamanian scholar Armando Fortune introduced the concept of Panama as a *sancocho,* understood as an inclusive *"mestizaje* from below" as opposed to the essentialist and exclusionary *crisol de razas* discourse, making the case for finally acknowledging the contributions of Afrodescendants, who had built the Canal to which the Panamanian republic owed its very existence. (Pulido Ritter, "Panamá es un sancocho'" 10). In his study of Afro-Panamanian popular culture, Peter Szok has argued that foreign influences from "Black Atlantic culture" have triggered a process of "re-Africanization" among black Panamanians, native and West Indian, who "demonstrated little interest in creating essentialist notions about the past but instead have focused on the formation of a contemporary sense of blackness, drawing strength from things as rumba, Afro-Brazilian soccer stars, reggae, hip-hop, and soul music. [...] Especially among younger generations, who look to the present for their inspiration, these foreign elements have offered a viable means of strengthening blackness in Latin America [...]" (8).

Whereas most interviewed *combos* musicians saw themselves as artists and not as activists, the music they played and the black aesthetics they helped to popularize had significant political implications for the anti-racist struggle in Panama, as Alberto Barrow claims:

> Claro ellos no estaban en la cosa política, pero obviamente lo que hacían tenía un sentido. Ellos estaban en la música pero ellos usaban afro. Quizás no elaboraban sobre la conexión, pero por qué usaban afro? Si te dicen que fue nada más que una moda, asumamos que era una moda que tenía un sentido. Aunque no sean consciente de ello, ellos no pueden desconectarlo. Mientras ellos tocaban sus congas y cantaban música soul, la policía estaba correteando a negros para cortarles el cabello. (Barrow)[61]

---

60 "Blacks of Caribbean descent, although they are the ones who have marked it most with their presence, especially in the cities of Panama and Colón, have not been part of this idea of a romantic nation that stands in opposition to transnationality" (Pulido Ritter, "Modernidad en movimiento" 23).

61 "Of course they were not in the political thing, but obviously what they were doing had a meaning. They were into music but they used Afro. Maybe they didn't elaborate on the connection, but why did they wear Afro? If they tell you it was nothing more than a fashion trend, let's assume it

The versatility by which the *combos* switched between African American, Afro-Caribbean and Afro-Latin American styles not only troubled homogenizing notions of a Hispanic mestizo nation, it also helped to forge integration between Panama's two black communities that had been pitted against each other in the discourse of nationalists such as Materno Vásquez and Laurenza: *afro-antillanos* and *afro-coloniales*. *Combos* such as The Exciters, The Silvertones, Los Mozambiques, and Los Soul Fantastics were integrated by members of both formerly antagonized communities and released sounds that were the product of hybridity and cross-fertilization. These processes questioned the nationalist idea of assimilation in which the Anglophone minority group had to adapt to the customs and traditions of the host nation, and forget about other "musics of the soul" (Laurenza 117). While African American influences were particularly strong among *afro-antillanos*, the Afro also became popular among Hispanic Afro-Panamanians and both, black and white Panamanians, were into soul music – even more so when it was performed in Spanish as in Little Francisco Greaves' "Necia de mi corazón" and many other Latin soul releases that followed. In the same vein, Afro-Caribbean musicians like Francisco "Bush" Buckley, who became Panama's leading salsa performer in the 1970s, demonstrated that specific musical skills were not a matter of biological roots but rather a result of the sociohistorical conditions that enabled interethnic transculturation. These processes heralded developments in Panama's black movement which has also been guided by the goal of overcoming cleavages between Hispanic and Caribbean-descended Afro-Panamanians and forge unity in their struggles against persistent forms of anti-black racism in Panama. As Carlos Castro noted on the role of the combos for integration:

> La música de los combos nacionales ayudó mucho a la integración de la población afroantillana al contexto nacional por medio de la música. La música sirvió de puente para destruir muchas de esas concepciones racistas que dividían el negro antillano, del negro criollo, el negro que habla español, él que es chombo, que habla inglés. Los combos nacionales una de funciones positivas es que sirve de elemento de integración de la comunidad afro. (*personal interview*)[62]

---

was a fashion trend that had a meaning. Even if they are not aware of it, they can't disconnect it. While they were playing their congas and singing soul music, police was running around cutting black people's hair" (Barrow).

62 "The music of the *combos nacionales* helped a lot in the integration of the Afro-Caribbean population to the national context through music. The music served as a bridge to destroy many of those racist conceptions that divided the Caribbean black, the Creole black, the black that speaks Spanish, the one that is chombo, the one that speaks English. One of the positive functions of the national combos is that it serves as an element of integration of the Afro community" (Castro, *personal interview*).

The imperial project of the Panama Canal not only bridged two oceans and paved the way for the rise of the U.S. as a global power. It also brought contradicting forms of racial oppression and anti-racist responses into contested dialogues. The crossing and non-crossing of racialized boundaries has been the overarching theme of these interactions. While the two involved state actors repeatedly engaged in efforts to prevent people and ideas from crossing boundaries – the U.S. trying to keep Panamanians out of the Canal Zone and blacks behind the color line; Panamanian nationalists denying West Indians first-class citizenship and struggling against African American influences – the Afrodescendant peoples affected by these policies consistently explored the emancipatory potential of engaging in border-crossing dialogues and movements as manifested in practices of black transnationalism that developed between and within both communities. The parallel struggles against Jim Crow segregation in the Canal Zone and the U.S., and exclusive Panamanian nationalism based on *mestizaje* discourses reinforced transnational identification and solidarity between Panamanians of West Indian descent and African Americans.

6.3 Black Rio: Soul as a Threat to National Security and *democracia racial*

Until the mid-1970s, Brazil's national media hadn't paid any attention to what was perceived as another short-lived dance craze of Rio's black youth without any political connotations. An article published in July 1976 by journalist Lena Frias in the national magazine *Jornal do Brasil* changed things. It was a five-page dossier titled "Black Rio – O orgulho (importado) de ser negro no Brasil" ["The (imported) pride of being black in Brasil"], which not only gave name to the movement formerly known as *Black Soul*, but also portrayed it as a cheap intent of Brazilian blacks to imitate their "cousins from Harlem" (1), arguing that Black Rio was "un-Brazilian" because of introducing racial hatred to a country where racism didn't exist (ibid.). In the aftermath of the Frias article, a heated national debate on the perils of Black Rio evolved.

Gilberto Freyre, whose *Casa Grande e Senzala* (1933) had laid the foundations for Brazilian *democracia racial* discourse, participated in the debate. In an article from 1976, titled "Atenção, brasileiros", he warned of the threat African American influences from the U.S. posed to Brazil's national security as well as to national identity. According to Freyre, Black Rio was the intent to import a foreign and hostile ideology which introduced U.S. style racial hatred to a country where members of all races co-existed peacefully, and racial belonging did not matter. He cautioned Afro-Brazilians to be aware of "americanos de cor" [Americans of color] from the

North, who had allegedly come to Brazil on a secret mission to make them abandon their happy and fraternal samba rhythms for sounds of melancholy and revolt from the U.S. (Hanchard, *Orpheus and Power* 115).

The dismissive reactions against soul and Black Rio from representatives of the nationalist right-wing military regime and leftist intellectuals alike proved that "Soul trampled on a long-cherished contrast at the heart of Brazilian national identity: racist United States versus racially tolerant Brazil," as Paulina Alberto acknowledges (20). The Black Rio debate exposed how the politics of racial comparison with the U.S. were crucial to the construction of *democracia racial* as a nationalist Brazilian identity discourse. According to the anti-imperialist perspective of Brazilian intellectuals which dismissed the alienated, colonialized character of those Brazilian cultural productions which were based on foreign models, the diffusion of soul from the United States among Afro-Brazilian youth represented a hostile penetration of authentic national *culturas populares* (Alberto 20). In line with this ideology, popularized under the regime of Getúlio Vargas in the 1930s and 1940s, the predominantly white critics from the left and the right agreed that the militancy and black assertiveness related to Black Rio was totally out of place in a "paraíso racial" like Brazil. They declared Afro-Brazilians dancing to imported soul music as lacking any kind of authenticity and alien to the cherished folkloristic expressions of *brasilidade*, as represented in nationalized Afro-Brazilian forms as carnival, samba, and capoeira (Alberto 20).

After its coup against the democratically elected government of João Goulart in 1964, the military regime had increased efforts to portray Brazil internationally as a vanguard country in terms of interracial coexistence – a policy for which the appropriation of Afro-Brazilian culture, as a sign of national unity, was crucial. The strictly apolitical and traditionalist celebration of black culture adopted by the national elites contrasted sharply with the U.S.-inspired politicized notions of defiant blackness as featured in Black Rio (Hanchard, *Orpheus and Power* 114). As a consequence, the *bailes black,* as large congregations of Afro-Brazilians exposed to the subversive influences of rebellious blacks from the North, were increasingly treated as a matter of national security. Anxious about the consequences of a raised awareness on matters of racial discrimination and the inspiration of black people revolting against their sociopolitical marginalization, the military regime unleashed its repressive apparatus on the movement in the late 1970s. Secret police documents of the notorious *Departamento da Ordem Política e Social* (DOPS) have been found, which prove that the Black Rio movement was under surveillance because of allegations of using foreign money from U.S. black nationalist organizations for subversive activities directed at instigating a race war in Brazil, the *bailes black* constituting their major recruitment base (Pedretti). In an intelligence report, a secret agent commented that "a group of black youngsters with high intellectual level is being created in Rio, which intends to generate a climate of hostility between whites and blacks ... led by a black American who controls the money that seems to arrive from outside, possibly from the United States" (qtd. in Medeiros, "Black Rio" 246). Other documents contained observations that the Black Rio participants "get inspiration from the Black Panthers from the United States" and that "the radicals are promoting a recruitment campaign among the Soul Club habitues" (ibid.) From 1975 on, the police started to crack down heavily on the movement, infiltrating it with secret agents, frequently raiding soul parties and arresting organizers and DJs, as was the case with Dom Filó and members of the soundsystem *Black Power* who were interrogated due to allegations of having been financed by a "negro americano" in order to launch a clandestine resistance movement (Oliveira).

Whereas the main preoccupation of conservative nationalists and the military rulers was Black Rio's subversive potential, the repudiation of the Brazilian left was based on their anti-imperialist ideology, which did not allow them to see U.S. influences as anything but a hostile penetration of national cultures. In the years prior to the coup, leftist intellectuals at the *Instituto Superior de Estudos Brasileiros* had developed a discourse of "alienation vs. authenticity" for categorizing contemporary cultural productions. They criticized the alienated, colonialized character of those Brazilian cultural productions which were based on imitating foreign models – a critique, which already had been directed against the avant-garde Tropicalía movement for its playful blending of local genres with foreign influences as rock, jazz, and soul. From this perspective, which was hegemonic in Brazil's left throughout the 1970s, Black Rio was a classic case of U.S. cultural imperialism, destined to undermine a revolutionary class consciousness among the black working-class and to destroy authentic *cultura popular* as represented by samba. Furthermore, the distribution of soul music was depicted as part of a neo-colonial publicity campaign for securing new markets in the periphery (Alberto 20). To leftist critics, Black Rio "represented a betrayal of Brazil's true cultural patrimony by people of color who, embracing foreign Soul instead of national samba, were shirking their duties as cheerful caretakers of an appropriate, authentic Afro-Brazilian heritage" (28), as Paulina Alberto notes.

In their nationalist rejection of U.S. influences, no difference was made between Washington's imperial foreign policy towards the Latin American "backyard" and the impact of counterhegemonic black liberation movements from the U.S. The leftists' critique of Brazil's soul movement was articulated by the journalist Roberto Moura in his "Carta aberta ao Black-Rio Instituto Superior de Estudos Brasileiros" [Open letter to Black Rio], in which he denounced Black Rio as "an insidious neocolonialist advertising campaign, aimed only at creating a subject to consume the surplus of an outside production. [...] It is clear that this social cluster

186 — 6 Soul vs. *cultura nacional*

is not thinking; it's being thought. From the outside in. If suddenly comes an order stimulating them to wear some other kind of clothing, they will take off the jacket and weird shoes" (qtd. in Medeiros, "Black Rio", 247).

In its hostility toward U.S. Black Power influences on Rios's black youth, Brazil's anti-imperialist left, antiracist by self-definition, manifested a deep paternalism regarding the Afro-Brazilian community and its cultural productions. Under the guise of progressive politics, much of the Brazilian left defended the *democracia racial* myth of Brazil as a country without racism in which only class differences mattered, shedding light on the persistence of racist hierarchies in contemporary Brazil (Stam and Shohat 113–117, 183 ff.). The white-dominated Brazilian left's neglect of black issues mirrored the failure of traditional Marxist movements and parties in other multiethnic societies to acknowledge the specific patterns of race-based discrimination – an omission which proved to be a decisive factor for the emergence of new social movements in the African diaspora from the 1970s on (Mullings).

The reactions to Michael Hanchard's pioneering study *Orpheus and Power* (1994) in which he also explores the significance of soul music and Black Power on black consciousness movements in Brazil, reveal the salience of anti-Afro-Americanism in the hostility towards practices of black transnationalism in Latin America which are equated with U.S. imperialism. In the essay "On the Cunning of Imperialist Reason" (1999), French sociologists Pierre Bourdieu and Loic Waquant accused Hanchard of acting as an agent of imperialism, arguing that *Orpheus and Power* represented a "brutal ethnocentric intrusion" (88) of U.S. concepts of race into a racially tolerant Brazilian context and therefore a manifesto of the "Mcdonaldization" of the local debates. In the same vein, Brazilian anthropologist José Jorge de Carvalho argues that transnational approaches to blackness in the Americas disregard global power relations and reproduce the neocolonial dominance of the Anglo-Saxon world over Africa, Latin America and the the Caribbean by cementing the hegemonic role of Anglophone African American intellectuals and artists:

> Aun cuando el Harlem sea un ghetto de la ciudad de Nueva York, la cultura popular allí generada se globaliza a través del circuito norteamericano de los medios y afecta las comunidades negras de América Latina y el Caribe del mismo modo neocolonial con que la cultura occidentalizante hollywoodiana nos afecta a todos, blancos y negros, en nuestro países. [...] hay una dimensión en la cual se unen Hollywood y la cultura afroamericana. (Carvalho 15–16).[63]

---

63 ["Even if Harlem is a New York City ghetto, the popular culture generated there is globalized through the North American media circuit and affects the black communities of Latin America and

This essentializing perspective contrasted progressive Latin American societies with the United States as a monolithic bloc, the imperialist, racist and homogenizing Other, from which a sharp demarcation was necessary in order to preserve national self-determination. In this worldview African Americans were not seen as voices of a counter-discourse but as compliant agents in the imperialist contamination of autochthonous folk cultures in the Third World.

6.4 Analyzing Soul in Latin American Contexts

The hemispheric dissemination of soul and its implications for local Afro-Latin American identity constructions and anti-racist movements was by no means a uniform process. Rather, it was strongly shaped by locally, nationally, culturally, linguistically, socially, and historically divergent conditions and constellations. The emergence of Latin boogaloo was the product of the "alliance of survival" (Torres 3) that the coexistence of African Americans and children of Puerto Rican immigrants in the most socially and racially excluded neighborhoods of New York had produced – and accordingly was strongly shaped by U.S.-specific racial and social configurations that placed Latino immigrants of color and African Americans on the same lowest rung of the social pyramid. In Panama, on the other hand, the popularization of soul was the result of the emergence of a contact zone between Afro-Caribbean migrant communities and African American popular culture that had resulted from the construction of the Panama Canal and the establishment of a U.S.-occupied zone – a connection that was reinforced by the emergence of a transnational Afro-Caribbean Panamanian migrant community in New York. The Rio soul scene, unlike the other two cases, was not based on the direct encounter of diasporic subjects, but rather on the transnational dissemination and commercialization of U.S. cultural products. Although the conditions were very different in many respects, there were also various striking parallels in the reception history of soul at the three locations, which will be examined in the following.

The connection between the popularization of soul and the role of the United States as a society based on racial stratification on the inside and as the hegemonic power of the Western hemisphere on the outside represents a significant factor in the emergence of a inter-American soul movement, both in terms of the genesis of soul as a form of expression of the African American community and its intereth-

---

the Caribbean in the same neocolonial way that the Westernizing Hollywood culture affects all of us, black and white, in our countries. [...] there is a dimension in which Hollywood and Afro-American culture are united."] (Carvalho 15 f.).

nic, translocal, and transnational diffusion through migrations from the periphery to the metropolis, imperial construction projects to reinforce dominance in the region and the world, and the global penetration of the U.S. music industry in marketing its products. The interrelatedness of the diffusion of soul and U.S. capitalism and imperialism also explains, partly, another parallel that has come to light in analyzing the importance of soul for nationalist identity and new constructions of *afrolatinidad:* whenever soul spread in Afro-Latin American contexts, it was resoundingly rejected as a manifestation of U.S. cultural imperialism by local elites and intellectuals, from both the right and left spectrums. Under the pretext that soul was undermining authentic national cultures as a kind of "fifth column" (Laurenza) of the United States, its rejection was presented as part of the resistance to the neocolonial dominance of the U.S. empire. Widespread anti-U.S.-Americanism in much of Latin American societies, which had its roots in the actual role of Cold War-influenced U.S. foreign policy in supporting radical right-wing military dictatorships and suppressing left-wing and nationalist Latin American movements, can, however, only partially explain the hostility against soul.

Another, equally central reason lay in the specific Latin American racial regimes that, based on nationalist discourses of identity such as *mestizaje, democracia racial, crisol de razas* or *latinidad,* which claimed that racism was an exclusive problem of the United States while celebrating harmonious race relations in Latin America. In fact, the polarization of U.S. society on the basis of race served as a cautionary example to highlight the exemplary interethnic relations in the Latin American nations. This explains why Latin American nationalists were particularly sensitive to the reception of new black identity discourses formulated in the context of the Civil Rights and Black Power movements of the 1960s and 1970s which spread beyond U.S. borders through soul. Since the translation of soul was also accompanied by the appropriation of the aesthetic representations of blackness conveyed through this genre, an identification with the African American freedom struggle and, last but not least, a thematization of racism in Latin American contexts, the popularization of soul was perceived as a threat to the established regimes of racial subordination based on a concealment of racism and the tabooing of the affirmation of black identity.

As Afro-Latin American youth identified with a foreign movement which was perceived as an expression of black separatism shaped by U.S. racism, the popularization of soul also posed a threat to national unity and harmonious race relations in the eyes of its critics. Under the regime of Brazil's military dictatorship, fears that the influence of Black Power might incite local youth to militant resistance, following the example of their U.S. counterparts, led repressive organs of the state treat soul *bailes black* as a matter of national security. The police repression campaign against black Panamanians with an Afro youth under the Torrijos regime also showed the extent to which these influences were perceived as a threat. Deep-rooted forms of fear, distrust, and racism that characterize the relationship of Latin American societies to their black populations were hidden behind the façade of anti-imperialism directed against all political and cultural influences from the United States. In this sense, anti-Afro-Americanism, the resentment against U.S. black expressions, ideologies, and symbols, became a central modality of anti-black racism in Latin America.

Soul also challenged an essential element of Latin American *mestizaje* discourses that consisted in the paternalism with which Afro-Latin American musical traditions were assigned the role of folkloric representations of authentic national cultures. While the celebration of African retentions and traditions was officially accepted and often encouraged in this context, exchanges with other diasporic communities in the Americas, particularly African Americans, were rejected. By turning away from these traditions to the decidedly non-traditionalist and modern genre of soul, young people confirmed, in the eyes of many guardians of "authentic" folk cultures, the danger that this new form posed to national identity.

It is precisely because soul in many ways represented a break with homogenizing *mestizaje* and *latinidad* ideologies and the related traditionalist stereotypes that the genre has been so attractive to Afrodescendants throughout the Americas. The symbolic appropriation of U.S. forms of blackness as manifested in the consumption and translation of soul music and soul style provided diasporic youth movements with a means to break with dominant paternalistic and folkloristic identity concepts – and to articulate dissent against the neglected forms of Latin American racism. The empowering impulse of soul was significant for the formation of anti-racist movements and the emergence of inter-American networks of solidarity which connected formerly isolated Afro-Latin American communities with other sites of the African diaspora in their struggles for human rights. Practical and symbolical alliances between Afro-Latin Americans and African Americans in hemispheric sites of transculturation as Panama, Rio, or New York undermined homogenizing and nationalist discourses of *mestizaje*, as they foregrounded shared Afro-diasporic experiences of marginalization and resistance instead of the nation as identity framework.

This was of particular importance for migrant communities such as West Indians in Panama and Puerto Ricans in New York. Due to the different forms of xenophobia, racism, and nationalism they faced in the countries they lived in, identifying with African Americans, who were also excluded, provided an alternative reference. Soul functioned as an important platform for the creation of interethnic alliances in both contexts. This was also true for overcoming language barriers. Both Spanish-speaking Puerto Ricans in the United States and Anglophone Afro-Caribbeans in Panama were subject to forms of linguistic discrimination. Bridges were established via the bilingual Latin soul productions that emerged in both contexts, demonstrating soul's inclusive potential. While in the New York context Latin boogaloo songs in Spanish and English intonated the dialogues between Nuyoricans and African Americans, in Panama it was the bilingual *combos nacionales* productions that reflected the overcoming of divisions and resentments between Anglophone and Hispanophone Afro-Panamanians. In the light of persistent mechanisms of exclusion based on Eurocentric notions of national identity, these processes represented an integration from below in which soul music enhanced collaboration and exchange with other diasporic groups on the basis of shared experiences with different forms of white supremacy: in New York between Puerto Rican migrants and African Americans, in Panama between the descendants of Caribbean immigrants and native Panamanians.

By encouraging the assumption of afro-diasporic identifications as an alternative to the hegemonic nationalist and folkloristic identity discourses, the border-crossing dissemination of soul contributed to the emergence of new hemispheric constructions of *afrolatinidad.* As was evident from the mid-1970s onward, dialogues with African American culture through soul were a major impetus for the proliferation of transnational genres such as reggae, salsa, and hip-hop, the growth of Afro-Latin American cultural and political movements throughout the region. Panama's *combos nacionales,* the emergence of Latin soul-boogaloo in New York City and the rise of an Afro-Brazilian soul movement in 1970s Rio, underline the pivotal role of black popular music in the forging of inter-ethnic alliances and the practice of hemispheric black transnationalism.

Conclusion

Following the traces of soul from its origins in urban black America to its popularization among Caribbean migrants in New York and Panama and Rio de Janeiro's Afro-Brazilian youth, it has become clear that the emergence and transnational dissemination of this musical form was closely linked to the anti-authoritarian, anti-colonial, and anti-racist struggles and the key role of U.S. countercultures that shaped the long global 1960s. The synchronicity that existed between the popularization of soul and the height of the African American freedom struggle in the United States and the interrelatedness between the transnationalization of the genre and the rise of Black Power-inspired articulations abroad suggest a congruence between music and movement. A hemispheric look at the historical relationship between musical form and sociopolitical articulation has shown that in the United States, soul music rather responded to and reflected on social changes such as the shift from Civil Rights to Black Power and the new expressions of black consciousness and militancy, while in contexts such as Spanish Harlem, Panama, and Rio de Janeiro, it was soul music itself that often provided crucial impetus for the formation of new movements. The border-crossing appeal of "soul" was related to the way it was embraced by Afrodescendants across the region not only as a musical genre but also as signifier for black achievement, resilience, and solidarity in the face of white supremacy and social exclusion. As activists in the United States, the Caribbean, and Latin America saw the mobilizing potential of soul, they tried to make use of the genre in their efforts to organize the anti-racist struggle. While soul had significance beyond entertainment in all contexts, the implications and debates surrounding its popularization, its relationship to blackness and its role as a product of U.S. popular culture were heavily shaped by the specifities of the local and national settings in which these processes took place, hinting at the use of a transnational and comparative perspective in the analysis of the form.

In the United States, black cultural nationalists, initially critical of the commercialist Western popular culture associated with soul, laid claims on the genre as "poetry of the Black revolution". With soul singers like James Brown and songs like "Say It Loud – I'm Black and I'm proud", the ideals and aesthetic symbols of black pride and masculinity propagated by black nationalists gained an unprecedented public stage and popularity. The intersections between soul and essentialized notions of blackness led a number of proponents of a Post-Soul Aesthetic, to interpret soul as a kind of synonym for those forms of narrow nationalism, ethnic particularism, and masculinism that needed to be overcome in the sense of a liberation from its limitations and homogenizing identity ascriptions. As has become clear throughout this study, soul was, however, very much like the Black Power

https://doi.org/10.1515/9783110665550-009

movement it rose in unison with, much more heterogeneous and flexible than the binary juxtapositions of both black cultural nationalist as well as Post-Soul interpretations were able to capture. Like Black Power, soul was often portrayed as a manifestation of black separatism, when in fact, the appeal of both, the movement and the genre, transcended the African American community and served as a platform for transnational and interethnic collaboration. Sylviane Diouf and Komozi Woodard argued that wherever "youth were denied full citizenship or where governments questioned their very humanity, activists claimed the language of Black Power in the fight for their human rights" (x) – a statement that also holds true for soul music which was, as is argued here, one of the languages through which Black Power reached other constituencies.

A closer look at the heterogeneous messages and meanings of soul for African American women, entertainers, activists, immigrants from Latin America and the Caribbean, as well as communities of color beyond U.S. borders has shown that both the romanticizing interpretation of soul as the ultimate expression of Black America united in a struggle against the U.S. white power structure as well as its dismissal as a symbol of retrograde black separatism fall short. Various scholars have already contributed anti-essentialist interpretations that point to the complex character of soul as a genre and discourse through which the historical-social conditionality of black struggles, but also intra-black differences are negotiated. Most of these approaches have been, however, limited by a U.S.-centered nation-based methodology. Inspired by the impetus of the recent decades to overcome national exceptionalisms and divisions between research areas, toward the transnationalization of African American Studies and the inclusion of hemispheric perspectives in the growing field of African Diaspora Studies, this study has attempted to take up these approaches and focus on some of the gaps in research on soul. In this spirit, this book has been guided by the intention to provide further insights into the multilayered dimensions of soul as a genre and a concept that harbored commercialist, patriarchal, essentialist, and nationalist tendencies at the same time as it was working-class, feminist, universalist, transnational, diasporic, and cosmopolitan.

Wherever soul emerged, it became a site of contestation on the meanings of race. As the language and aesthetics of soul were closely related, though not identical, to the rise of black nationalism in the 1960s, the hemispheric perspective adopted here has also provided new insights into the different implications of blackness in the Americas. As the popularization of Black Power through the consumption and translation of soul has shown, some elements of black nationalism, such as black group-solidarity and the affirmation of ethnic pride, have proven to be adaptable in other contexts. The border-crossing networks of solidarity that were forged through these flows hint at the fact that ideas of black nationalism were not diametrically opposed to but rather closely interrelated with the practice of black internationalism. Following Appadurai's model of ethno-, media-, and ideoscapes, the mobility associated with *hemispheric soulscapes* enabled the transnational dissemination of black nationalist imaginaries, contributing to emergence of "diasporic public spheres."

These processes were by no means unidirectional or homogenous imitations of the U.S. model. Rather, the dynamics in each of the soul scenes under scrutiny were shaped significantly by specific historical, social, cultural and racial configurations, hinting at the fluidity and flexibility of soul and blackness addressed in Hanson's concept of "aural blackness". The emancipatory potential of soul lay precisely in its capacity to cross imperial, national, ethnic, cultural, and linguistic boundaries and serve as a tool for the articulation of dissent with the status quo in the most diverse locations. This became especially apparent in Latin American contexts where soul music defied essentialist and folkloristic attributions about what national cultures had to represent. The translation of this foreign form and the associated cosmopolitan practices of appropriating symbols and discourses from abroad and developing a sense of belonging to a transnational community were crucial in the intersecting struggles of Afrodescendants and Caribbean migrants for self-determination across the Americas.

Underscoring the contradictory and multidimensional character of both, soul and Black Power, its transnational diffusion was often related to the adoption of essentialized notions of blackness related to U.S. black nationalism while at the same time evidencing a hybrid and flexible approach to racial and national identity. While the positive assertion of black identity propagated by soul in the face of anti-black racism was a central reason for its popularity among Afrodescendants from across the hemisphere, the spread of soul among Caribbean immigrants in New York and Panama also revealed its anti-essentialist and inclusive dimensions. In both contexts, bilingual soul became an important medium of integration through which minorities discriminated on the basis of language entered into dialogue with other marginalized groups. In this sense, it is also worth noting that some of the protagonists of New York Latin soul, such as Joe Cuba, Joey Pastrana, Ray Barretto, and Pete Rodriguez, were non-black Nuyoricans who embraced African American culture through soul. In Panama, the *combos nacionales* contributed to the overcoming of divisions between Caribbean and native black communities. As the research has shown, the encounters of migrants as translocal actors played a central role in the translation of discourses and musical forms from one context to another, reflected, for example, in the emergence of collaborations between Nuyoricans and Afro-Panamanians in the Afro-Latin soul scenes of New York and Panama. Thus, the mobility of soul enabled Black Power symbols and slogans to travel to other localities where they were employed for different, locally specific means, connecting diverse formerly separated populations with the idioms and expressions of the African American freedom struggle in defiance of Latin American nationalisms – a practice that I have defined as Black Power cosmopolitanism.

This confluence of two at first glance mutually exclusive philosophies – Black Power as an assertion of black particularity and cosmopolitanism as the universal idea of the equality of all people as citizens of the world – is based on theories of black cosmopolitanism as a cosmoplitanism from below that acknowledge the rootedness of global struggles against inequality in local traditions of resistance and thus understands mobilizations based on shared experiences of racism not as a counterpart but as an elementary part of a universal struggle for freedom. The urban contact zones studied here were sites of diverse manifestations of a diasporic cosmopolitanism in which different racialized and migrant communities interacted with each other on the basis of shared experiences of exclusion, thereby gaining an understanding that their identities were shaped less by biological origin and national identity than by intersecting race-, class-, and gender-based mechanisms of oppression. The flexible appropriation of various elements of other cultures and movements, as demonstrated by the emergence of Afro-Latin Soul, unfolded its liberating potential by evading the demands for purity and authenticity formulated by nationalist discourses of identity. Precisely because Afro-Latin Soul was neither pure nor traditional, but hybrid and modern, and thus a provocation of established norms, this form became a "site of resistance" (Winter) and contestatory cosmopolitanism in the various contexts considered.

Thus, this study has demonstrated how the emergence of soul among non-African American groups challenged U.S.-centered notions of the genre as an expression of narrow black nationalism and essentialism, shedding light on the cosmopolitanism of soul. Ironically, when Afro-Panamanians, Afro-Brazilians and Nuyoricans started to follow the latest soul releases and to produce Afro-Latin soul sounds on their own, they put some of the very aspirations into practice that advocates of the Post-Soul Aesthetic hoped to achieve by overcoming "soul". By participating in a modern, urban, and highly commercialized youth movement from abroad, they "troubled" essentialized and traditionalist notions of Afro-Latin blackness and challenged the racialized expectations in black popular culture in a way that was, in the words of Bertram Ashe, "either unlikely or unseemly in earlier Black artistic eras" (614). By refusing to cherish local folk traditions, be it in Panama, Rio de Janeiro or Spanish Harlem, Afro-Latin American soul dancers and musicians educated themselves by a mix of international and local cultures in the spirit of Ellis' 'new Black aesthetic', demonstrating that "Blackness is constantly in flux" (235). What Greg Tate said about the protagonists of the Post-Soul Aesthetic also holds true for the pioneers of soul in 1960s and 1970s Afro-Latin America: "These are artists for whom Black consciousness and artistic freedom are not mutually exclusive but complementary, for whom 'Black culture' signifies a multicultural tradition of expressive practices" (207).

While the call for a Post-Soul Aesthetic in the United States was related to the wish of overcoming the essentialist constraints of narrow black cultural nationalism, in Latin American contexts it was soul itself which provided dissident voices with the opportunity to opt out of the homogenizing and exclusionary confines of nationalist ideologies such as *mestizaje, latinidad, panameñidad, democracia racial* and the related expressions of anti-Afro-Americanism. The transnational, cosmopolitan, and non-essentialist dimension of soul turned the genre into an attractive alternative to traditionalist, paternalistic and folkloristic notions of national culture in Latin American contexts. Soul served as a platform in the forging of alliances that contributed to the blossoming of anti-racist movements and new hybrid popular music genres throughout Latin America in the 1970s and beyond. The emergence of new notions of *afrolatinidad* was a direct result of these inter-American dialogues.

As the key role of women in the more recent manifestations of *afrolatinidad* demonstrates, the post-soul period in Afro-Latin America also saw important steps toward overcoming the male dominance that characterized the settings considered here in the 1960s and 1970s. Hopefully, future research will devote more attention to the perspectives and experiences of Afro-Latin American women in the music scenes and social movements of this period than this study was able to. A focus on the impact of Black Power discourses and soul styles among Afro-Latinas promises insights that will deepen our understanding of the importance of hemispheric dialogues in the 1960s and 1970s to the emergence of transnational black feminism across the Americas in the decades that followed.

Sources

Works Cited

Alberti, Verena, and Amilcar Araujo Pereira. *Histórias do movimento negro no Brasil.* Rio de Janeiro: Pallas, 2007.

Alberto, Paulina. "When Rio Was Black: Soul Music, National Culture, and the Politics of Racial Comparison in 1970s Brazil." *Hispanic American Historical Review*, vol. 89, no. 1, 2009, 3–39.

Alberto, Paulina, and Jesse Hoffnung-Garskof. "'Racial Democracy' and Racial Inclusion – Hemispheric Histories". *Afro-Latin American Studies – An Introduction*, ed. Alejandro de la Fuente and George Reid Andrews. Cambridge: Cambridge UP, 2018, 264-316.

Almada, Sandra. *Abdias Nascimento – Retratos do Brasil Negro*, São Paulo: Selo Negro, 2009

Alvarez, Luis and Daniel Widener. "Brown-Eyed Soul: Popular Music and Cultural Politics in Los Angeles." *The Struggle in Black and Brown: African American and Mexican American Relations during the Civil Rights Era*, ed. Brian Behnken. Lincoln: University of Nebraska Press, 2011.

Anderson, Benedict. *Imagined communities: reflections on the origin and spread of nationalism,* London. Verso, 1991.

Andrews, George Reid. "Black Movements in Latin America, 1970–2000", *Black Power in Hemispheric Perspective: Movements and Cultures of Resistance in the Black Americas*, eds. Wilfried Raussert and Matti Steinitz, New Orleans and Trier: WVT/New Orleans UP, 2022. 157–172

Andrews, George Reid. *Afro-Latin America, 1800–2000.* Oxford: Oxford University Press, 2004.

Anthias, Floya: "Methodological Nationalism versus Methodological Transnationalism: Moving beyond the Binary", 2009, Online: http://www.socant.su.se/polopoly_fs/1.30452.1320939981!/FloyaAnthiaspapers.pdf (May 8, 2023).

Aparicio, F. R. "La India, La Lupe and Celia: Toward a Feminist Genealogy of Salsa Music". *Disciplines in the Line: Feminist Research on Spanish, Latin American, and U.S. Latina Women*, ed. A. J. Cruz, R. Hernandez-Pecoraro & J. Tolliver. Newark, Delaware: Juan de la Cuesta, 2003, 37–57.

Appadurai, Arjun. *Modernity at Large – Cultural Dimensions of Globalization*, Minneapolis: University of Minnesota Press, 2000.

Appiah, Kwame Anthony. *The Ethics of Identity*, Princeton: Princeton University Press, 2007.

Asante, Molefi Kete. *The Afrocentric Idea*, Philadelphia: Temple University Press, 1987.

Asante, Molefi Kete: "Review of *Against Race*". *Journal of Black Studies*, vol. 31, 2001, 848–849.

Ashe, Bertram D. "Theorizing the Post-Soul Aesthetic: An Introduction". *African American Review*, vol. 41, no. 4, 2007, 609–623.

Atkins, E. Taylor. "The Funky Divas Talk Back: Dialogues about Black Feminism, Masculinity, and Soul Power in the Music of James Brown", *Popular Music and Society*, vol. 38, no. 3, 2015, 337–354.

Baraka, Amiri (LeRoi Jones). *Blues People.* New York: William Morrow, 1963.

Baraka, Amiri (LeRoi Jones). *Black Music.* New York: William Morrow, 1967.

Béhague, Gerard. "Bridging South America and the United States in Black Music Research." *Black Music Research Journal*, vol. 22, no. 1, 2002, 1–11.

Béhague Gerard (ed.). "Introduction". *Music and Black Ethnicity: The Caribbean and South America*, Miami: University of Miami, 1994.

Biesanz, John. "Race Relations in the Canal Zone". *Phylon*, vol. 11, no. 1, 1950, 23–30.

Boggs, Vernon. "Rhythm 'n' Blues, American Pop and Salsa: Musical Transculturation". *Latin Beat Magazine*, vol. 2, no. 1, 1992, 16–19.

https://doi.org/10.1515/9783110665550-010

Sources

Bourdieu, Pierre and Loïc Wacquant. "On the Cunning of Imperialist Reason". *Theory, Culture, Society,* vol. 16, no. 1, 1999, 31–58.

Boyce-Davies, Carole and Angelique V. Nixon (2021) "Caribbean Global Movements". *The Black Scholar,* vol. 51, no. 2, 2021, 1–7.

Boyce-Davies, Carole. "Revisiting Black Marxism: Key Texts in the Study of the African Diaspora", webinar hosted by *Association for the Study of the Worldwide African Diaspora* (October 23, 2020), Online: https://www.youtube.com/watch?v=u76OX FYBYxk (May 8, 2023).

Brown, David-Luis. *Waves of Decolonization – Discourses of Race and Hemispheric Citizenship in Cuba, Mexico, and the United States.* Duke UP, 2008.

Brown, Patrice C. "The Panama Canal – The African American Experience". *Federal Records and African American History,* vol. 29, no. 2, 1997, Online: https://www.archives.gov/publications/pro logue/1997/summer/panama-canal, (March 1, 2023).

Brooks, Daphne. "Planet Earth(a): Afrocosmopolitanism, Sonic Transnationalism & the Diasporic Politics of Eartha Kitt's Cabaret". *Cornbread and Cuchifritos: Ethnic Identity Politics, Transnationalization, and Transculturation in American Urban Popular* Music, ed. Wilfried Raussert and Michelle Habell-Pallán, Trier: Wissenschaftlicher Verlag Trier, 2011, 111–126.

Brooks, Daphne. "Nina Simone's Triple Play". *Callaloo,* vol. 34, no. 1, 2011, 176–197.

Brown, Timothy Scott, and Andrew Lison, eds. *The Global 1960s in Sound and Vision – Media, Counterculture, Revolt,* New York: Palgrave Macmillan, 2014.

Bryce-Laporte: "Crisis, Conterculture, and Religion among West Indians in the Canal Zone". *Blackness in Latin America and the Caribbean – Social Dynamics and Cultural Tansformations,* vol 1, ed. Norman E. Whitten and Arlene Torres, Indianapolis: Indiana University Press, 100–118.

Burgos Jr., Adrián. "'The Latins from Manhattan' – Confronting Race and Building Community in Jim Crow Baseball, 1906–1950." *Mambo Montage – The Latinization of New York,* ed. Agustín Laó-Montes and Arlene Dávila. Columbia UP, 2001, 73–95.

Bush, Roderick D. *The End of White World Supremacy – Black Internationalism and the Problem of the Color Line,* Philadelphia: Temple UP, 2009.

Butler, Kim: "Defining Diaspora, Refining a Discourse". *Diaspora: A Journal of Transnational Studies,* vol. 10, no. 2, 2001, 189–219.

Cabanillas, Francisco. "The Musical Poet, A session with Victor Hernández Cruz". *Centro Journal,* vol. XVI, no. 2, 2004, 34–41.

Carvalho, José Jorge de. *Las culturas afroamericanas en Iberoamérica: Lo negociable y lo innegociable.* Bogotá: Universidad Nacional de Colombia, 2005.

Castillo-Garsow, Melissa, and Jason Nichols, eds. *La Verdad: An International Dialogue on Hip Hop Latinidades.* Columbus: Ohio State University Press, 2016.

Castro, Carlos. "Notas al margen a propósito de la Panameñisima Reina Negra". *La Antigua* vol. 20, 1982, 171–178.

Chivallon, Christine. "Beyond Gilroy's Black Atlantic: The Experience of the Black Atlantic", *Diaspora,* vol. 11, no. 3, 2002, 359–382.

Chrisman, Laura. "Journeying to death: Gilroy's Black Atlantic". *Race & Class,* vol. 39, no. 2, 1997, 51–64.

Chrisman, Laura, Farah Jasmine Griffin and Tukufu Zuberi (eds.). "Introduction to 'Transcending Traditions' Special Issue of The Black Scholar". *The Black Scholar,* vol. 30, vol. 3/4, 2000, 2–3.

Clifford, James. *Routes – Travel and Translation in the late Twentieth Century,* Cambridge: Harvard University Press, 1997.

Collins, Patricia Hill. *Black Feminist Thought: Knowledge, Consciousness, and the Politics of Empowerment.* New York: Routledge, 1991.

Conniff, Michael. *Black Labor on a White Canal: Panama, 1904–1981.* Pittsburgh: U of Pittsburgh P, 1985.

Corinealdi, Kaysha. "Envisioning Multiple Citizenships: West Indian Panamanians and Creating Community in the Canal Zone Neocolony." T*he Global South*, vol. 6, no. 2, 2013, 87–106.

Corinealdi, Kaysha. *Panama in Black: Afro-Caribbean World Making in the Twentieth Century.* Duke UP, 2022.

Corinealdi, Kaysha. "When Panama came to Brooklyn", Online: https://www.publicbooks.org/when-panama-came-to-brooklyn/#fn-50837-23 (May 15, 2023).

Craft, Renée Alexander. *When the Devil Knocks – The Congo Tradition and the Politics of Blackness in Twentieth-Century Panama*, Columbus: Ohio State University Press, 2015.

Da Silva, Jonatas C. "História de lutas negras." *Escravidão e invenção da liberdade – Estudos sobre o negro no Brasil*, ed. João José Reis. Editora Brasiliense: São Paulo, 1988.

Davis, Angela. *Women, Culture, and Politics.* New York: Random House, 1989. *Culture.* New York: Routledge, 2013.

Davis, Stephen M. *Reggae Bloodlines: In Search of the Music and Culture of Jamaica.* New York: Da Capo Press, 1992.

De la Fuente, Alejandro, and George Reid Andrews (eds.). *Afro-Latin American Studies – An Introduction.* Cambridge: Cambridge UP, 2018.

Diawara, Manthia. "The 1960s in Bamako: Malick Sidibé and James Brown", *Black Cultural Traffic: Crossroads in Global Performance and Popular Culture*, ed. Harry J. Elam and Kennell Jackson, University of Michigan Press, 2005, 242–264.

Diouf, Sylviane A., and Komozi Woodard. "Introduction." *Black Power 50*, ed. Sylviane Diouf, and Komozi Woodard. New York: The New Press, 2016, vii–xiii.

Dixon, Aaron. *My People are Rising: Memoir of a Black Panther Party Captain*, Haymarket Books, 2012.

Diniz, Andre. *Black Rio nos anos 70: a grande África Soul.* Rio de Janeiro, Numa Editora, 2022.

Dj Lynnée Denise. "The Afterlife of Aretha Franklin's 'Rock Steady:' A Case Study in DJ Scholarship," *The Black Scholar*, vol. 49, no. 3, 2019, 62-72.

Donoghue, Michael. *American Encounters/Global Encounters: Borderland on the Isthmus: Race, Culture, and the Struggle for the Canal Zone.* Durham: Duke UP, 2014.

Dombrowski, Diana. "Interview with Irwin Frank", Samuel Proctor Oral History Program (2011), Online: http://ufdc.ufl.edu/AA00013377/00001/pdf?search=black+%3 dstudents, (March 1, 2023).

Du Bois, W. E. B. *The Souls of Black Folk*, New York: Penguin, 1903.

Duke, Dawn. "Black Movement Militancy in Panama; SAMAAP's Reliance on an Identity of West Indianness." *Latin American and Caribbean Ethnic Studies* vol. 5, no. 1, 2010, 75–83.

Duke, Lynne. "Silver Tones and Golden Arches". *Los Angeles Times* (March 19, 2002), online: https://www.latimes.com/archives/la-xpm-2002-mar-19-lv-pianoman19-story.html (May 8, 2023).

Dulitzky, Ariel. "A Region in Denial: Racial Discrimination and Racism in Latin America." *Neither Enemies nor Friends: Latinos, Blacks, Afro-Latinos*, ed. Anani Dzidienyo and Suzanne Oboler. London: Palgrave, 2005, 39–59.

Duany, Jorge. *The Puerto Rican Nation on the Move – Identities on the Island and in the United States.* The U of North Carolina P, 2002.

Dunn, Christopher. *Contracultura: Alternative Arts and Social Transformation in Authoritarian Brazil.* Chapel Hill: University of North Carolina Press, 2016.

Dzidzienyo, Anani and Suzanne Oboler, eds. *Neither Enemies nor Friends: Latinos, Blacks, Afro-Latinos.* Palgrave, 2005.

Dzidzienyo, Anani, and Suzanne Oboler. "Flows and Counterflows: Latinas/os, Blackness, and Racialization in Hemispheric Perspective." *Neither Enemies nor Friends: Latinos, Blacks, Afro-Latinos*, ed. Anani Dzidzienyo and Suzanne Oboler. New York: Palgrave, 2005, 3 – 35.

Edwards, Brent Hayes. *The Practice of Diaspora: Literature, Translation, and the Rise of Black Internationalism.* Cambridge: Harvard University, 2003.

Elam, Harry Justin, et al. *Black Cultural Traffic: Crossroads in Global Performance and Popular Culture.* University of Michigan Press, 2005.

Ellis, Trey. "The New Black Aesthetic". *Callaloo*, vol. 38, 1989, 233 – 243.

Enck-Wanzer, Darrel, ed. *The Young Lords – A Reader.* New York: New York UP, 2010.

Espinoza Agurto, Andrés. *Salsa Consciente: Politics, Poetics, and Latinidad in the Meta-Barrio.* East Lansing: Michigan UP, 2022.

Eyerman, Ron, and Andrew Jamison. *Music and Social Movements: Mobilizing Traditions in the Twentieth Century.* Cambridge: Cambridge UP, 1998.

Eze, E. Chukwudi. "Transcending Traditions." *Black Scholar*, vol. 30, no. 3/4, 2000, 18 – 22.

Fared, Grant. "Wailin' Soul: Reggae's Debt to Black American Music." *Soul – Black Power, Politics, and Pleasure*, ed. Monique Guillory and Richard C. Green. New York: New York UP, 1998, 56 – 74.

Featherstone, David. "Black Internationalism, Subaltern Cosmopolitanism, and the Spatial Politics of Antifascism." *Annals of the Association of American Geographers*, vol. 103, no. 6, 2013, 1406 – 1420.

Feldstein, Ruth. "I Don't Trust You Anymore": Nina Simone, Culture, and Black Activism in the 1960s." *The Journal of American History* vol. 91, no. 4 (Mar. 2005), 1349 – 1379.

Fernández, Johanna. "The Young Lords: Its Origins and Convergences with the Black Panther Party". Online: https://www.ibiblio.org/shscbch/ribb/lords-origins.pdf (May 12, 2023).

Fernández, Johanna. *The Young Lords: A Radical History.* Chapel Hill: The U of North Carolina P, 2020.

Fila-Bakabadio, Sarah. "Against the empire: the Black Panthers in Congo, insurgent cosmopolitanism and the fluidity of revolutions." *African Identities*, vol. 16, no. 2, 2018, 146 – 160.

Fisher Fishkin, Shelley."Crossroads of Cultures: The Transnational Turn in American Studies – Presidential Adress to the American Studies Association, November 12, 2004," *American Quarterly*, vol. 57, no. 1, 2005.

Flores, Juan. *From Bomba to Hip Hop: Puerto Rican Culture and Latino Identity.* New York: Columbia UP, 2000.

Flores, Juan. *Salsa Rising: New York Latin Music of the Sixties Generation.* New York: Oxford UP, 2016.

Flores, Juan, and Miriam Jiménez, "Triple Consciousness? Approaches to Afro-Latino Culture in the United States." *Latin American and Caribbean Ethnic Studies*, vol. 4, no. 3, 2009, 319 – 328.

Flores-Rodríguez, Ángel G. "The Young Lords, Puerto Rican Liberation, and the Black Freedom Struggle – Interview with José "Cha Cha" Jiménez." *OAH Magazine of History*, vol. 26, no. 1, 2012, 61 – 64.

Fluck, Winfried, Donald E. Pease, John Carlos Rowe (eds.). *Re-framing the Transnational Turn in American Studies.* Hanover: Dartmouth College Press, 2011.

Ford, Tanisha C. *Liberated Threads: Black Women, Style, and the Global Politics of Soul.* UNC Press Books, 2015.

Fontaine, Pierre-Michel. "Research in the Political Economy of Afro-Latin America." *Latin American Research Review*, vol. 15, no. 2, 1980, 111 – 41.

Freitag, Ulrike and Achim von Oppen (eds.). *Translocality. The Study of Globalising Processes from a Southern Perspective*, Leiden & Boston: Brill Academic Publishers, 2010.

Freyre, Gilberto. "Atenção, Brasileiros." *Diário de Pernambuco* (May 15, 1977).

Frias, Lena. "Black Rio: o orgulho (importado) de ser negro no Brasil." *Jornal do Brasil.* (July 7, 1976), 1–5.

García, David. Arsenio Rodríguez and the Transnational Flows of Latin Popular Music. Philadelphia: Temple University Press, 2006.

García Peña, Lorgia. Translating Blackness: Latinx Colonialities in Global Perspective. Durham, London: Duke University Press, 2022.

George, Nelson. *The Death of Rhythm and Blues*, New York: Penguin, 1988.

Giacomini, Sonia Maria. *A alma da festa – família, etnicidade e projetos num clube social da Zona Norte do Rio de Janeiro – O Renascença Clube.* Rio de Janeiro: IUPERJ, 2006.

Gilroy, Paul. *There Ain't No Black in the Union Jack.* Routledge, 1987.

Gilroy, Paul. *The Black Atlantic – Modernity and Double Consciousness.* London: Verso, 1993.

Glasser, Ruth. *My Music Is My Flag: Puerto Rican Musicians and their New York Commmunities, 1917–1940.* U of California P, 1995.

Glick Schiller, Nina. "Beyond the Nation-State and Its Units of Analysis: Towards a New Research Agenda for Migration Studies. Essentials of Migration Theory." *Working Papers – Center on Migration, Citizenship and Development*, 33, Bielefeld, 2007.

Glick Schiller, Nina. "Diasporic Cosmopolitanism: Migrants, Sociabilities and City-Making." *Whose Cosmopolitanism? Critical Perspectives, Relationalities and Discontents*, ed. Nina Glick Schiller and Andrew Irving, New York, Oxford: Berghahn Press, 2014, 103–120.

Gonzalez, Juan. *Harvest of Empire: A History of Latinos in America.* Penguin, 2011.

Grant, Nathan. "Notes of a Prodigal Son: James Baldwin and the Apostasy of Soul." *Soul – Black Power, Politics, and Pleasure*, ed. Monique Guillory and Richard C. Green. New York: New York UP, 1998, 32–44.

Greene, Julie. *The Canal Builders: Making America's Empire at the Panama Canal.* New York: Penguin Books, 2009.

Grosfoguel, Ramón, and Chloé Georas. "Latino Caribbean Diasporas in New York." *Mambo Montage – The Latinization of New York*, ed. Agustín Laó-Montes and Arlene Dávila, Columbia UP, 2001, 97–118.

Guralnick, Pete. *Sweet Soul Music: Rhythm and Blues and the Southern Dream of Freedom.* New York: Harper and Row, 1986.

Guridy, Frank André. *Forging Diaspora – Afro-Cubans and African Americans in a World of Empire and Jim Crow*, Chapel Hill: The U of North Carolina P, 2010.

Guridy, Frank André, and Juliet Hooker. "Currents in Afro-Latin American Political and Social Thought." *Afro-Latin American Studies – An Introduction*, ed. Alejandro de la Fuente and George Reid Andrews. Cambridge: Cambridge UP, 2018, 179–221.

Guzmán, Will. "Miriam Jiménez Román (1951–2020)". Online: https://www.blackpast.org/african-ameri can-history/miriam-jimenez-roman-1951-2020/, (May 3, 2023).

Guzmán, Pablo "Yoruba". "Before People Called Me A Spic, They Called Me a Nigger." *The Afro-Latin@ Reader – History and Culture in the United States*, edited by Miriam Jiménez & Juan Flores, Duke UP, 2010. 235–243.

Haas, Astrid, ed. *The Harlem Renaissance in an Inter-American Perspectiv*, special issue *fiar – Forum for Inter-American Research*, vol. 7, no. 2, 2014.

Hall, Stuart. "Cultural identity and diaspora", *Identity: Community, Culture, Difference*, ed. Jonathan Rutherford, London: Lawrence Wishart, 1990, 222–237.

Hanchard, Michael. *Orpheus and Power – The Movimento Negro of Rio de Janeiro and São Paulo, Brazil, 1945–1988*. Princeton: Princeton University Press, 1994.

Hanchard, Michael. "Black Transnationalism, Africana Studies, and the 21st Century". *Journal of Black Studies*, vol. 35, no. 2, 2004, 139–153.

Hanson, Michael. "Suppose James Brown Read Fanon: The Black Arts Movement, Cutural Nationalism, and the Failure of Popular Musical Praxis." *Popular Music*, vol. 27, no. 3. 2008, 341–365.

Hebdige, Dick. *Cut 'N' Mix: Culture, Identity and Caribbean Music.* Routledge, 2003.

Hernandez, Rod. "Latin Soul: Cross-Cultural Connections between the Black Arts Movement and Pocho-Che", *New Thoughts on the Black Arts Movement*, ed. Lisa Gail Collins and Margo Natalie Crawford, New Brunswick: Rutgers University Press, 2006, 333–348.

Herskovits, Melville Jean. *The Myth of the Negro Past.* New York, London: Harper & Brothers, 1941.

Hill-Collins, Patricia. *Black Feminist Thought: Knowledge, Consciousness and the Politics of Empowerment.* New York: Routledge, 1991.

hooks, bell. *Rock My Soul: Black People and Self-Esteem.* New York: Washington Square Press, 2003.

Ingram, James D. "Cosmopolitanism from Below: Universalism as Contestation." *Critical Horizons*, vol. 17, no. 1, 2016, 66–78.

Irving, Eduardo. "Tras la pista de los combos nacionales." *Talingo/La Prensa* 399 (January 14, 2001), 8–13.

Jackson, Richard. *Black Writers and Latin America – Cross-Cultural Affinities*, Washington D.C.: Howard University Press, 1998.

Joseph, Peniel E. "The Black Power Movement: A State of the Field." *The Journal of American History*, vol. 96, no. 3, 2009, 751–776.

Jiménez, Miriam and Juan Flores, eds. *The Afro-Latin@ Reader – History and Culture in the United States.* Duke UP, 2010.

Johnson, Cedric. *Revolutionaries to Race Leaders: Black Power and the Making of African American Politics.* Minneapolis: U of Minnesota P, 2007.

Kaltmeier, Olaf. "Inter-American perspectives for the Rethinking of Area Studies." *Fiar*, vol. 7, no. 3, 2014, 171–182.

Kelley, Robin D.G. "How the West was One: On the Uses and Limitations of Diaspora." *The Black Scholar*, vol. 30, no. 3/4, 2000, 31–35.

Kelley, Robin D.G. and Tiffany Ruby Patterson. "Unfinished Migrations: Reflections on the African Diaspora and the Making of the Modern World." *African Studies Review*, vol. 43, no. 1, 2000, 11–45.

Kelley, Robin D.G. *Freedom Dreams: The Black Radical Imagination.* Boston: Beacon Press, 2002.

Kunow, Rüdiger. "American Studies as Mobility Studies: Some Terms and Constellations." *Re-framing the Transnational Turn in American Studies*, ed. Winfried Fluck, Donald E. Pease, John Carlos Rowe. Hanover: Dartmouth College Press, 2011, 245–264.

Kurasawa, Fuyuki. "Cosmopolitanism from Below: Alternative Globalization and the Creation of a Solidarity without Bounds." *European Journal of Sociology*, vol. 45, no. 2, 2004, 233–255.

Kurlansky, Mark. *Ready for a Brand New Beat – How "Dancing in the street" Became the Anthem for a Changing America.* New York: Riverhead Books, 2013.

Laó-Montes, Agustín and Arlene Dávila. *Mambo Montage – The Latinization of New York.* New York: Columbia University Press, 2001.

Laó-Montes, Agustín. "Afro-Latinidades and the Diasporic Imaginary." *Iberoamericana* 17, 2005, 117–130.

Laó-Montes, Agustín. "Hilos descoloniales – Trans-localizando los espacios de la diáspora africana." *Tabula Rasa*, vol. 7, 2007, 47–79.

Laó-Montes, Agustín. "Cartografía del campo político afrodescendiente en América Latina." *Debates sobre ciudadanía y políticas raciales en las Américas Negras*, ed. Claudia Rosero-Labbé et. al. Bogotá: Universidad Nacional de Colombia, 2010, 279–316.

Laó-Montes, Agustín. *Contrapunteos diaspóricos: Cartografías políticas de Nuestra Afroamérica.* Bogotá: Universidad Externado, 2020.

Lapidus, Benjamin. *New York and the International Sound of Latin Music, 1940-1990.* Jackson: University Press of Mississippi, 2020.

Laurenza, Roque Javier: "Un eco de tantanes (Reflexiones en torno al no. 5 de la Revista Nacional de Cultura)." *Revista Nacional de la Cultura*, vol. 7/8,1977, 100–117.

Leymarie, Isabelle. *Cuban Fire: The Story of Salsa and Latin Jazz.* New York: Bloomsbury Continuum, 2003.

Lewis, Earl. "To Turn As on A Pivot: Writing African American History into a History of Overlapping Diasporas." *The American Historical Review*, vol. 100, no. 3, 1995, 765–787.

Lipsitz, George. *Dangerous Crossroads – Popular Music, Postmodernism, and the Politics of Place.* London: Verso, 1994.

Lipsitz, George. "Review of The Black Atlantic." *Social Identities*, vol. 1, no. 1, 1995, 193–201.

Lordi, Emily J. *Black Resonance: Iconic Women Singers and African American Literature.* New Brunswick: Rutgers UP, 2013.

Lordi, Emily J. *The Meaning of Soul – Black Music and Resilience since the 1960s* (Durham and London: Duke University Press, 2020.

Lowe de Goodin, Melva. "El idioma inglés y la integración social de los panameños de origen afro-antillano al carácter nacional panameno." *Revista Nacional de Cultura*, Número Cinco, 1976, 22–44.

Luciano, Felipe. "The Song of Joe B." *New York Magazine*, vol. 4, no. 43, 1971, 49–55.

Mahler, Anne Garland. *From the Tricontinental to the Global South: Race, Radicalism, and Transnational Solidarity.* Durham: Duke UP, 2018.

Maloney, Gerardo. "Malcolm X: significado de su Lucha a favor del negro." *Estrella de Panama* (May 28, 2017), Online: https://www.laestrella.com.pa/nacional/170528/x-lucha-favor-malcom-signi ficado (May 15, 2023).

Maloney, Gerardo. *Los Gay Crooners,* Documentary, Panama, 2020.

Materno Vásquez, Juan. *El país por conquistar: La tesis del país integral.* Bogotá: Internacional de Publicaciones, 1974.

Materno Vásquez, Juan. "La nacionalidad panameña – concepto jurídico y concepto histórico-político." *Revista Nacional de Cultura*, vol. 9/10 (1977/78), 83–93.

Marable, Manning. "Blackness beyond Boundaries – Navigating the Political Economies of Global Inequality." *Transnational Blackness: Navigating the Global Color Line*, ed. Manning Marable and Vanessa Agard-Jones, New York: Springer, 2008.

Martin, Waldo. *No Coward Soldiers: Black Cultural Politics in Postwar America.* Cambridge: Harvard UP, 2005.

Marx, Anthony. *Making Race and Nation. A Comparison of South Africa, the United States, and Brazil,* Cambridge: Cambridge University Press, 1999.

Masiki, Trent, and Regina Marie Mills. "Introduction: Bridging African American and Latina/o/x Studies." *The Black Scholar*, vol. 52, no. 1, 2022, 1–4.

Marcus, George E. "Ethnography in/of the World System: The Emergence of Multi-Sited Ethnography." *Annual Review of Anthropology*, vol. 24, 1995, 95–117.

Matutino. "Clamando Justicia Condenan Discriminación Racial Zoneita" (October 23, 1972).

Maultsby, Portia K. "Soul." *African American Music*, ed. Mellonee V. Burnim and Portia K. Maultsby. New York: Routledge, 2015, 277–298.

McCann, Bryan. "Black Pau: Uncovering the History of Brazilian Soul." *Journal of Popular Music Studies* vol. 14, 2002, 33–62.

Medeiros, Carlos Alberto. "Black Rio: Music, Politics, and Black Identity". *Black Power in Hemispheric Perspective: Movements and Cultures of Resistance in the Black Americas*, ed. Wilfried Raussert and Matti Steinitz. New Orleans and Trier: WVT/New Orleans University Press, 2022, 239–249.

Meehan, Kevin. *People Get Ready: African American and Caribbean Cultural Exchange.* Jackson: UP of Mississippi, 2010.

Mitchell, Tony, ed. *Global Noise: Rap and Hip Hop Outside the USA.* Middletown: Wesleyan University Press, 2001.

Morales, Iris. *Through the Eyes of Rebel Women, The Young Lords 1969–1976*, New York: Red Sugar Cane Press, 2016.

Moreno, Jairo. "Bauzá–Gillespie–Latin/jazz: difference, modernity, and the Black Caribbean". South Atlantic Quarterly vol. 103, no. 1, 2004, 81–99.

Mullings, Leith, ed. *New Social Movements in the African Diaspora – Challenging Global Apartheid.* New York: Palgrave Macmillan. 2009.

Munro, Martin. *Different Drummers – Rhythm and Race in the Americas.* Berkeley: University of California Press, 2010.

Murch, Donna. "The Many Meanings of Watts: Black Power, 'Wattstax,' and the Carceral State." *OAH Magazine of History* vol. 26, no. 1, 2012, 37–40.

Neal, Larry. "The Black Arts Movement." *The Drama Review*, vol. 12, no. 4, 1968, 29–39.

Neal, Mark Anthony. *Soul Babies: Black Popular Culture and the Post-Soul Aesthetic.* New York: Routledge, 2002.

Neal, Mark Anthony. *What the Music Said: Black Popular Music and Black Public Culture.* New York: Routledge, 2013.

Nwankwo, Ifeoma. "The Promises and Perils of U.S. African American Hemispherism: Latin America in Martin Delany's Blake and Gayl Jones's Mosquito." *Hemispheric American Studies: Essays Beyond the Nation*, ed. Caroline Levander and Robert Levine. New Brunswick: Rutgers UP, 2008. 187–204.

Nwankwo, Ifeoma. "Introduction: Making Sense, Making Selves. Afro-Latin Americans of British Caribbean Descent." *Latin American and Caribbean Ethnic Studie*s, vol. 4, no. 3, 2009, 221–230.

Nwankwo, Ifeoma. *Black Cosmopolitanism: Racial Consciousness and Transnational Identity in the Nineteenth-Century Americas.* Philadelphia: U of Pennsylvania P, 2014. Print.

Ogbar, Jeffrey O.G. *Black Power: Radical Politics and African American Identity*, Baltimore: Johns Hopkins UP, 2004.

Ogbar, Jeffrey O.G. "Puerto Rico en mi corazón, The Young Lords, Black Power and Puerto Rican Nationalism in the U.S., 1966–1972." *Centro Journal*, vol. 1, 2006, 67–74.

Ogbar, Jeffrey O.G. "Rainbow Radicalism. The Rise of the Radical Ethnic Nationalism." *The Black Power Movement – Rethinking the Civil Rights-Black Power Era*, edited by Peniel. E Joseph, Routledge, 2006, 193–228.

Ogbar, Jeffrey O.G. "The Looks." *Black Power 50*, ed. Sylviane A. Diouf and Komozi Woodard. New York: The New Press, 2016, 125 – 136.

Oliveira, Iris. "Imprensa Alternative e o 'movimento negro' nos anos de 1970." Text presented at *5° Encontro Regional Sul de História da Mídia*. Alcar Sul, 2014.

Okosun, Kensedeobong Blessed. "Soul music and Sisterhood as expressions of Black Power." *Black Power in Hemispheric Perspective: Movements and Cultures of Resistance in the Black Americas*, ed. Wilfried Raussert and Matti Steinitz, New Orleans and Trier: WVT/New Orleans University Press, 2022, 223 – 237.

Opie, Frederick. *Upsetting the Apple Cart – Black-Latino Coalitions in New York City from Protest to Public Office*, New York: Columbia University Press, 2014.

Ostendorf, Berndt. "Americanization and Anti-Americanism in the Age of Globalization." *North-Americanization of Latin America? Culture, Gender, and Nation in the Americas*, ed. Hans-Joachim König and Stefan Rinke. Stuttgart: Verlag Hans-Dieter Heinz, 2004,19 – 45.

Parker, Jason. "'Capital of the Caribbean': The African American-West Indian 'Harlem Nexus' and the Transnational Drive for Black Freedom, 1940 – 1948." *The Journal of African American History*, vol. 89, no. 2, 2004, 98 – 117.

Palombini, Carlos. "Notes on the Historiography of *Música Soul* and *Funk Carioca*." *Historia Actual Online*, vol. 23, 2010, 99 – 106.

Panama Canal Spillway: "R. of P. Decrees Ban on Long Hair", (April 10, 1970).

Paschel, Tianna. "Rethinking Black Mobilizations in Latin America." *Afro-Latin American Studies – An Introduction*, ed. Alejandro de la Fuente and George Reid Andrews. Cambridge: Cambridge UP, 2018. 222 – 263.

Patterson, Sandra. "H.O.G." *Afro-Panamanian Newsletter*, September 2010.

Pedretti, Lucas. *Dançando na mira da ditadura. Bailes soul e violência contra a população negra nos anos 1970*, Rio de Janeiro: Arquivo Nacional, 2022.

Pelegrini, Sandra and Amanda Palomo Alves. "'Black is beautiful': arte, identidade e política na obra musical de Tony Tornado (1970)", Online: https://de.scribd.com/document/406613057/Amanda-Palomo-Alves-e-Sandra-Pelegrini (May 15, 2023).

Pereira, Amilcar. *O mundo negro. Relações raciais e a constituição do movimento negro contemporâneo no Brasil*. Rio de Janeiro: Pallas, 2013.

Pereira, Malin, "'The Poet in the World, the World in the Poet': Cyrus Cassells's and Elizabeth Alexander's Versions of Post-Soul Cosmopolitanism." *African American Review*, vol. 41, no. 4, 2007), 709 – 725.

Pérez Price, Ariel René. *Pionero: La historia de Luis Russell*. Panama: Miss Hilda Press, 2021.

Pinho, Osmundo Santos de Araujo. *O Mundo Negro – Hermenêutica Crítica da Reafricanização em Salvador.* Salvador: UNIAFRO, 2010.

Posnock, Ross. "The Dream of Deracination: The Uses of Cosmopolitanism." *American Literary History*, vol. 12, no. 4, 2000, 802 – 818.

Prahlad, Anand. *Reggae Wisdom: Proverbs in Jamaican Music*. Jackson: University Press of Mississippi, 2001.

Priestley, George. "Antillean Panamanians or Afro-Panamanians? Political Participation and the Politics of Identity During the Carter-Torrijos Treaty Negotiations." *Transforming Anthropology*, vol. 12, no. 1/2, 2004, 50 – 67.

Pulido Ritter, Luis. "Notas sobre Eric Walrond: La inmigración caribeña y la transnacionalidad literaria en Panamá: una excursión por las calles de la memoria, la reflexión y los espacios en movimiento." *Intercambio*, vol. 6, 2008, 175 – 180.

Pulido Ritter, Luis. "Lord Cobra: del cosmopolitismo decimonónico y del folklorismo al cosmopolitismo diaspórico", *Istmo* 20 (2010), http://istmo.denison.edu/n20/articulos/22-pulido_luis_form.pdf, 1–24 (June 26, 2024).

Pulido Ritter, Luis. "Modernidad en movimiento: transitismo, cosmopolitismo y transnacionalidad en la ciudad letrada panameña", *Istmo* 21 (2010), http://istmo.denison.edu/n21/articulos/4-pulido_ritter_luis_modernidad_form.pdf, 1–31 (June 26, 2024).

Pulido Ritter, Luis. "'Panamá es un sancocho': Armando Fortune y el mestizaje en la identidad cultural panameña." *Istmo*, vol. 23, 2011, 1–24.

Putnam, Lara. "Nothing Matters but Color – Transnational Circuits, the Interwar Caribbean, and the Black International", *From Toussaint to Tupac: The Black International since theAge of Revolution*, ed. Michael O. West, William G. Martin, and Fanon Che Wilkins. Chapel Hill: University of North Carolina Press, 2009, 107–129.

Putnam, Lara. *Radical Moves: Caribbean Migrants and the Politics of Race in the Jazz Age.* Chapel Hill: The University of North Carolina Press, 2013.

Putnam, Lara. "Jazzing Sheiks at the 25 Cent Bram: Panama and Harlem as Caribbean Crossroads, circa 1910–1940." *Journal of Latin American Cultural Studies*, vol. 25, no. 3, 2016, 339–359.

Quinn, Kate, ed. *Black Power in the Caribbean.* Gainesville: UP of Florida, 2014.

Ramsey, Guthrie P., Jr. *Race Music – Black Cultures from Bebop to Hip Hop.* Los Angeles: U of California P, 2003.

Ratcliff, Anthony. "Black Writers of the World, Unite!" *The Black Scholar*, vol. 37, no. 4, 2008, 27–38.

Raussert, Wilfried and Michelle Habell-Pallán, eds. *Cornbread and Cuchifritos – Ethnic Identity Politics, Transnationalization, and Transculturation in American Urban Popular Music.* Trier: Wissenschaftlicher Verlag Trier, 2011.

Raussert, Wilfried, and John Miller Jones, eds. *Traveling Sounds. Music, Migration, and Identity in the U.S. and Beyond.* Berlin: LIT Verlag, 2008.

Raussert, Wilfried. "Ethnic Identity Politics, Transnationalization and Transculturation in American Urban Popular Music: Inter-American Perspectives", in: *Cornbread and Cuchifritos: Ethnic Identity Politics, Transnationalization, and Transculturation in American Popular Music*, ed. Wilfried Raussert and Michelle Habell-Pallán, Trier: WVT & Arizona State University: Bilingual Press, 2011, 1–25.

Raussert, Wilfried. "Narrating African American Migrations: Mobile Voices and Shifting Narrative Strategies." *Verbum et Lingua*, vol. 3, 2014, 8–21.

Raussert, Wilfried, ed. *Theorizing Hemispheric American Studies.*" *fiar* vol. 7, no. 3, 2014.

Raussert, Wilfried. "Mobilizing America/América: Toward Entangled Americas and a Blueprint for Inter-American 'Area' Studies." *Fiar*, vol. 7, no. 3, 2014, 59–97.

Raussert, Wilfried, and Matti Steinitz, eds. *Black Power in Hemispheric Perspective: Movements and Cultures of Resistance in the Black Americas*, New Orleans and Trier: WVT/New Orleans University Press, 2022.

Redmond, Shana L. *Anthem – Social Movements and the Sound of Solidarity in the African Diaspora*, New York: New York UP, 2014.

Reed Jr., Adolph. "Black Particularity Reconsidered." *Is it Nation Time? Contemporary Essays on Black Power and Black Nationalism*, ed. Eddie S. Glaude Jr. Chicago: U of Chicago P, 2001.

Reichardt, Ulfried: "Globalisierung, amerikanische (populäre) Musik und das Versprechen von Freiheit: Cage, Madonna und Rap." *Globaler Gesang vom Garten der Freiheit – Anglo-amerikanische Populärmusik und ihre Bedeutung für die US-Außenpolitik*, ed. Werner Kremp and David Sirakov, Trier: Wissenschaftlicher Verlag Trier, 2008, 103–115.

Reina, Antonio. "The Debonairs." *Afro-Panamanian Newsletter* (October 2013).

Ribeiro, Rita Aparecida da Conceição. "Errância e Exílio na Soul Music: do movimento Black-Rio nos anos 70 ao Quarteirão do Soul em Belo Horizonte, 2010." *Tempo e Argumento*, vol. 2, 2010, 154–180.

Richardson, Jill Toliver. *The Afro-Latin@ Experience in Contemporary American Literature and Culture*, New York Palgrave Macmillan, 2016.

Risério, Antônio. *Carnaval Ijexá – Notas sobre afoxés e blocos do novo carnival afrobaiano.* Salvador: Currupio, 1981.

Rivera, Raquel, Wayne Marshall & Deborah Pacini Hernandez, eds.. Reggaeton. Durham: Duke University Press, 2009.

Rivera, Raquel Z. *New York Ricans From the Hip Hop Zone.* New York: Springer, 2003.

Rivera, Raquel Z. "Hip Hop, Puerto Ricans, and Ethnoracial Identities in New York." *Mambo Montage – The Latinization of New York*, ed. Agustín Laó-Montes and Arlene Davila. New York: Columbia UP, 2001. 235–262.

Rivera-Rideau, Petra. "'Cocolos Modernos': Salsa, Reggaetón, and Puerto Rico's Cultural Politics of Blackness". Latin American and Caribbean Ethnic Studies vol. 8; no. 1, 2013, 1–19.

Rivero, Yeidy. *Tuning Out Blackness: Race and Nation in the History of Puerto Rican Television.* Duke UP Books, 2005.

Rivero, Yeidy. "Bringing the Soul: Afros, Black Empowerment, and Lucecita." *The Afro-Latin@ Reader: History and Culture in the United States*, ed. Miriam Jiménez Román and Juan Flores. Durham: Duke UO, 2009, 343–357.

Roberts, John Storm. *The Latin Tinge: The Impact of Latin American Music on the United States.* Oxford UP, USA, 1999.

Robinson, Cedric J. *Black Marxism: The Making of the Black Radical Tradition.* London: Zed Books, 1983.

Rondón, César Miguel. *The Book of Salsa: A Chronicle of Urban Music From the Caribbean to New York City.* Univ of North Carolina Press, 2008.

Roth, Julia. "Translocating the Caribbean, Positioning Im/Mobilities: The Sonic Politics of Las Krudas from Cuba." *Mobile and Entangled America(s)*, ed. Maryemma Graham and Wilfried Raussert, Routledge, 2016, 103–123.

Russell, Carlos E. "Exclusive Interview with Brother Malcolm X." *Liberator* vol. 4, no. 5 (May 1964), 12–16.

Salazar, Max. *Mambo Kingdom: Latin Music in New York.* New York: Schirmer Trade, 2002.

Sánchez-Coll, Israel, and Ian Seda. "Boogaloo y Sing – A – Ling. Un repaso histórico en sus 40 años." *Herencia Latina*, Feb 2005. Web. 15 Jan. 2018.

Sansone, Livio. *Blackness without Ethnicity: Constructing Race in Brazil.* New York: Palgrave Macmillan, 2003.

Saukko, Paula. *Doing Research in Cultural Studies – An Introduction to Classical and New Methodological Approaches.* London: Sage, 2003.

Saunders, Tanya. *Cuban Underground Hip Hop: Black Thoughts, Black Revolution, Black Modernity.* Austin: U of Texas P, 2015.

Seale, Bobby. *Seize the Time – The Story of the Black Panther Party and Huey P. Newton*, Baltimore: Black Classic Press, 1991.

Seigel, Micol. *Uneven Encounters: Making Race and Nation in Brazil and the United States.* Durham: Duke UP, 2009.

Sebadelhe, Zé Octavio and Luiz Felipe de Lima Peixoto. *1976: Movimento Black Rio*, Rio de Janeiro: José Olympio, 2016.

Shelby, Tommie. "Two Black Nationalisms." *Political Theory* vol. 31, no. 5, 2003, 664–692.

Sheriff, Robin. *Dreaming Equality: Color, Race, and Racism in Urban Brazil.* Piscataway: Rutgers University, 2001.

Slate, Nico, ed. *Black Power Beyond Borders.* New York: Palgrave Macmillan, 2012.

Slate, Nico, ed. *Colored Cosmopolitanism: The Shared Struggle for Freedom in the United States and India.* Cambridge: Harvard UP, 2017.

Smethurst, James. "A Soul Message – R & B, Soul, and the Black Freedom Struggle." *The Routledge History of Social Protest in Popular Music.* Jonathan C. Friedman, New York: Routledge, 2013, 108–120.

Smith Fernández, Alberto: "El Afro-Panameño Antillano frente al concepto de la Panameñidad." *Revista Nacional de Cultura*, Número Cinco (1976), 45–60.

Smith, Suzanne. *Dancing in the Street: Motown and the Cultural Politics of Detroit.* Cambridge: Harvard UP, 2000.

Smith, Michael Peter, and Luis Eduardo Guarnizo. *Transnationalism From Below.* Transaction Publishers, 1998.

Stam, Robert and Ella Shohat. *Race in Translation – Culture Wars Around the Postcolonial Atlantic.* New York: New York University Press, 2012.

Steinitz, Matti. "Black Power in a paraíso racial? The Black Rio movement, U.S. Soul music, and Afro-Brazilian mobilizations under military rule (1970–1976)." *Politics of Entanglement in the Americas: Connecting Transnational Flows and Local Perspectives*, ed. Lukas Rehm, Jochen Kemner, Olaf Kaltmeier, WVT Wissenschaftlicher Verlag, 2017, 13–30.

Steinitz, Matti. "'Calling Out Around the World' – How Soul music transnationalized the African-American freedom struggle." *Sonic Politics. Music and Social Movements in the Americas from the 1960s to the Present*, ed. Wilfried Raussert and Olaf Kaltmeier, Routledge, 2019.

Steinitz, Matti. "We got Latin Soul! Transbarrio Dialogues and Afro-Latin Identity Formation in New York's Puerto Rican Community during the Age of Black Power (1966–1972)." *Human Rights in the Americas*, ed. Luz Kirschner, Maria Herrera Sobek, and Francisco Lomeli.New York/London: Routledge, 2021, 243–262.

Steinitz, Matti. "Soulful Sancocho: Soul Music and Practices of Hemispheric Black Transnationalismin 1960s and 1970s Panama." *The Black Scholar* vol. 52, no. 1, 2022, 15–26.

Steinitz, Matti. "Hemispheric Ambassador of Black Power: Carlos E. Russell and the Practice of Pan-Afro-Americanism between New York and Panama." *Black Power in Hemispheric Perspective: Movements and Cultures of Resistance in the Black Americas*, ed. Wilfried Raussert and Matti Steinitz, New Orleans and Trier: WVT/New Orleans University Press, 2022.

Steinitz, Matti, and Juan Suárez Ontaneda. "Sonido y movimiento: música popular y transnacionalismo negro en las Américas". *PerspectivasAfro* vol. 3, no. 2, 2024, 202–211.

Stephens, Michelle. "Black Transnationalism and the Politics of National Identity: West Indian Intellectuals in Harlem in the Age of War and Revolution." *American Quarterly*, vol. 50, no. 3, 1998, 592–608.

Stephens, Michelle. "Re-imagining the Shape and Borders of Black Political Space." *Radical History Review*, vol. 87, 2003, 169–82.

Stephens, Michelle. "What Is This Black in Black Diaspora?" *Small Axe* vol. 13, no. 2, 2009, 26–38.

Stephens, Michelle. *Black Empire: The Masculine Global Imaginary of Caribbean Intellectuals in the United States, 1914–1962.* Durham: Duke UP, 2005.

Stephenson Watson, Sonja. "Are Panamanians of Caribbean Ancestry an Endangered Species? Critical Literary Debates on Panamanian Blackness in the Works of Carlos Wilson, Gerardo Maloney, and Carlos Russell." *Latin American and Caribbean Ethnic Studies* vol. 4, no. 3, 2001, 231–254.

Stephenson Watson, Sonja. *The Politics of Race in Panama – Afro-Hispanic and West Indian Discourses of Contention.* Gainesville: University Press of Florida, 2014.

Sterling, Cheryl, C. A. "Bleque Pau, Black Bailes and the Perfor(n)ormative in AfroBrazilian Cultural Space", Online: http://avery.cofc.edu/wp-content/uploads/2012/08/sterling.pdf (June 1, 2016).

Stewart, Alexander. "Make It Funky: Fela Kuti, James Brown and the Invention of Afrobeat." *American Studies*, vol. 52, no. 4, 2013, 99–118.

Stewart, James. "Message in the Music: Political Commentary in Black Popular Music from Rhythm and Blues to Early Hip Hop." *The Journal of African American History*, vol. 90, no. 3, 2005, 196–225.

Stokes, Martin. "Globalization and the Politics of World Music." *The Cultural Study of Music – A Critical Introduction*, ed. Martin Clayton, Trevor Herbert, and Richard Middleton. New York: Routledge, 2003. 297–308.

Stolzoff, Norman *Wake the Town and Tell the People: Dancehall Culture in Jamaica.* Durham: Duke University Press, 2000.

Storey, John: *Cultural Studies and the Study of Popular Culture – Theory and Methods.* Athens: University of Georgia Press, 1996.

Street, Joe. *The Culture War in the Civil Rights Movement.* Gainesville: UP of Florida, 2007.

Sullivan, Denise. *Keep on Pushing: Black Power Music from Blues to Hip-Hop.* Chicago: Lawrence Hill Books, 2011.

Swan, Quito. "Transnationalism." *Keywords for African American* Studies, ed. Erica R. Edwards, Roderick A. Ferguson and Jeffrey O. G. Ogbar, New York: NYU Press, 209–213.

Szok, Peter. *Wolf Tracks: Popular Art and Re-Africanization in Twentieth-Century Panama.* Oxford: University Press of Mississippi, 2014.

Tate, Greg. "Cult Nats Meet Freaky Deke." *Flyboy in the Buttermilk: Essays on Contemporary America.* New York: Simon & Schuster, 1992, 198–210.

Taylor, Keeanga-Yamahtta. *How We Get Free: Black Feminism and the Combahee River Collective.* Chicago: Haymarket Books, 2017.

Thayer, Allen. "Black Rio – Brazilian Soul and DJ Culture's Lost Chapter." *Wax Poetics*, vol. 16, 2006, 89–106.

Thies, Sebastian, and Josef Raab, eds. *E Pluribus Unum? National and Transnational Identities in the Americas.* Berlin: Lit Verlag, 2009.

Thomas, Lorrin. *Puerto Rican Citizen: History and Political Identity in Twentieth-Century New York City.* University of Chicago Press, 2010.

Thomas, Piri. *Down These Mean Streets.* Knopf, 1967.

Torres, Andrés. *Between Melting Pot and Mosaic – African Americans and Puerto Ricans in the New York Political Economy.* Temple University Press, 1995.

Torres-Saillant, Silvio. "One and Divisible: Meditations on Global Blackness." *Small Axe*, vol. 29, no. 13–2, 2009, 4–25.

Touré. Askia. "Afro-American Youth and the Bandung World." *Liberator* vol. 5, no. 2, 1965.

Twickel, Christoph. "Reggae in Panama: Bien Tough." *Reggaeton*, ed. Raquel Z. Rivera, Wayne Marshall, and Deborah Pacini Hernandez, Durham: Duke University Press, 200, 81–87.

Tyson, Timothy B. *Radio Free Dixie: Robert F. Williams and the Roots of Black Power.* U of North Carolina Press, 2009.

210 —— Sources

Valdés, Vanessa. *Diasporic Blackness: The Life and Times of Arturo Alfonso Schomburg*. New York: SUNY Press, 2017.

Van Deburg, William. *New Day in Babylon – The Black Power Movement and American Culture*. Chicago: The University of Chicago Press, 1992.

Vianna, Hermano. *O Mundo Funk Carioca*. Rio de Janeiro: Jorge Zahar Editor, 1988.

Vincent, Rickey. *Party Music: The Inside Story of the Black Panthers' Band and How Black Power Transformed Soul Music*. Chicago: Chicago Review Press, 2013.

Wade, Peter. *Race and Ethnicity in Latin America*. London: Pluto Press, 1997.

Wald, Gayle. "Soul's Revival – White Soul, Nostalgia, and the Culturally Constructed Past." *Soul – Black Power, Politics, and Pleasure*, ed. Monique Guillory and Richard C. Green. New York: New York University Press, 139–158.

Wang, Oliver. "Singin' some Soul", Online: https://fania.com/record/singin-some-soul/, (May 12, 2023).

Ward, Brian. *Just my Soul Responding – Rhythm and Blues, Black Consciousness and Race Relations*. London: Routledge, 1998.

Ward, Brian. "Jazz and Soul, Race and Class, Cultural Nationalists and Black Panthers. A Black Power debate revisited." *Media, Culture, and the Modern African American Freedom Struggle*, ed. Brian Ward. Gainesville: University of Florida Press, 2001, 161–196.

Werner, Craig. *A Change Is Gonna Come – Music, Race & the Soul of America*. Ann Arbor: University of Michigan Press, 2006.

Werner, Craig. *Higher Grounds – Stevie Wonder, Aretha Franklin, Curtis Mayfield, and the Rise and Fall of American Soul*. New York: Penguin Random House, 2007.

West, Michael O., and William G. Martin. "Introduction: Contours of the Black International From Toussaint to Tupac." *From Toussaint to Tupac: The Black International since the Age of Revolution*, ed. Michael O. West, William G. Martin, and Fanon Che Wilkins. Chapel Hill: University of North Carolina Press, 2009, 1–44.

Winant, Howard. "Foreword – A New Hemispheric Blackness." *Comparative Perspectives on Afro-Latin America*, ed. Kwame Dixon and John Burdick. Gainesville: University of Florida Press, 2012, ix–xiv.

Woodard, Komozi. *A Nation within a Nation: Amiri Baraka (LeRoi Jones) and Black Power*, Chapel Hill: U of North Carolina P, 1999.

Westerman, George W. "School Segregation in the Panama Canal Zone." *Phylon*, vol. 15, no. 3, 1954, 276–287.

We Like It Like That. Documentary directed by Mathew Ramirez Warren, 2014.

Yelvington, Kevin. "The Anthropology of Afro-Latin America and the Caribbean: Diasporic Dimensions." *Annual Review of Anthropology*, vol. 30, 2001, 227–60.

Young, Cynthia. "Havana up in Harlem: LeRoi Jones, Harold Cruse, and the Making of a Cultural Revolution." *Science & Society* vol. 65, no. 1, 2001, 12–38.

Yudice, George: *The Expediency of Culture – Uses of Culture in the Global Era*. Durham, London: Duke University Press, 2003.

X, Malcolm. *By Any Means Necessary*. New York: Pathfinder Press, 1970.

Zeleza, Paul Tiyambe. "Rewriting the African Diaspora: Beyond the Black Atlantic." *African Affairs*, vol. 104, no. 414, 2005, 35–68.

Zentella, Ana Celia. "A Nuyorican's view of our History and Language(s) in New York, 1945–1965." *Boricuas in Gotham – Puerto Ricans In The Making of New York City*, ed. Gabriel Haslip-Viera et al. New York: Markus Wiener Publishers, 2004, 21–34.

Zien, Katherine. "Race and Politics in Concert: Paul Robeson and William Warfield in Panama, 1947–1953." *The Global South*, vol. 6, no. 2, 2013, 107–129.

Discography

Anderson, Vickie. "The Message from the Soul Sisters", King, 1970, single.

Arroyo, Joe. "La Rebelión", Discos Fuentes, 1987, single.

Ballard, Hank. "How You Gonna Get Respect (When You Haven't Cut Your Process Yet)", King, 1968, single.

Barbara and Gwen. "Right On", New Chicago Sound, 1970, single.

Barretto, Ray. "El Watusi", Columbia, 1963, single.

Barretto, Ray. *Latino Con Soul*, Fania, 1967, LP

Barretto, Ray. "Soul Drummers", Fania, 1968, single.

Barretto, Ray. "A Deeper Shade Of Soul", Fania, 1969, single.

Barretto, Ray. "Together", Fania, 1970, single.

Barretto, Ray. "New York Soul", Fania, 1970, single.

Barretto, Ray. "Right On", released on *Barretto Power*, Fania, 1970.

Barretto, Ray. "Power", released on *Barretto Power*, Fania, 1970

Bataan, Joe. "Gypsy Woman", Fania, 1967, single.

Bataan, Joe. "Ordinary Guy", released on *Gypsy Woman*, Fania, 1967, LP.

Bataan, Joe. "It's a Good Feeling (Riot)", Fania, 1968, single.

Bataan, Joe. "Freedom", released on *Poor Boy*, Fania, 1969, LP.

Bataan, Joe. "Young, Gifted, and Brown", released on *Singin' Some Soul*, Fania, 1969, LP.

Bataan, Joe. "Unwed Mother", released on *Singin' Some Soul*, Fania, 1969, LP.

Bataan, Joe. "Shaft", released on *Saint Latin's Day Massacre*, Fania 1972, LP.

Bataan, Joe. "Para Puerto Rico Voy", released on *Saint Latin's Day Massacre*, Fania 1972, LP.

Bataan, Joe. "Peace, Friendship And Solidarity", Mericana, 1974, single.

Bataan, Joe. "Rap-O Clap-O", Salsoul, 1979, single.

Beachers, The. "Black Soul", Loyola, year unknown, single

Beachers, The. "Africa Caliente", Loyola, year unknown, single.

Bender, Harvey and the Groovemakers. "You Got Soul Girl (You Are Super Bad)", Sally Ruth, year unknown, single.

Brown, James. "Papa's Got a Brand New Bag", King, 1965, single.

Brown, James. "America is My Home", King, 1968, single.

Brown, James. "Say It Loud – I'm Black and I'm Proud", King, 1968, single.

Brown, James. "I Don't Want Nobody to Give Me Nothing (Open Up The Door I'll Get It Myself)", King, 1969, single.

Brown, James. "Soul Power", King, 1971, single.

Brown, James. "All For One", released on *Reality*, Polydor, 1974, LP

Brown, Sammy. "Vietnam (You Son of Gun)", Grassroots Records, 1973, single.

Bush Y Su Nuevo Sonido Salsa. "Puerto Rico y Panama", released on *El Mundo Latino*, Continental Discos, 1982, LP.

Byrd, Bobby. "I Know You Got Soul", King, 1971, single.

Clarke, Frederick. "Soul Chombo", released on *Chombo's Show*, Loyola, 1972, LP.

Collins, Lyn. "Women's Lib", released on *Think (About It)*, People, 1972, LP.

Colón, Johnny. "Boogaloo Blues", Cotique, 1967, single.

Colón, Willie and Hector Lavoe. "La Murga", Fania, 1972, single.

Congenial Four, The. "Freedom Song", Capitol Records, 1970, single

Cooke, Sam. "A Change Is Gonna Come", RCA Victor, 1965, single.

Cuba, Joe. "To Be With You", Seeco, 1962, single.

Cuba, Joe. *El Alma del Barrio – The Soul of Spanish Harlem*, 1964, Tico, LP.

Cuba, Joe. "El Pito (I'll Never Go Back To Georgia)", Tico, 1966, single.

Cuba, Joe. "Bang! Bang!", Tico, 1966, single.

Cuba, Joe. "Alafia", Tico, 1966, single.

Cuba, Joe. "Hey Joe, Hey Joe (Hey Girl Hey Girl)", Tico, 1967, single.

Dyke & The Blazers. "We Got More Soul", Original Sound, 1969, single.

Exciters, The. "The Bag", Loyola, 1968, single.

Exciters, The. "The Brown", Loyola, 1968, single.

Exciters, The. "Sock It To Me/Different Strokes", Sally Ruth, 1968, single.

Exciters, The. "Stop Look Listen", Sally Ruth, year unknown, single.

Exciters, The. "Ojos Verdes", Loyola, 1969, single.

Exciters, The. *Exciters' ...Potpourri*, Panavox, 1972, LP.

Four Tops, The. "Reach Out I'll be There", Motown, 1966, single.

Franklin, Aretha. "Respect", Atlantic, 1967, single.

Franklin, Aretha. "To Be Young, Gifted and Black", Atlantic, 1972, single.

Gay Crooners, The. "Soul Man", Discos Musart, year unknown, single.

Gaye, Marvin. "What's Going On?", Motown, 1971, single.

Goombays, The. "Soul Power", Sally Ruth, year unknown, single.

Goombays, The. "Black Tribute", released on *Story Book,* Carlos Records, ear unknown, LP.

Greaves, Little Francisco. "Necia de mi Corazón", Sally Ruth, 1966, single.

Guzman, George. "Hierba Buena (Good Grass)", Fania, 1968, single.

Happy Sound, The. "Soul Girl", Loyola, year unknown, single.

Hebrew Rogers. "Can't Buy Soul", Original Sound, year unknown, single.

Ilê Aiyê. "Que Bloco è Esse?", released on *Canto Negro*, PolyGram, 1984, LP.

Impressions, The. "Gypsy Woman", ABC-Paramount, 1961, single.

Impressions, The . "Keep On Pushing", ABC-Paramount, 1964, single.

Impressions, The. "People Get Ready", ABC-Paramount, 1965, single.

Invaders, Los. "Soul Invasion", label and year unknown, single.

Jackson, Jesse. "Introduction", released on *The Living Word (Wattstax 2)*, Stax, 1973, LP.

Jackson, J.J. "Do the Boogaloo", Polydor, 1966.

Johnson, Syl. "Different Strokes", Twilight, 1967, single.

Johnson, Syl. "Is It Because I'm Black", Twilight, 1969, single.

Kako & His Orchestra. "Negro Soy", released on *Sock It To Me Latino*, Musicor Records, 1968, LP

King Combo, Gerson. "Mandamentos Black", released on *Gerson King Combo*, Polydor, 1977, LP.

Knight, Jean. "Mr. Big Stuff", Stax, 1971, single.

Latinaires, The. "Creation", released on *Camel Walk*, Fania, 1968, LP.

Latinaires, The. "Afro-Shingaling", released on *Camel Walk*, Fania, 1968, LP.

Latinaires, The. "Panama", released on *Like It Is*, Cotique, 1970, LP.

Lord Cobra. "Black Man", released on *Lord Cobra And Pana-Afro Sounds*, Tamayo, 1978, LP.

Lebron Brothers. "Let's Get Stoned", released on *The Brooklyn Bums*, Cotique, 1968, LP.

Luciano, Felipe. "Jíbaro, My Pretty Nigger", released on *The Last Poets – Right On! Original Soundtrack.* Juggernaut Records, 1971.

Lymon, Frankie & The Teenagers. "Why Do Fools Fall In Love", Gee, 1955, single.

Machito and his Orchestra. "Tangá", Mercury, 1951, single.

Main Ingredients, The. *Black Seeds*, RCA-Victor, 1971, LP.

Mayfield, Curtis. "Miss Black America", released on *Curtis*, Curtom, 1970, LP.

Nat Turner Rebellion. *Laugh To Keep From Crying*, Chrysalis, 2019. LP.

Orchestra Harlow. "Be Free", released on *El Exigente*, Fania, 1967, LP.

Orquesta Olivieri. *A Swingin' Combination,* Speed, 1968, LP.

Reeves, Martha, and The Vandellas. "Dancing in the Streets", Motown, 1964, single.

Pacheco, Johnny and Pete "El Conde" Rodriguez. "Moreno", Fania, 1972, single.

Palmieri, Charlie. "Panama's Bugalu", released on *Latin Bugalu,* Atlantic, 1968, LP.

Palmieri, Eddie. "The African Twist", Tico, 1968, single.

Palmieri, Eddie. "Justicia", released on *Justicia*, Tico, 1969, LP.

Palmieri, Eddie. *Harlem River Drive*, Roulette, 1971, LP.

Panama, Joe. *The Explosive Sound of Joe Panama*, Decca, 1967, LP.

Panama, Joe. "My People", Tico, 1972, single.

Pastrana, Joey. "Afro Azul", Cotique, 1968, single.

Persuaders, The. "Black Power", Taboga, year unknown, single.

Pucho & The Latin Soul Brothers. *Tough!* Prestige, 1966, LP.

Pucho & The Latin Soul Brothers. *Saffron & Soul.* Prestige, 1967, LP.

Pucho & The Latin Soul Brothers. *Shuckin' And Jivin,* Prestige, 1967, LP.

Puente, Tito. "Black Brothers", released on *Tito Puente And His Concert Orchestra*, Tico, 1973.

Robles, Ralph. "Soul Gritty", released on *Main Man / El Bravissimo*, Fania, 1969, LP.

Rivera, Ismael. "El Nazareno", Tico, 1974, single.

Rivera, Ismael. "Las Caras Lindas". Tico, 1978, single.

Rodriguez, Pete. *Latin Boogaloo*, Alegre, 1966, LP.

Rodriguez, Pete. "I Like it Like That", Alegre, 1967, single.

Sabater, Jimmy. "Times Are Changin'", Tico, 1969, single.

Sam and Dave. "Hold On! I'm Coming!", Stax, 1966, single.

Santamaría, Mongo. "Watermelon Man", Battle, 1963, single.

Santamaría, Mongo. "We Got Latin Soul", Columbia, 1969, single.

Silvertones, Los. "Oh...! Gee", Padisco, 1969, single.

Silvertones, Los. "Tamborito Swing", Padisco, 1969, single.

Simone, Nina. "Missisippi Goddam", Philipps, 1964, single.

Simone, Nina. "To Be Young, Gifted and Black", RCA Victor, 1969, single.

Soul Fantastic, Los. "Soul Train", Taboga, year unknown, single.

Soul Revolution. "Mi Bella Panama", Sally Ruth, year unknown, single.

Staple Singers, The. "Brand New Day", Stax, 1970, single.

Starr, Edwin. "War", Motown, 1970, single.

Simone, Nina. "Get Ready", Motown, 1966, single, single.

Simone, Nina. "Message from a Black Man", Motown, 1970, single.

TNT Band. "Musica Del Alma", Cotique, 1969, single.

Tornado, Toni. "Sou Negro", Odeon, 1970, single.

Tornado, Toni. "Se Jesus Fosse Um Homem De Cor (Deus Negro)", Continental, 1976, single.

Weeks, Ralph. "Something Deep Inside", Sta4rs, year unknown, single.

214 —— Sources

Weeks, Ralph. "Algo Muy Profundo", Sally Ruth, year unknown, single.
Weston, Kim. "Lift Every Voice and Sing", released on *The Living Word (Wattstax 2)*, Stax, 1973, LP.
Whitney, Marva. "It's my Thing", King, 1970, single.

Compilations

The NuYorican Funk Experience, Nascente, 2000, LP.
Latin Soul – New York Barrio Grooves 1966–1972, Nascente, 2003, LP.
Broasted Or Fried: Latin Breakbeats, Basslines & Boogaloo, Harmless, 2000, LP.
Freak Off: Latin Breakbeats, Basslines & Boogaloo, Harmless, 2001, LP.
Brown Sugar: Latin Breakbeats, Basslines & Boogaloo, Harmless, 2002, LP.
Samba Soul 70!, Ziriguiboom, 2001, LP.
Black Rio – Brazil Soul Power 1971–1980, Strut, 2002, LP.
Panama! Latin, Calypso and Funk on the Isthmus 1965–75, Soundway, 2006, LP.
Panama! 2 Latin Sounds, Cumbia Tropical & Calypso Funk On The Isthmus 1967–77, Soundway, 2009, LP.

Personal Interviews

Aponte, Carlos. September 17, 2018 (New York).
Barrow, Alberto. April 3, 2017 (Panama City).
Bataan, Joe. September 18, 2018 (New York)
Bonilla, Benny. September 17, 2018 (New York).
Boxhill, Stanley. April 3, 2017 (Panama City).
Brown, Carlos. April 3, 2017 (Panama City).
Brown, Henry "Pucho". September 22, 2018 (Middletown, NY).
Castro, Carlos. April 10, 2017 (Panama City).
Codrington, Bruce. March 31, 2017 (Panama City).
Dafé, Carlos. April 9, 2019 (Rio de Janeiro).
Dixon, Cobo. April 9, 2017 (Panama City).
Duncan, Alejandro. April 4, 2017 (Colón).
Gallimore, Lloyd. March 31, 2017 (Panama City).
García, Mauro. April 4, 2017 (Colón).
Grenald, Carlos. April 4, 2017 (Colón).
Harris, Irving. April 3, 2017 (Colón).
Johnson, Tito. September 29, 2018 (New York).
King, Ernie. April 2, 2017 (Panama City).
King Combo, Gerson. April 7, 2019 (Rio de Janeiro).
Luciano, Felipe. November 12, 2022 (telephone interview).
Lowe de Goodin, Melva. March 31, 2017 (Panama City).
Maloney, Gerardo. March 30, 2017 (Panama City).
Medeiros, Carlos Alberto. April 2, 2019 (Rio de Janeiro).
Melendez, Papoleto, September 26, 2018 (New York).
Miller, Selvia. April 7, 2017 (Colón).

Oliveira Filho, Asfilófio de. April 6, 2019 (Rio de Janeiro).
Oliver-Velez, Denise. September 13, 2018 (telephone interview).
Russell, Carlos. March 28, 2017 (Panama City).
Paulinho Black Power, April 2, 2019 (Rio de Janeiro).
Sanabria, Bobby. September 11, 2018 (New York).
Sealy, Ines. March 29, 2017 (Panama City).
Stewart, Judith. April 8, 2017. (Panama City).
Sidney Alma Negra, April 7, 2019 (Rio de Janeiro).
Weeks, Ralph, September 13, 2018 (telephone interview).
Wilson de Bryan, Dosita. April 8, 2017. (Panama City)

Appendix

Fig. 1: Ad for a regular show by Joe Panama and his band at Bronx jazz club Blue Morocco (1955).

Fig. 2: Joe Cuba Sextet, *Joe Cuba presents the Velvet Voice of Jimmy Sabater*, Tico (1967); Jimmy Sabater on the right.

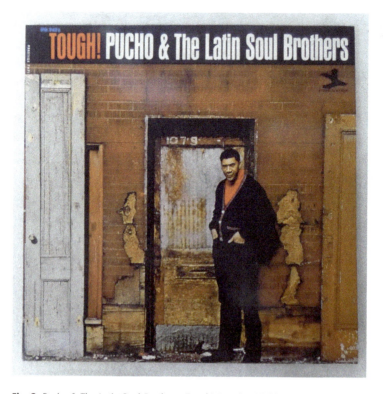

Fig. 3: Pucho & The Latin Soul Brothers, *Tough!*, Prestige (1966).

Fig. 4: Pete Rodriguez, *I Like It Like That,* Alegre Records (1966); Benny Bonilla on the far left.

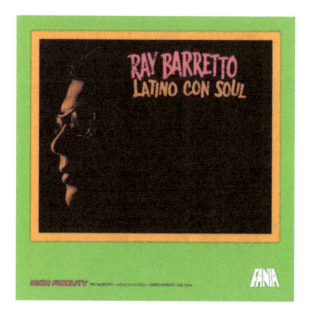

Fig. 5: Ray Barretto, *Latino Con Soul*, United Artists (1967).

Fig.6: Joe Bataan, *Riot!* Fania (1968).

Fig. 7: Felipe Luciano (center) with The Original Last Poets (1969).

Appendix — 223

Fig. 8: Young Lords newspaper *Palante*, (February 1971); Denise Oliver center left.

Fig. 9: Cover live album, *Young Lords Organization Benefit at the Apollo, Harlem* (April 1970).

Fig. 10: *Combos Nacionales* in Panama. "Onda Nueva Records congratulates all the bands who participated in the Soul Festival..." (*Crítica*, May 6, 1971).

Fig. 11: After returning from New York, Ernie King (later known as Kabir) from Colón became popular as one of Panama's leading soul singers with The Soul Invaders and Los Fabulosos Festivals (photo: 1973).

Fig. 12: Melva Lowe grew up in the Canal Zone, graduated in the United States in 1968, and returned to Panama in the early 1970s where she became involved in the Afro-Panamanian movement as a writer, educator and co-founder of Sociedad de Amigos del Museo Afro-Antillano (SAMAAP) (1972).

Fig. 13: The Astronauts from Gamboa were one of the many doo-wop vocal groups that emerged throughout the Canal Zone in the early 1960s, playing mostly for GIs on the U.S. military posts.

Fig. 14: The Exciters (aka Los Dinámicos Exciters) became the most successful soul band in the *combos nacionales* era. Singers: Joaquín Moore and Toribio Samuels, on the far right: band leader and bass player Carlos Brown (1971).

Fig. 15: "The Pressure Man": Carlos Brown, bandleader of The Exciters (1972).

Fig. 16: In the early 1970s, The Exciters introduced "Miss Soul" ("Reina Soul") beauty pageants during carnival season featuring Afro-Panamanian women with natural hair. This ad announces the "coronation" of "Miss Soul" 1972, Sonja Stultz, featuring live appearances by The Exciters, The Festivals and Ralph Weeks from New York (*Crítica*, February 10, 1972).

Appendix — 229

Fig. 17: After several attempts and overcoming many obstacles, The Exciters succeeded in bringing James Brown to Panama in 1972. *(Crítica,* October 30, 1972).

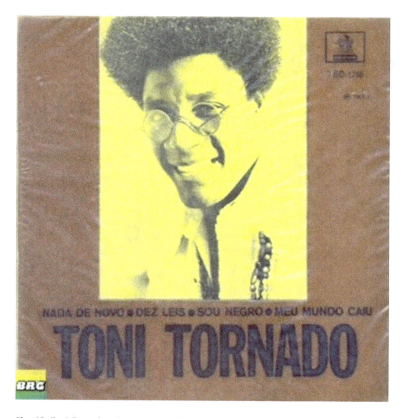

Fig. 18: Toni Tornado, "Sou Negro", Odeon (1970).

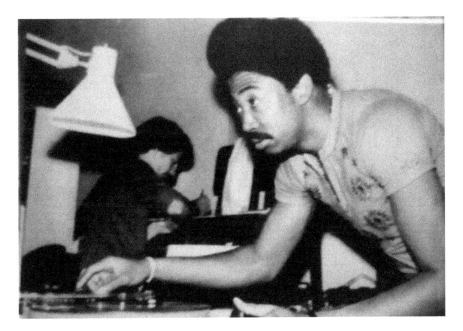

Fig. 19: With their sound system *Black Power*, DJs Paulão (front) and Paulinho were among the most successful of the Black Rio movement (1973).

Fig. 20: In the early-to-mid 1970s, Dom Filó (left) established his *Soul Grand Prix* sound system a site of black empowerment, attracting activists like Carlos Alberto Medeiros who saw the potential of soul music to mobilize Afro-Brazilian youth (1974).

Fig. 21: *Baile black*, Rio de Janeiro (1976).

Index

Abernathy, Ralph   126
Abolição (band)   165
Acción Reivindicadora del Negro Panameño (ARE-NEP)   150, 156
African American Studies   5, 22, 27, 30 – 33, 35 – 36, 39, 48, 50 – 55, 78, 192
African Diaspora Studies   27, 35, 39, 51, 78, 192
Afro (hairstyle)   20, 25 – 26, 58, 64 – 66, 71, 101, 109, 112, 117, 133, 141, 146 – 147, 151 – 152, 154, 160 – 161, 163 – 164, 167, 170, 172, 174, 181 – 182, 189, 194
afrobeat   10, 24
Afrocentrism   12, 30, 32, 34, 38, 40 – 41, 57 – 58, 68
Afro-Cuban   4, 10, 85 – 88, 94, 95, 101, 143, 171, 172
Afro-Latin American Studies   5, 27, 49 – 53
afrolatinidad   5, 7, 21, 27, 51 – 54, 115, 174, 188, 190, 195
Afro-Latin Soul   2, 4 – 7, 11, 14, 23, 28, 80, 85, 193
Afro-Puerto Rican   1, 3, 2, 49, 79, 80, 84 – 85, 111, 170
Albizu Campos, Pedro   114
Alegre Records   93, 104, 219
Ali, Muhammad   2, 10, 69, 132, 172
Allen, Carlos   143
Alma Negra (sound system)   5, 6, 162
Americanization   9, 205
Anderson, Vickie   66, 71, 73, 74
anti-Afro-Americanism   11, 13 – 14, 28, 169, 173, 175, 186, 189, 195
anti-U.S.-Americanism   132, 171, 173, 188
anti-essentialism   42, 76, 173, 192 – 193
anti-imperialism   13 – 14, 20, 28, 117, 131, 141, 158, 170, 184 – 186, 189
anti-West Indian sentiment   17, 120, 124, 150, 152, 174, 176, 179
Aponte, Carlos   81, 83 – 85, 91
Apollo Theatre   89, 108, 224
Appadurai, Arjun   8, 26, 197
Araújo Lima, Sidney. *see Dr. Sidney*
Arias, Arnulfo   120, 123 – 124, 131, 176

Armstrong, Louis   10
Arosemena, Justo   155
Arroyo, Joe   173
Ascots, The   139
Asociación Afro-Panameña   146, 153
Asociación de Profesionales, Obreros y Dirigentes de Ascendencia Negra (APODAN)   150
Astronauts, The   137, 144 – 145, 226
Atlantic Records   24, 56
Averne, Harvey   96
Azuquita, Camilo   130, 144

baile funk   11, 168
bailes black   5, 136, 158, 162 – 166, 179, 184, 188, 232
Ballard, Hank   64, 66, 161
Banda Black Rio   161
Baraka, Amiri   56 – 60, 67, 70, 75, 160
Barbados   17, 118, 121, 129, 131, 151
Barbara and Gwen   69 – 70
Barretto, Ray   4, 88, 97, 101, 193, 220
Barrow, Alberto   6, 17, 132, 135 – 136, 147 – 149, 152, 181 – 182
Bataan, Joe   6, 23, 79, 94, 99 – 109, 221, 224
Bauzá, Mario   1, 10, 85
bebop   85
Belafonte, Harry   10
Bell, Archie   98
Ben, Jorge   162
Big Boy   163
bilingualism   90, 96, 101, 108, 112, 143, 190, 193
Black Arts Movement   28, 38, 56 – 58, 62, 76 – 77, 79, 111, 113, 115, 129, 156
black internationalism   6, 10, 14 – 15, 22, 29, 31 – 32, 35, 37 – 38, 41 – 42, 48, 53, 67, 113, 116, 118, 193, 198
"Black is beautiful" (slogan)   64, 77, 114, 147, 155, 160, 163 – 164, 175
black nationalism   8, 12, 27 – 28, 30, 32, 37 – 42, 45, 49, 53, 56 – 59, 61 – 62, 65 – 66, 71 – 73, 75 – 77, 110, 112, 120, 166, 169, 191 – 195

https://doi.org/10.1515/9783110665550-012

234 —— Index

Black Panther Party (BPP)   28, 32, 38–39, 42, 45, 48, 60, 64, 67–70, 72, 80, 91, 92, 107–108, 110, 113–115, 114, 133, 160–162, 185
Black Power   2–3, 5–14, 16–18, 20–21, 25–28, 30–33, 35, 37–40, 42, 48, 50, 52, 54, 56–58, 61–68, 70–77, 80, 89, 91–93, 97–98, 107–108, 110, 112–115, 117, 129, 131–134, 140, 143, 146–148, 150, 153, 156, 158–161, 164–167, 169, 172, 180, 184–186, 188, 191–194
black radical tradition   14, 31, 45
Black Solidarity Day   129
black transnationalism   3, 19, 27, 29–30, 35–36, 38, 41–42, 48–50, 52–53, 55, 174, 180, 186, 190
Blades, Rubén   130, 144, 156
Bland, Bobby   58
blocos afros   167
Bobo, Willie   87, 89
Bocas del Toro   119, 142, 143
Bonet, Pete   98
Bonilla, Benny   6, 83, 87–88, 94, 98, 114, 143–144, 219
Booker T. & The MGs   143
Bourdieu, Pierre   186
Boxhill, Stanley   139
brasilidade   184
Brazil   3, 5–6, 11–12, 14, 20–21, 24–25, 54, 136, 158–161, 164, 166, 184, 186
Bronx   1, 11, 83–84, 87, 98, 106
Brooklyn   127–130
Brown, Carlinhos   167
Brown, Carlos   6, 139, 141, 144–148, 226–228
Brown, Elaine   69
Brown, Henry see *Pucho & The Latin Soul Brothers*
Brown, H. Rap   60, 112, 155
Brown, James   3, 10, 19–20, 28, 58, 61–66, 68–69, 73, 80, 95, 98, 104, 106, 117, 135, 145, 147–149, 155, 158, 165, 172, 175, 191, 230
Bryce-Laporte, Roy   122, 156
Buckley, Francisco "Bush" 144, 182
Byrd, Bobby   66

calypso   10, 24, 117, 121, 136, 139, 142–145, 153, 175

capitalism   7, 18, 28, 31, 33, 42, 53, 65, 67–68, 114, 188
Cardoso, Fernando Henrique   159
Caribbean Studies   54
Carlos, John   62
Carlos, Roberto   161
Carmichael, Stokely   33, 60, 71, 91, 112, 155, 160–161, 166
Carvalho, José Jorge   186
Castillero Calvo, Alfredo   178
Castro, Carlos   121, 137, 147, 182
Centro de Estudos Afro-Asiáticos (CEAA)   166
cha-cha-cha   1, 89, 98–99
Chan, Eduardo "Balito"139
Charles, Ray   2–3
Chess Records   24
Chi-Lites, The   69, 141
Civil Rights Movement   2–3, 5, 12, 20, 25, 38, 42, 50, 56, 59, 61, 71–72, 75, 77, 85, 91, 107, 117, 125–128, 129, 133, 159, 164, 169, 188, 191
Clark, Kenneth B. 129
Clarke, Frederick   140
Cleaver, Eldridge   48, 151, 166
Codrington, Bruce   133, 146–148
Cold War   13, 31, 120, 188
Cole, Nat King   90, 137
Coleman, Ornette   58
Cold War   13, 31, 164, 188
Collins, Lyn   71, 73–74, 149, 229
Colón   10, 16–17, 19, 24, 48, 88, 116–122, 124, 126, 129–131, 133–135, 137–139, 142, 144, 146–148, 150, 181
Colón, Johnny   4, 82, 93–94, 96, 104–105
Colón, Willie   143–144
Coltrane, John   58
combos nacionales   5, 14, 22, 24, 117, 135–147, 149–150, 152, 175, 181–182, 190, 193
communism   33, 36, 72
Concerned Brothers   134
Congreso de la Cultura Negra de las Américas   157
Congressional Black Caucus   130
Cooke, Sam   59, 68, 91, 137–138
Corea, Chick   89
Cortijo, Rafael   144

cosmopolitanism   6, 11 – 12, 17, 27, 29, 37 – 38,
    40, 42 – 49, 53, 78, 117, 119, 122, 126, 142,
    194
Cotique Records   93, 104
counterculture   13, 19, 39, 96, 115, 167, 174
crisol de razas   123, 176, 181, 189
Cristal, Pancho   93, 104
Crowns, The   116, 137
Cruz, Celia   94, 101, 172
Cuba   15, 16, 54, 85, 88, 117, 121, 136, 172
Cuba, Joe   1, 2, 4, 89 – 94, 98, 105, 130, 171,
    193, 217
cumbia   24, 143, 145

Dafé, Carlos   6, 214
Davis Jr., Sammy   2, 137
Davis, Angela   18, 39, 45, 72, 108 – 109, 129,
    151
Davis, Betty   71
Debonairs, The   135
decolonization   15 – 16, 29, 33, 45, 48, 122, 131
Dells, The   91
democracia racial   7, 13, 20, 40, 50, 78, 158 –
    161, 164 – 165, 167, 183 – 184, 195
Departamento da Ordem Política e Social (DOPS)
    184
diaspora   9 – 12, 16, 18, 20 – 21, 24, 27, 29 – 31,
    33 – 36, 38 – 41, 49 – 51, 53, 55, 63, 78, 84,
    113, 115, 125 – 126, 128, 133, 156 – 158, 169,
    174, 186, 189, 192
Diggers, The   116, 135
Diggers Descendants, The   139
Dixon, Cobo   120
DJs   3, 6, 14, 24 – 25, 61, 65, 100, 133, 135, 137,
    162, 163, 185
Dom Filó   6, 163 – 164. 185, 231
doo-wop   86, 87, 94, 116, 137 – 138, 142, 144
Douglas, Emory   67, 68
Douglass, Frederick   155
Dramatics, The   149
Dragons, The   79, 83, 103
Dr. Sidney   6, 162
Drifters, The   95
Du Bois, W.E.B. 30, 31, 37, 45, 48, 51, 126, 155,
    175
Duncan, Quince   3
Dyke & The Blazers   66, 98

essentialism   12, 33, 39 – 40, 42, 46 – 47, 50,
    194
exceptionalism   12, 29 – 30, 39, 50 – 51, 55, 78
Exciters, The   5, 117, 133, 136, 139, 141 – 142,
    144 – 149, 182, 226 – 229

Fábregas, José Isaac   176
Fania All-Stars   10, 101, 144, 172
Fania Records   24, 93, 100 – 102, 104, 109, 130,
    171 – 172, 221
Fanon, Frantz   45, 46, 62, 166
Feliciano, Cheo   90, 101, 171 – 172
feminism   33, 36, 45, 71, 73, 195
Fernandes, Florestan   159
Festivals, The   5, 117, 141 – 142, 145, 149, 224,
    228 – 229
Flack, Roberta   23, 71
Flag Riots   131
Flores, Juan   4 – 5, 10, 20, 51, 92, 95, 99 – 100,
    171
folklorization   8, 19, 50,170, 184, 189 – 1900,
    193 – 195
Fortune, Armando   181
Four Tops, The   58, 91, 141
Franklin, Aretha   2 – 3, 23, 66, 71 – 73, 91, 99, 158
Frente Negra Brasileira   159, 168
Freyre, Gilberto   158, 159, 183
funk   4, 10 – 11, 24, 49, 61 – 62, 69, 77, 87, 89,
    94 – 95, 98, 142, 161 – 162, 165

Gallimore, Lloyd   143
Garret, Vernon   66
Garvey, Marcus   2 – 3, 33, 38, 54, 112, 119 – 120,
    135, 143, 155, 175
Gay Crooners, The   137
Gaye, Marvin   58, 65, 70, 91
Gerson King Combo   6, 161, 165
Ghetto Records   101. 109
Gil, Gilberto   161, 167
Gillespie, Dizzy   10, 85, 90, 130
Gilroy, Paul   9, 19, 24, 30 – 31, 33, 37, 39 – 41, 46
Giovanni, Nikki   72
globalization   8 – 9, 15, 26, 29, 33 – 34, 42
gold and silver roll   122 – 123, 126
Golden Boys, The   137
Goldner, George   104
González, Juan   81, 83 – 84, 223

236 —— Index

Goodin, Orville 152
Goombays, The 140, 142
Gordy, Berry 65
gospel 56, 59, 133, 137
Greaves, Lester 126 – 127
Greaves, Little Francisco 127, 139, 182
Grenald, Carlos 142, 143
Groove Makers, The 139
guajira 94, 96
Guaycucho 146, 151
Guillén, Nicolás 3
Guzmán, George 94, 96
Guzmán, Pablo "Yoruba" 79, 80, 96, 110, 113, 115, 173, 223
Gyemant, Roberto Ernesto 24, 138, 141

H.O.G. (radio station) 133, 139
Hall, Stuart 33, 53
Hampton, Fred 68, 110, 114
Hancock, Herbie 88
Happy Sound, The 139
Harlem 1, 11, 16 – 17, 25, 36, 41, 49, 54, 79 – 81, 83 – 84, 86 – 91, 94, 96, 98 – 99, 102 – 104, 110, 112 – 114, 119 – 120, 126, 129, 137, 160 – 161, 170, 183, 186, 192, 194
Harlem Renaissance 17, 41, 49, 54, 119
Harlem River Drive (album) 99
Harlem Writers Guild 129
Harlow, Larry 96, 101
Harris, Irving 137
Havana 16, 19, 94, 119
Hayes, Isaac 56, 65, 66, 108
Hebrew Rogers 66
Hemispheric Black Studies 22, 53 – 55
Heres brothers 138, 139, 145
Hernández Cruz, Victor 90, 96, 115
Hesitations, The 66, 69
highlife 10, 24
hip-hop 9, 11, 18, 20 – 21, 24, 49, 59, 74, 92, 112, 168, 173 – 174, 181, 190
Holiday, Billie 71

Ilê Aiyê 167
imperialism 7, 9, 13, 15 – 16, 22, 33, 43 – 44, 50, 52 – 53, 67, 78, 80, 150, 175, 180, 185 – 186, 188
Impressions, The 58 – 59, 79, 104, 149

Innis, Cecil 134
Instituto de Pesquisa da Cultura Negra (IPCN) 166
Instituto Nacional 132
Instituto Soul 146
Instituto Superior de Estudos Brasileiros 185
Inter-American Studies 8, 27, 53
Invaders, The [Los Soul Invasores] 116, 117, 142, 224

J.B.'s, The 66, 73, 117, 149, 229
Jackson Five, The 149
Jackson, Jesse 56, 65 – 66, 129 – 130, 150, 166
Jamaica 16 – 17, 54, 116, 118, 121, 129, 131, 136, 151
James, C.L.R 45
James, Etta 91
jazz: 1, 11, 17, 56 – 58, 68 – 69, 86 – 89, 91, 111, 119, 121, 133, 161, 172, 185
Jim Crow 15, 50, 80, 90, 122 – 123, 125, 126, 131, 134, 150, 156, 183
Jiménez Román, Miriam 3
Jiménez, "Cha Cha" 110
Jiménez, Nick 90
Johnson, Syl 66, 67, 69, 145
Johnson, Tito 121, 124
Jones, Claudia 45
Jones-Shafroth Act 15, 81
Jordan, Louis 90

Kain, Gylan 111 – 112, 222, 224
Kako and his Orchestra 130, 144, 174
Karenga, Ron 58, 67 – 68
Kennedy, John F. and Robert 2 – 3
King, Coretta 156
King Records 24
King, B.B. 138
King, Ben E. 56
King, Ernie 6, 116 – 117, 135, 137, 141 – 142, 149, 226
King, Martin Luther 2 – 3, 12, 42, 56, 61, 70, 72, 106 – 107, 129, 133, 155 – 156, 160, 176
Kingston 16, 19
Kitt, Eartha 49
Knight, Gladys 23, 95, 104
Knight, Jean 74

Korean War 120–121
Kuti, Fela 10

La Lupe 23, 94, 143
Lakas, Demetrio 146
language discrimination 82, 125, 153–154, 170, 173, 176–179, 193
Last Poets, The 79, 108, 112–113, 222, 224
Latin American Studies 22, 50, 55
Latin boogaloo 1, 4, 10, 14, 22, 24, 79–80, 88, 90–91, 93–102, 104–105, 110–111, 113–115, 117, 130, 136, 142–145, 170–174, 187, 190
Latin jazz 1, 10, 81, 85, 90, 101, 174, 234
Latinaires, The 98, 144
latinidad 7, 13, 51, 170, 188–189, 195
Laurenza, Roque Javier 156, 176–180, 182
Lavoe, Hector 143–144
Lebrón Brothers 96
Lee, Warren 70
Lemos, Ademir 162
Lesseps, Ferdinand de 118
Levy, Morris 92, 93, 100
Liberator 129
Lord Cobra 119, 143
Lord Panama 10, 143
Love, Warmth, and Affection 130, 146
Lowe de Goodin, Melva 6, 17, 23, 125, 133–134, 152–153, 157, 174, 176, 225
Loyola Records 24, 139, 145
Luciano, Felipe 6, 54, 79, 83–84, 86, 91, 100, 110–112, 115, 130, 173, 222–224
Lumpen, The 68, 69
Lymon, Frankie 86, 87, 137
Lyons, Mary Queenie 69
Lyrics, The 116, 137

Machito 1, 10, 85–87, 89, 100–101
Maia, Tim 161
Main Ingredients, The 66
Makeba, Miriam 65
Maloney, Gerardo 6, 17, 134–137, 142, 150, 156
mambo 1, 10, 86–88, 92, 95–96, 98–99, 101, 141, 171
Marley, Bob 11
Marshall, Thurgood 126
Martinique 118

Marxism 31–32, 45
Masucci, Jerry 100, 102, 104, 105
Materno Vasquéz, Juan 131, 141, 152–154, 156, 174–180, 183
Mayfield, Curtis 59, 66, 68–70, 104, 114, 141
McSween, Cirilo 130–131, 150
Medeiros, Carlos Alberto 6, 12, 163–164, 166–167, 185, 231
Medici, Emilio 162
Meléndez, Mickey 110
Meléndez, Papoleto 115
Mendes, Sergio 161
Menezes, Margareth 167
Mercury, Daniela 167
mestizaje 7, 13, 34, 40, 50, 78, 82, 151, 156, 170, 173–174, 181, 183, 188–189, 195
Mighty Sparrow 10, 114
migration 2, 4–5, 9, 15–17, 19, 22, 26, 28–29, 33–34, 51–53, 80–81, 85, 116, 118, 120, 128
Miller, Selvia 23, 124, 131, 134
Miranda, Ismael 96
Miranda, Santos 87
Miss Soul Queen [La Reina Soul] 145, 147–148, 228
mobility 4, 8–9, 18–19, 22, 25, 28, 42, 45, 47–48, 52, 75, 126, 161, 175, 193
modernity 19, 30–31, 33–36, 42–43, 47–48, 85, 169
Modestin, Yvette 157
Morales, Eusebio 155
Morales, Iris 115
Morejón, Nancy 3
Motown Records 24, 60, 65, 69, 72, 98, 101
Motta, Ed 164
Moura, Roberto 186
Movimento Negro Unificado (MNU) 167
Mozambiques, Los 142, 143, 182
Mr. Funky Santos 162

NAACP 56, 126, 127, 129
Nascimento, Abdias 159, 160
Nat Turner Rebellion, The 70
nationalism 14, 20–21, 24, 29, 29, 33, 44, 46–47, 50, 55, 122–123, 141, 152, 155–156, 175, 183, 189, 191
Neal, Larry 57–59, 62
Nelson, David 112. 222, 224

238 —— Index

New Orleans   10, 19, 60, 116, 119
Newton, Huey   70, 91
night of fun   135, 136
Nixon, Richard   68
Noite do Shaft   163 – 164, 231
Nuyorican identity   14, 79, 83 – 91, 95 – 96, 99,
   110 – 115

Oliveira Filho, Asfilófio de. *see Dom Filó*
Oliver, Denise   6, 23 – 24, 110, 113, 115, 129, 173,
   223
Olodum   167
Orquesta Olivieri   95

Pabón, Tony   94, 98
Pacheco, Johnny   100, 101, 104, 105, 173
Padmore, George   45
Palladium Ballroom   86, 93
Palm Gardens Ballroom   92
Palmieri, Eddie   99, 142, 173
pan-Africanism   10, 14, 30, 33, 40, 120, 143
Panama   1 – 7, 10 – 11, 14, 16 – 17, 21 – 22,
   24 – 25, 28, 54, 78, 80, 88 – 90, 98, 116 – 121,
   123 – 135, 137 – 154, 156 – 157, 169, 172, 175 –
   183, 187, 189 – 191, 193 – 195
Panama Canal   1, 5, 14, 16 – 17, 22, 116 – 135,
   13, 139, 142, 144 – 148, 150, 152 – 154, 176,
   180 – 181, 183, 187
Panama City   118, 124, 126, 131, 133, 135, 137 –
   139, 142, 143, 145, 147
Panama Tribune   125
Panama, Joe   1 – 2, 4 – 5, 80, 88 – 90, 130, 217
panameñidad   154, 155, 174, 177, 181, 195
Parker, Charlie   99, 144
Partido Revolucionario Democrático   131
Pastrana, Joey   94, 99, 193
paternalism   8, 14, 27, 43, 186,189, 195
patriarchy   18, 23, 76
Payne, Freda   70
Persuaders, The   140
Pickett, Wilson   106, 458
Pietri, Pedro   114, 115, 224
Platters, The   137
Playboys, The   137
Porras, Belisario   155
Post-Soul   5, 54, 74 – 76, 78, 191, 192, 194, 195
Pozo, Chano   10, 85

Priestley, George   127, 128, 130, 132, 150
Preudhomme, David. *see Panama, Joe*
Pucho & The Latin Soul Brothers   1 – 2, 6,
   88 – 90, 218
Puente, Tito   1, 10, 80, 82, 85 – 86, 88 – 89, 94,
   99 – 101, 121, 124, 130
Puerto Rico   15 – 16, 20, 54, 81, 86, 88, 99 –
   100, 103, 108, 113, 115, 117, 128, 136, 144,
   169 – 170, 172 – 174
punk   24

R&B   1, 4, 58, 90, 95, 100, 121, 137, 172, 197
rainbow coalitions   68, 110, 113, 114
Ramos, Tito   82
rap   109 – 110
Ray, Richie   94, 141
Redding, Otis   65, 72, 91
Reeves, Martha and The Vandellas   58, 60
reggae   11, 18, 21, 24, 49, 181, 190
reggaetón   11
Regina, Elis   161
Remón-Eisenhower Treaty   127
Renascença Clube   163
Revista Nacional de Cultura   153, 156, 176
Revolutionary Action Movement   38, 42, 51
Ripperton, Minnie   71
Rivera, Héctor   94
Rivera, Ismael   145, 173
Roach, Max   58, 85
Robeson, Paul   17, 31, 45, 126 – 127
Robinson, Smokey   91, 95, 137, 138
Robles, Ralph   94
rock   69, 86, 97 – 98, 125, 141 – 142, 162, 185
rock'n'roll   121
Rodney, Walter   45
Rodriguez, Arsenio   10
Rodriguez, Pete   4, 83, 88, 93 – 94, 98, 105,
   143, 193, 219
Rodríguez, Pete "Conde"   101, 172 – 173
Rodriguez, Tito   86, 99
Roena, Roberto   101, 144, 172
Ron Coloniales, Los   137
Roosevelt, Theodore   16
Ross, Diana   23, 71
rumba   10, 121, 181
Russell, Carlos   110, 112, 129 – 131, 147, 150, 156
Russell, Luis   10, 17, 130

S.C.N. [radio station]   137, 139
Sabater, Jimmy   1–2, 87, 89–90, 92, 97, 217
Sally Ruth (label)   24, 139, 143
salsa   10, 20–21, 24, 49, 80, 86, 101, 108–109, 117, 130, 136, 141–145, 156, 171–173, 182, 190
Salsa Soul Sisters   109
Sam and Dave   65, 91, 140
samba   11, 24, 121, 141, 159, 162–165, 167, 184–185
samba reggae   11
San Juan   19, 119
Sanabria, Bobby   81, 83–86, 95–96, 101
Sanabria, Izzy   95–96
Santamaria, Mongo   4, 88–89, 98, 101, 130
Santana   142
Santiago, Adalberto   104
Scott-Heron, Gil   59, 75
Seale, Bobby   67, 69, 91, 160
Sealy, Ines   135–136, 148
Selassie, Haile   143
Seybold, John   127
Shabazz, Atillah   156
Sharpton, Al   63
Shaw, Marlena   70
Shepp, Archie   58
Silvertones, The   142–143, 182
Simonal, Wilson   161
Simone, Nina   23, 49, 59, 65–66, 68–69, 71, 73, 102
Sinatra, Frank   137
Skyliners, Los   137
slavery   18–19, 29, 38, 43–44, 53, 143, 160
Sly & The Family Stone   69
Smith Fernández, Alberto   17, 133, 146, 153–156, 175–180
Smith, Bessie   71
Smith, Mauricio   130
Smith, Tommie   62
Student Non-Violent Coordinating Committee (SNCC)   60, 64, 65, 91, 112
soca   11
Sociedad de Amigos del Museo Afro-Antillano de Panamá (SAMAAP)   157
Sociedade de Intercâmbio Brasil-África (SIMBA)   166

solidarity   3, 7, 12–13, 19, 21, 37–38, 40, 42, 46–47, 49, 76, 93, 99, 103, 109, 111, 114–115, 122, 129, 132, 141, 164, 173, 183, 189, 191–192
son   1, 96, 101, 117, 141, 171
Sonora Ponceña   144
Soul Fantastic, The   5, 137, 140, 142, 228
Soul Grand Prix (sound system)   5, 163–164, 231
Soul Revolution, The   140
Soul Senders, The   66
soul style   19, 64–65, 101, 114, 133, 139, 141, 171–172, 189
Spanish-American War   15, 81, 103, 116
Spinners, The   172
Staple Singers, The   56, 69
Staple, Ricardo   137–138
Starr, Edwin   65, 70
Stax Records   24, 56, 65, 143
Stewart, Judith   127
Stewart, Waldaba   127
Sugar Hill Gang   109
Supremes, The   58, 68

Taboga (label)   24, 139
Tate, Greg   75, 194
Teatro Experimental do Negro   159
Temptations, The   3, 65, 69, 91, 95, 137–138, 141, 158
Terrace, Ray   94
Terrell, Tammi   91
Third World   12, 32, 37, 39, 91, 106, 113, 125, 159, 187
Thomas, Carla   65, 71
Thomas, Piri   85, 115
Tico Records   2, 92–93, 104, 217
Till, Emmett   129
Típica   73, 144
Tjader, Cal   88
TNT Band, The   82, 98
Tornado, Toni   23, 160–161, 230
Torrijos, Omar   117, 130–131, 138, 140–141, 146–153, 174–175, 189
Torrijos-Carter Treaties   130, 150, 152
Touré, Askia   59
Transnational American Studies   8
Tropicalía   185

Turner, Tina   71, 137
Twilights, The   116, 137

U.S. army   120, 131–133, 137, 139, 141, 144, 145
U.S. empire   15–16, 59, 82, 188
Umbra   115
União Black (band)   165
United Fruit Company   16
United Public Workers of America (UPWA)   126
universalism   42–44, 46

Valentin, Bobby "Mr. Soul"   94
Vargas, Getúlio   184
Veloso, Caetano   161, 167
Versus   167
Viceroys, The   83, 90
Vietnam War   62, 70, 120, 132, 151
Voices of East Harlem, The   69

Walrond, Eric   17, 119
Waquant, Loic   186
Warwick, Dionne   58
Washington, Booker T.   155
Washington, Dinah   137
Watts Prophets   59
Wattstax   56, 66, 164, 166
Weeks, Ralph   6, 23, 72, 145–146, 228

Wells, Mary   58
Westerman, George   122, 126, 134
Weston, Kim   56, 66
Wetherborne, Egbert   146, 151
white supremacy   7, 13, 18, 29–31, 38, 43, 53, 58, 60–61, 66, 73, 114, 133, 150, 190–191
Whitney, Marva   71, 73, 74
Williams, Robert F.   68
Wilson de Bryan, Dosita   132
Wilson, Carlos Guillermo   3
Withers, Bill   10, 172
Wood, Hugo   133
World War II   31, 37, 81, 103, 120, 123, 125, 126
Wright, Richard   45

X, Malcolm   2–3, 42, 57, 59, 61, 63, 68–70, 89, 112, 114–115, 116, 129, 133, 151, 155–156, 160, 166

Young Rascals, The   69, 108, 224
Young, Sidney   126
Youngs Lords   6, 14, 79–80, 83, 108, 110–111, 113–115, 129–130, 156, 173–174, 223–224

Zamot, Johnny   94
Zapata Olivella, Manuel   3